DATE DUE

BRODART   Cat. No. 23-221

Environment and Experience

Environment and Experience

*Settlement Culture
in Nineteenth-Century Oregon*

Peter G. Boag

University of California Press
Berkeley · Los Angeles · Oxford

University of California Press
Berkeley and Los Angeles, California

University of California Press, Ltd.
Oxford, England

©1992 by
The Regents of the University of California

Library of Congress Cataloging-in-Publication Data

Boag, Peter G.
    Environment and experience : settlement culture in nineteenth-century Oregon /
Peter G. Boag.
        p.   cm.
    Includes bibliographical references and index.
    ISBN 0-520-07719-9 (alk. paper)
    1. Calapooia River Valley (Or.)—Historical geography.   2. Land
settlement—Oregon—Calapooia River Valley—History—19th century.
3. Human geography—Oregon—Calapooia River Valley—History—19th
century.   I. Title.
F882.L7B62   1992
979.5'35—dc20   92-12931
                                                                                CIP

Printed in the United States of America

9 8 7 6 5 4 3 2 1

In Memoriam
Elizabeth Ellen Oster Horand

Contents

Illustrations

Tables

Acknowledgments

In the winter of 1983–84 I first approached Richard Maxwell Brown, of the University of Oregon, with my desire to trace the history of the relationship between humans and the landscape on the local level in the Pacific Northwest. From that moment, Professor Brown has been a constant and enthusiastic supporter of my work. His guidance, his generosity with time and advice, and his willingness to let me stand on my own helped me turn my then rather amorphous ideas into a dissertation, and now into the book before you. I owe to Professor Brown more than I can express in words.

As with any project of this type, many people lent their assistance, and I wish to thank them. Dennis "Whitey" Lueck taught me much of what I know about ecology and greatly increased my awareness of, and appreciation for, the natural environment. In the writing of early drafts of this manuscript, Whitey also provided editorial assistance, reining in my often rambling prose. Carlos A. Schwantes, of the University of Idaho, offered thoughtful suggestions and encouraged me through the publishing process. Local historians of the Calapooia—Patricia Hoy Hainline, Margaret Standish Carey, and Richard R. Milligan—opened their personal files to me and also pointed out numerous other little-known and sometimes privately owned sources. I am especially thankful to a very kind and caring anonymous reviewer for the University of California Press, who had an important influence on the final version of this book. I am indebted, too, to the many historians who have gone before me and on whose work I drew for this study.

A number of friends, colleagues, family members, and teachers either lent moral support or read various forms of my manuscript and offered their thoughtful criticisms. They include the late Mary Anteaux, Edwin R. Bingham, Ross Bunnell, Stephanie Christelow, Glen A. Love, Nancy McFadden, Paul C. Pitzer, and Louise C. Wade. I am also grateful to Anne Montgomery not only for reading and commenting on my manuscript but also for our frequent hikes in the Oregon outdoors. Our saunter through the Willamette Valley's Finley National Wildlife Refuge, on a beautiful fall day in October 1987, enabled me to overcome one of my bouts with writer's block and move on to produce chapter 1. I also thank my parents, E. Guy and Olga M. Boag, for their love and support through the various stages of this undertaking.

During my years of work on this project I also received support from the graduate schools and departments of history at both the University of Oregon and Idaho State University. The staffs at the University of Oregon's Knight Library, the Oregon Historical Society, the Oregon State Library and Archives, and the Lane County and the Linn County Historical Museums all aided me in my research. I need to make special mention of the local history and genealogical contributors to the Brownsville (Oregon) Community Library. Because of their determination that records of their ancestors be maintained and made available, that otherwise small library contains a wealth of information without which this study would have been impossible. I especially thank Nancy Lane, former librarian there, for giving me free access to the collection.

I am also indebted to the various editors at the University of California Press who worked with me and my manuscript. Specifically, I wish to thank Lynne Withey, Sandria B. Freitag, Pamela MacFarland Holway, and Dan Gunter.

Finally, I am thankful that this project took me away from the desk and computer, outside libraries and archives, and onto the land. I will fondly remember the countless times I traveled to the Calapooia and into other areas of the Willamette Valley, went for walks, viewed the landscape, and tried to understand the landscape's side of the story.

Introduction

One late summer day in 1854, Wilson Blain, Presbyterian minister and early Oregon settler, left his home in the Calapooia Valley—a region of the larger Willamette Valley and the setting for this study—to journey to the neighboring valley to the south, the Mohawk. His purpose was to observe the progress of settlement there. That day, Blain and his traveling companion followed the only route connecting the two valleys: an old "Indian trail" that headed up a small creek into the forest and across the rugged ridge separating the Calapooia from the Mohawk. In the 1980s, while researching this study, I often visited the Calapooia. As a matter of convenience, from my home in Eugene I usually traveled Interstate 5 down the Willamette Valley. But for a change, on one of those trips I took the longer back route, which followed, though in reverse, Blain's trail of 1854. From Eugene, I drove up the Mohawk and then crossed the dividing ridge and descended into the Calapooia. The old Indian path is now a paved, two-lane highway. Enclosed within an automobile, I traveled this route in a matter of minutes, easily speeding across small rivers and creeks that Blain must have found difficult to ford safely—whereas my trip required virtually no physical exertion. Only because Blain was on my mind did I consider the rugged nature of the terrain. Also, around many a bend in the road I came on mixtures of fresh clearcuts and recently planted stands of timber. The forest is also cut through by a large corridor draped with high-power, electrical transmission wires. Here and there along the route I also chanced on modern homes, lawns, and driveways. My experience on the Calapooia landscape was, in short, much different from Blain's, which took place about five generations before mine.

I undertook this study in an attempt to answer questions about the relationship between nineteenth-century Euro-American settlers and western landscapes and the environment. I chose the Euro-American settlement community of the Calapooia Valley specifically, and the Willamette Valley generally, as the laboratory in which to find these answers. My initial questions were simple. What was the environmental experience and perception of early settlers in the West? And how did their experience and perception change over time with changes in landscape, environment, and settlement? In the process of examining these questions, a whole set of other questions arose. I began to wonder how the environmental experience of Euro-Americans in the Far West of the Willamette Valley differed from their experiences on previous American frontiers, particularly in cis-Appalachia.[1] What effect did Native Americans have on the environment and landscape that Euro-American settlers encountered, and how did the activities of Native Americans influence the settlers' thoughts and feelings? My study is therefore an investigation into the origins of, and the changes in, the western American environment, Euro-Americans' initial reaction to this environment, and the changes over time in the relationship between them (and their descendants) and the western landscape in the nineteenth century.

During my research I examined the vast historical and cultural literature concerning the nature of early Americans' intellectual relationship with the environment. I reacted strongly against the older interpretive tradition represented by scholars such as Hans Huth, Arthur A. Ekirch, Jr., and Roderick Nash, who place western pioneers at the center of an ongoing battle with the "wilderness." This interpretation, which is no longer accepted, argues that colonists and settlers saw the American wilderness as a threat to their survival and that its strange and fearful inhabitants (both real and imaginary) challenged their moral integrity.[2] In his classic *Wilderness and the American Mind*, Nash summed up the attitude westering Americans held toward their environmental surroundings: "In the morality play of westward expansion, wilderness was the villain, and the pioneer, as hero, relished its destruction."[3] Furthermore, this interpretation of the wilderness and settler relationship argues that a positive wilderness ethic emerged in this country only during the early and mid nineteenth century. It first appeared with a group of romantic poets and writers, such as William Cullen Bryant and James Fenimore Cooper, and painters of the Hudson River School, such as Thomas Cole and Frederick Church. It found its fullest expression among the Transcendentalists, with Henry David Thoreau often cited as the most important example. Unfortunately, this argument therefore has maintained that appreciation of wilderness was limited to intellectuals—that actual frontierspeople lived too close to the wilderness to enjoy it.

Another group of cultural-environmental historians has questioned the basic black-and-white assumption of the wilderness interpretation. One strand of this scholarly tradition—exemplified by Henry Nash Smith, Leo Marx, and, more recently, Barbara Novak—suggests that the romantic categories of the primitive and the pastoral, which dominated environmental interpretation in the eighteenth and nineteenth centuries, have had greater influence on their history and thought than has the concept of wilderness. One can safely draw the conclusion, furthermore, that the categories of the primitive and the pastoral suggest a more positive intellectual relationship between Americans and the environment than does the wilderness interpretation.[4]

Another strand in this debate is represented by Lee Clark Mitchell. Mitchell has eloquently argued that the positive view that Euro-Americans held about nineteenth-century westward expansion "masked the other side of progress: empire building required the destruction of a wilderness." Once Americans became aware of this devastation, many traveled West to record the last vestiges of a "vanishing wilderness" in paintings, novels, and poetry.[5] Mitchell, as opposed to earlier scholars concerned with the wilderness concept, declares that the roots of this feeling of loss extend deep into various levels of society. However, like supporters of the discarded wilderness interpretation, Mitchell also concentrates on the responses of America's intellectuals, artists, and writers to the western environment.

Together, these various interpretations reveal that the relationship between the Euro-American mind and the environment is multifaceted, often contradictory, and certainly not black-and-white. None of these studies has tackled the human intellectual-environmental relationship from a community perspective. To date, several superb environmental studies from a community approach have concentrated on social, economic, and ecological issues, but they have passed over the cultural-intellectual component of the relationship between the human and the land and thus also the relationships among the social, economic, and ecological aspects and the cultural and intellectual aspects.[6]

This study attempts both to begin to fill this void and to bridge interpretive gaps. A community history, it focuses on a variety of social, environmental, and intellectual relationships. The study is divided into three sections. Part 1 discusses the natural and Native American forces that created the Willamette Valley environment, outlines explorers' reactions to that environment, and sketches the cultural-environmental background of the Euro-American settlers who came to the Willamette, and specifically the Calapooia, in the mid nineteenth century. Part 2 considers early Euro-American settlers' material and intellectual responses and adjustments to the Calapooia and Willamette environment. Part 3 outlines the economic and consequently environmental changes settlers caused in the Calapooia and Willamette. The final chapter sums up answers to questions the study has posed and assesses how the connections among environmental, cultural, and social change affected the psychology of late nineteenth-century Calapooia and Willamette Valley residents.

This study demonstrates that the western settlers brought to their encounter with the environment a variety of cultural beliefs about wilderness, the primitive, and the pastoral and that much of their response to and interaction with the environment was positive. It also looks at environmental forces that acted independently of both Native Americans and Euro-American settlers and thus examines how environment and landscape shapes humans' cultural interpretations and beliefs. It reveals that the western experience changed over time and from place to place, as different environments shaped human activities differently. Also, this work demonstrates that the cultural history of the Calapooia settlers is a history with a pattern—a pattern woven into the movement of people on the landscape. Finally, this study attempts to reconnect the human mind with the land and to offer us lessons about our own relationship with the environment.

PART ONE

A Landscape and Its People

CHAPTER I

Valley of the Long Grasses

Prehistorically, the Willamette Valley's native peoples annually burned the valley floor to maintain a vegetative cover that provided foods necessary for their diet. This burning created in the valley large meadows interspersed with oak woodlands. Dense forests developed only in the foothills and along streams and rivers, where cooler and moister conditions prevailed, limiting the effects of fire. This was the Willamette Valley landscape that Canadian artist Paul Kane painted in 1847, before extensive white settlement (figure 1).

The natives' use of fire in the valley encouraged the vigorous growth of tall grasses such as tufted hairgrass (*Deschampsia caespitosa*), sloughgrass (*Beckmannia syzigachne*), meadow barley (*Hordeum brachyantheum*), and bluegrass (*Poa pretensis*), some of which reached several feet in height. The native peoples called these long grasses *kalapuya*. When Europeans came to the valley of the long grasses, they used this Native American word to refer to the Willamette's people, thus dubbing them the Kalapuya.[1]

Mid nineteenth-century Euro-American settlers found long grasses probably the most striking feature of the Willamette and Calapooia Valley landscape and remembered them for many years:

> In the early days the tall, rank grass covered all this valley. We would turn out our cattle on the valley and they would immediately be lost in the tall grass which reached higher than their backs. In looking for cattle it was impossible to find them by sight. It was necessary to listen for their bells, and when they were lying down to rest during the heat of the day, one might pass within a few feet without finding them.[2]

Figure 1.   Paul Kane, *The Walhamette River from a Mountain*. The Canadian artist Paul Kane rendered this painting of the mid Willamette Valley about thirty miles south of Oregon City in early January 1847. The painting shows extensive prairies interspersed with large patches of forest; no Euro-American settlements are shown. The middle and northern portions of the Willamette Valley had more extensive forested areas than did the southern portion, where the Calapooia is located. Courtesy of the Royal Ontario Museum, Toronto.

Long grasses composed only one environmental element of the Willamette and Calapooia valleys that natives and nature wove together into a complex landscape. Understanding the natural history of this landscape, and the effect of the Kalapuya people on it, is requisite to comprehending the drama Euro-American settlers staged on it after their arrival in the mid nineteenth century.

NATURAL HISTORY

Some fifty million years ago, the Pacific Northwest had a tropical climate. At that time, the landmass that later became the Willamette Valley lay completely submerged under the warm waters of the Pacific Ocean, whose tides lapped at the base of the ancient western Cascade Mountains. Roughly thirty million years ago, the ocean's waters began to subside to the west as huge basalt flows and folding and faulting uplifted new mountains, the Coast Range, from the floor of the Pacific.

The submerged Willamette Valley now lay between two mountain chains, acting as a catch basin for eroding sediment. During the next twenty-five million years, the Willamette Valley landmass slowly rose, the inland sea that covered it drained, and the present river valleys formed (map 1).[3]

About ten million years ago, basalt lava flowed and solidified across the northern outlet to the valley. The relatively modest flow of the Willamette River has been unable to breach this impediment, and thus over the millennia rich river alluvia of clay, silt, sand, and gravel collected behind it in the huge trough that is now the Willamette Valley. The ancient basalt flow forms a cliff over which the Willamette River plunges some fifty feet (figure 2).[4]

Roughly one million years ago, the earth's surface cooled, creating in North America a continental ice sheet that spread southward from the Arctic zone into the northernmost reaches of the Pacific Northwest. In high mountainous zones of the region, such as in the Cascades east of the Willamette, large alpine glaciers formed. Although these glaciers did not descend to the Willamette Valley lowlands, streams issuing from them carried yet more sediment down to the valley. At the end of this cool cycle, glaciers and the continental ice sheet retreated, releasing huge quantities of water and inundating the entire Willamette Valley with inland seas up to one hundred feet deep. By the time of the next glacial advance some sixty thousand years ago, however, the Willamette had once again been drained of its waters.[5]

During this next ice age, the advancing continental glacier dammed a fork of the Columbia River far to the northeast of the Willamette Valley, in what is now northeastern Washington and northern Idaho. Behind it formed a large lake. Several times as this ice sheet retreated, weakened, and broke before forming again, huge floods swept down the Columbia River. Because precipitous banks restricted the Columbia's flow downstream from its confluence with the Willamette River, floodwater carrying chunks of glacial ice washed all the way back to the southern portion of the Willamette Valley. Each time floodwater backed up into the Willamette, it destroyed the natural vegetation and deposited huge amounts of silt and even some large boulders.[6]

While the land was still marshy, only slowly draining from this cycle of flooding, a warming and drying period in the climate encouraged the growth of tree species such as Douglas fir (*Pseudotsuga menziesii*), Sitka spruce (*Picea sitchensis*), and western hemlock (*Tsuga heterophylla*) in

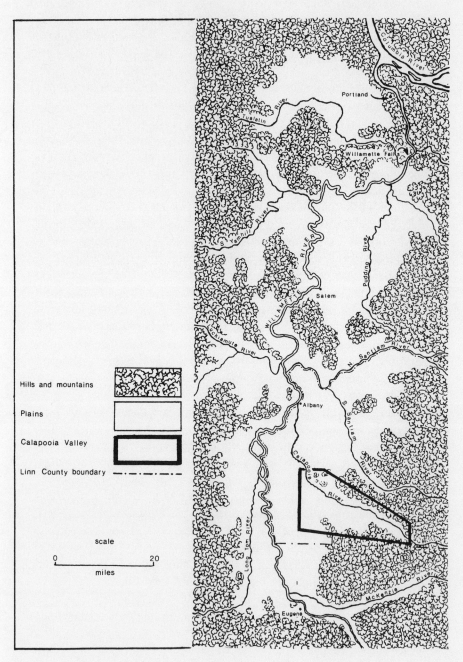

Hills and mountains

Plains

Calapooia Valley

Linn County boundary — · — · —

scale

0   20

miles

Portland

Tualatin River

Willamette Fall

Yamhill River

Pudding River

WILLAMETTE RIVER

Salem

Luckiamute River

N. Santiam River

·Albany

S. Santiam River

Calapooia River

Long Tom River

McKenzie River

·Eugene

Columbia River

Map 1.   The Willamette Valley.

Figure 2. Willamette Falls, 1878. Source: Wallis Nash, *Oregon: There and Back in 1877.*

higher areas and along the edges of the Willamette Valley. On the well-drained foothills surrounding the valley grew grand fir (*Abies grandis*) and ponderosa pine (*Pinus ponderosa*).[7]

Beginning about eleven thousand years ago and continuing until about four thousand years ago, the Northwest's climate became yet drier and warmer. During this period, marshlands and lakes on the Willamette Valley's floor receded farther, more grasses appeared, and the more drought-tolerant western white oak (*Quercus garryana*) and California black oak (*Quercus kelloggii*) became the dominant tree species. Today, western white oak naturally occurs from Vancouver Island south into California's central valleys, and thus grows throughout the Willamette. The California black oak's range, however, extends only as far north as the very southern portion of the Willamette Valley. It does not occur naturally north of there.[8]

About six thousand years ago, the valley became dry enough to inhabit, and humans descended to the valley floor from the surrounding hills, which they had occupied for at least two thousand and possibly as much as four thousand years.[9] Although these people did not know it, their very act of moving from foothills to valley floor revealed a tension between human occupation and the natural features of the Willamette's landscape. Recognizing this tension, especially with regard to the role of foothills and valley floor, is central for understanding the life and thought of nineteenth-century Euro-American settlers.

Two thousand years after humans arrived on the Willamette's floor, the climate again changed, initiating a cooler and moister pattern that has persisted up through and beyond the arrival of Europeans in the Pacific Northwest at the end of the eighteenth century. This climatological pattern has continued to the present, though indications are that the Willamette Valley, like much of the West, is entering another drying and warming period. During the last four thousand years, a strong marine influence has marked the region's climate. Winters are especially wet, though coastal mountains to the west protect the valley from severe winds and driving rains that blow in from the ocean. Storms coming in off the Pacific drop much of their precipitation as they pass over the coastal chain. The valley, left with gentle yet persistent rains that fall from mid autumn to late spring, receives as little as thirty inches of rain on the Coast Range's eastern slopes, but as much as sixty inches along valleys such as the Calapooia that reach back into the foothills of the Cascade mountains on the eastern margin of the Willamette. As the warm, wet winter winds push up the high Cascades, they cool and drop their remaining moisture as rain and snow in annual amounts of up to 120 inches. The Cascades also act as a cordon against the dry, frigid continental winds that influence the winter over much of the North American landmass to the east of the Willamette. This barrier, coupled with the Pacific's warm winter storms, keeps valley temperatures moderate in winter, with a mean of forty degrees Fahrenheit during the coldest months. Snow does occasionally fall on the valley floor, though it rarely lingers. The predominantly southwest winter winds off the Pacific shift to the north in late spring, bringing a drier and warmer period when little if any precipitation falls and the mean temperature reaches sixty-seven, with occasional hot spells resulting in daily temperatures of over one hundred. This pattern continues until the rainy season begins again in mid autumn.[10]

Precipitation falling on the Willamette's bordering foothills and mountains eventually finds its way to the valley floor, whose great expanse slopes gently, almost imperceptibly to the north. Native Americans and early European settlers witnessed how the absence of relief in the Willamette Valley forced streams, creeks, and rivers, after breaking out of the foothills, to meander sluggishly across the valley in a series of braided channels, oxbows, sloughs, and sandbars, depositing their sediments on banks that rose slightly above the surrounding plain. Choked with debris, vegetation, and mud islands, streams and rivers of the Willamette often overflowed onto nearby flood plains, leaving standing water for many months of the year. Lack of relief and drainage, coupled with occasional winter snows in the valley and foothills that melt quickly, caused major floods at least every tenth season, sometimes as often as every fifth season during prehistoric times.[11]

This moderate, seasonally moist climate, along with the marshy conditions that have characterized the Willamette Valley for four thousand years, has in large part determined the flora that grow there and that greeted the earliest Euro-American settlers. These first settlers found along the Willamette River and its tributaries on the flat valley floor extensive gallery forests—often up to two miles wide—composed of Oregon ash (*Fraxinus latifolia*), cottonwood (*Populus trichocarpa*), willows (*Salix* spp.), red alder (*Alnus rubra*), and bigleaf maple (*Acer macrophyllum*), with Douglas fir and western red cedar (*Thuja plicata*) sprinkled throughout. Along smaller streams such as the Calapooia, the gallery forests narrowed. Along the foothills of the Willamette Valley flourished Douglas fir, grand fir, ponderosa pine, and incense cedar (*Calocedrus decurrens*), with western hemlock and western red cedar thriving in moister and cooler yet well-drained areas along upper foothills and streams. Hardwood trees such as bigleaf maple, western white oak, and madrone (*Arbutus menziesii*) also grew in the foothills. Their understory consisted of shrubs such as hazelnut (*Corylus cornuta*), ocean spray (*Holodiscus discolor*), and snowberry (*Symphoricarpos albus*), and along prairie edges, smaller plants such as cheat grass (*Bromus vulgaris*), Oregon grape (*Mahonia nervosa*), and tarweed (*Madia* spp.). Between the foothills and the gallery forests of the Willamette Valley grew extensive meadows composed mostly of grasses, flowers, and scattered oak trees, or oak savanna.[12]

Ecologists apply the term *climax* to the theoretically highest stage of ecological succession, or evolution, of a plant-animal community or ecosystem. At climax, the ecosystem is stable and self-perpetuating. Climax does occur in nature, but other natural factors, such as disease and fire, limit the stability, persistence, and extensiveness of a climax community. Had the Willamette Valley been left to "nature," its gallery and foothill forests of maple, Douglas fir, and grand fir would theoretically have eventually covered the valley floor as a climax community. However, the Native American inhabitants of the Willamette, in order to ensure an abundance of the plants and animals essential to their diet and culture, used fire to keep the valley's flora in a fire-maintained subclimax state of grasslands and oak groves for hundreds of years.[13]

THE KALAPUYA

The Kalapuya traditionally occupied the Willamette Valley between the basalt cliff forming the falls in the north to the Umpqua River basin bounding the south. Ethnologists divide the Kalapuya into three distinct groups. The Tualatin-Yamhill Kalapuya occupied the northern valley, the Yoncalla lived in the south into the Umpqua region, and the Santiam-McKenzie inhabited the greater portion of the central and southern Willamette. Ethnologists have further divided each of these main groups into smaller tribelets or bands that occupied separate tributary valleys to the Willamette, such as the Santiam, Luckiamute, Long Tom, McKenzie, and St. Mary's. Each of these bands spoke a slightly different dialect of the Kalapuya language. Along the banks and in the valley of what Euro-Americans dubbed the Calapooia River lived the people who spoke a dialect that linguists call Tsankupi. It must be pointed out that all dialects were fairly similar because of close contact between bands and because all lived in a landscape that was almost uniform throughout the valley of the long grasses.[14]

The Kalapuya have posed a special problem to anthropologists who attempt to categorize Native American cultures. Although the Kalapuya occupied a near-coastal environment, they depended on plants rather than fish and other seafood as a staple; thus, they occupy a place on the cultural spectrum overlapped by the Northwest Coast and Columbia River Plateau groups. Anthropologists have perhaps best described the Kalapuya culture as a modified blend of "primitive river phase" and "grassland" because of the nature of the Willamette Valley, which has both abundant streams and rivers and extensive prairies.[15]

Though historians and ethnologists have debated the point, the best analysis places the maximum Kalapuya population at about 13,500, or very roughly fifty people per one hundred square miles, during the last quarter of the eighteenth century. The availability of food, partly determined by the environment, limited the size of the Kalapuya population. The Kalapuya relied primarily on plants, less so on game, and almost not at all on fish. Plant resources of the Willamette provided a diet that was less varied and less nutritious than were the diets of other Northwest Coastal groups, such as the Kalapuya's northern neighbors the Chinook of the Columbia River and the Coastal Salish of Puget Sound. These latter two groups relied principally on relatively abundant and nutritionally rich salmon and other forms of sea life, which could support larger and more densely concentrated human populations. The Chinook and Coast Salish populations reached densities of perhaps four hundred people per one hundred square miles. Conversely, the Willamette environment provided more abundant food sources than did the desertlike Columbia Plateau and the desert Great Basin regions east of the Cascades. In the most extreme case, the Northern Paiute of the Great Basin may have reached a population density of only five people per one hundred square miles.[16]

On first consideration, it might seem surprising that, unlike other Northwest Coastal peoples, the Kalapuya did not rely on salmon and other fish for sustenance even though through their backyard flowed the Willamette River, which is, in terms of water volume, the tenth largest river in the United States. During prehistoric and much of early historic times in the Northwest (until Euro-Americans introduced fish ladders), few salmon actually came to the upper Willamette River because the basalt cliff on the very northern course blocked them from entering the valley. Only the smaller run of spring chinook could negotiate the falls, because at that time of year increased water flow from rain and melting snows allowed the strongest salmon to swim over the barrier. The much larger fall run of chinook and silver salmon, the latter of which migrate only in the autumn, returned to the Northwest's streams after the long, dry summers, when low water flow prevented them from negotiating the falls of the Willamette. Furthermore, the powerful Chinook tribe, the Kalapuya's neighbors to the north, controlled access to the falls, preventing other groups from harvesting any of the returning spring salmon.

Charles Wilkes, an explorer from the United States Navy, visited a Hudson's Bay Company trading post at the falls on 5 June 1841 and recorded in his journal the following observations about the Chinook fishing operation:

> At the time of our visit to the falls, the salmon fishery was at its height, and was to us a novel as well as an amusing scene. The salmon leap the falls; and it would be inconceivable if not actually witnessed how they can force themselves up, and after a leap of from ten to twelve feet retain their strength enough to stem the force of the water from above. About one in ten of those who jumped succeed in getting by. . . . I never saw so many fish collected together before; and the Indians are employed in taking them.

The Chinook did, however, allow the Kalapuya to gather eels that clung to the basalt cliffs behind curtains of cascading water. The Kalapuya also collected eels and fished for salmon at smaller waterfalls and rapids on the Willamette's tributary streams, such as the falls on the Calapooia. Often they fished at night, by the light of pitchwood torches, and took their catch back to camp to preserve it for winter storage through drying and smoking. In their fishing the Kalapuya used bone-tipped spears, woven basketwork traps, weirs, and fishing poles with hair for string and grasshoppers for bait. But again, this food source played a relatively limited role in the Kalapuya's diet.[17]

Instead, the Kalapuya relied on plants, vegetable produce, and, to a lesser extent, wild game. To maximize food and natural resources in an environment not as naturally abundant as the lower Columbia River and the coast, the Kalapuya followed a seasonal routine, moving through a variety of task-specific sites and manipulating the environment through the use of fire to ensure the availability of food and other resources necessary for their culture. In late summer, when a number of other Pacific Northwest tribes congregated at fishing sites to harvest salmon, the Kalapuya converged on the dry Willamette Valley meadows to set fire to its grasses in order to encourage the growth of camas (*Camassia* spp.), the staple of their diet. Camas, a member of the lily family, requires open prairie habitat. Because geographical and climatological factors make lightning strikes in the Willamette rare, the valley would naturally have become overgrown with forest, and the camas would have become extinct. But the Kalapuya's intentional burning of the prairies at the end of each summer eliminated the camas's competition: shrubs and the seedlings of climax species such as Douglas fir and bigleaf maple. Since the bulb of the camas lies hidden underground and dormant at the end of summer, fire cannot directly affect this vital portion of the plant. During the following spring, the bulb multiplies and sprouts, sending up tall green shoots with spikes of purple, blue, and sometimes white flowers. Grass buds, also underground and thus also protected from fire, sprout in fall and grow during the mild winter and spring, but provide no competition for the camas.[18]

David Douglas, an English botanist who arrived in the Willamette Valley in the autumn of 1826, noted of the aftermath of burning, "Most parts of the country burned; only in little patches and on the flats near the low hills that verdure is to be seen." A few days later he commented, "As I walked nearly the whole of the last three days, my feet are very sore from the burned stumps of low brush-wood and strong grasses." Not only did the earliest European and Euro-American visitors and settlers in the Willamette Valley remark on the immediate effects of the Kalapuya's use of fire, but they also left records of the actual process and scene of burning. On 15 September 1841, W. D. Brackenridge noted as he traveled out of the southern Willamette Valley, "day very fine but dense with smoke from prairies in vicinity." Jesse Applegate, nephew of the more famous settler by the same name, left the following description of his family's encounter with one of the last of the Kalapuya burnings, which occurred in the early 1840s:

> This season the fire was started somewhere on the South Yamhill, and came sweeping up through the Salt Creek gap. The sea breeze being quite strong that evening, the flames leaped over the creek and came down upon us like an army with banners. All our skill and perseverance were required to save our camp. The flames swept by on both sides of the grove; then quickly closing ranks, made a clean sweep of all the country south and east of us. As the shades of night deepened, long lines of flame and smoke could be seen. . . . On dark nights the sheets of flame and tongues of fire and lurid clouds of smoke made a picture both awful and sublime.[19]

By burning the Willamette Valley, the Kalapuya altered the environment, prevented the growth of dense and continuous forests, and maintained a subclimax ecosystem of extensive grasslands and broad camas prairies. These grasslands also supported a variety of wildflowers: larkspur (*Delphinium* spp.), cranesbill (*Geranium dissectum*), yarrow (*Achillea millefolium*), aster (*Aster* spp.), scarlet gilia (*Gilia* sp.), monkeyflower (*Mimulus* spp.), poppy (*Eschscholzia californica*), buttercup (*Ranunculus* spp.), tarweed (*Madia* spp.), balsam root (*Balsamorhiza sagittata*), and narrow-leafed mule's ear (*Wyethia angustifolia*). Thickets or small forests of fir and maple still flourished in isolated patches throughout the valley, usually on the cooler and moister northern slopes of buttes and hills and often along river and stream banks. The northern Willamette, slightly wetter and much more hilly than the very

flat and open southern portions of the valley, had more densely forested areas. And, of course, trees grew profusely on the valley's surrounding foothills.[20]

The point where two or more ecosystems—such as a prairie and a
forest—intersect is a transitional zone ecologists call an *edge* or
ecotone. Edges support the most diverse biological populations of the
environment because plant and animal species native to both ecosystems and the transitional zone itself can be found there. At the edge
between forest and prairie ecosystems, furthermore, waterflow from
springs improves, and here, too, grow a profusion of transitional species
of woody shrubs whose sprouts make up the primary food source for
deer, which tend to be browsers rather than grazers. The Kalapuya
consciously preserved edges both to support white-tailed and black-
tailed deer populations and to concentrate them in certain areas to make
hunting easier. Douglas noted, "Some of the natives tell me it is done for
the purpose of [indu]cing the deer to frequent certain parts to feed,
which they leave unburned." Lewis Judson wrote, "These fir groves had
been found necessary by the Indians to induce deer and other wild game
to stay in the valley. The groves were undisturbed by fire. . . . The
Indians burned right up to imaginary lines, but never was the fire allowed to go past or get out of hand. So some authority existed among
them because biennially the prairies were burned."[21]

Burning the Willamette Valley also increased production of acorns,
another important component of the Kalapuya diet. Fire has little effect
on mature western white and California black oak trees, whose corklike
bark resists relatively cool ground fires fueled only by dead grass and
low-growing shrubs. Charles Wilkes noted the resistance of oaks to fire
when he sojourned in the Willamette in September 1841: "The country
had an uninviting look from the fact that it had lately been overrun by
fire, which had destroyed all the vegetation except the oak trees, which
appeared not to be injured." Oak trees dotted the grasslands of the
valley in groves or as single stately trees. The natural growth habits of
oaks and their constant subjection to fire prevented them from forming
extensive, densely canopied forests in the valley. Without competition
from other trees, oaks produce not only more leaves but more acorns as
well. And burning grass cover in late summer allowed natives more
easily to find ripe acorns that had fallen beneath the trees. The Kalapuya
thus resembled the natives of the central valleys of California, who also
depended on the acorn as their staple.[22]

The Kalapuya used fire in other ways, too. For instance, they used it as a tool of the hunt. In a practice called the *battue*, Kalapuya men encircled a parcel of territory and set a ring of fire; as the flames came together, so, too, did game animals, trapped within the walls of fire. When the circle of fire became smaller yet, hunters entered the ring and selectively shot game. Natives performed the battue at the end of summer and beginning of fall, when deer are fattest and healthiest and grasses and brush driest. But the Kalapuya carefully did not overhunt those animals they considered best for breeding purposes. Two Kalapuya men recalled, "They preserved the best males, the very young and best animals, with care. They could always find enough to answer their purposes without exterminating the game."[23]

The Kalapuya also employed fire to clear and fertilize land for the growing of tobacco, which was their only cultivated crop in the modern sense. Douglas reported, "An open place in the wood is chosen where there is dead wood, which they burn, and sow the seed in the ashes. . . . Thus we see that even the savages on the Columbia know the good effects produced on vegetation by the use of carbon."[24] Douglas, a product of European culture, looked down on the Kalapuya as inferior, but his own evidence supports the fact that these people had a deep awareness of the environment and the ways to alter it for their continued benefit.

Though camas was the staple of the Kalapuya diet, one of this people's strategies for survival in the Willamette was not to depend wholly on one or a limited number of foods. Thus, they also collected acorns and more than fifty other plants, including *wappato* (*Sagittaria* spp.), a kind of tuber that grew along lake shores in the northern valley. Again, fire aided the Kalapuya in collecting these foods. For instance, it parched the heads and pods of sunflowers such as balsam root, *Wyethia*, and tarweed, making their seeds easily shaken loose and collected. The Kalapuya also included a variety of animals and insects in their diet, such as grasshoppers, whose baked bodies they collected after burning. And prairie burning enhanced habitat for game animals other than deer. Shortly after the fires of late summer and early autumn, rains returned to the Willamette, encouraging grasses to green up in the burned-over areas. Elk, moving down from mountains at this time, and migrating geese, swans, ducks, and other fowl in both fall and spring concentrated to graze on and feed among these fresh young grasses. This concentration made hunting much easier. In addition to this game, other meat sources for the Kalapuya included beaver, river otter, musk-rat, black bear, cougar, bobcat, rabbit, squirrel, and raccoon. The Kalapuya's diversity of food sources guaranteed security.[25]

The Kalapuya maximized resources for their survival through burning and reliance on a great variety of foods. Both these strategies made up components of their larger, complex approach to survival: seasonal movements. In moving seasonally to different ecosystems of the valley and surrounding hills and mountains, the Kalapuya avoided relying on, and thereby overusing, certain food sources. The Kalapuya also moved to various sites to gain access to a wide variety of animals and plants that provided other materials necessary for their culture. Different seasons and landscapes provided different types of food and resources.

In winter the Kalapuya congregated in seasonally permanent villages located among willow, maple, and cottonwood thickets that bordered large streams such as the Calapooia. There they occupied large, rectangular, cedar bark and plank lodges, architecturally similar to the cedar plank houses of other coastal tribes from northern California to southern Alaska. Since western red cedar did not grow in some of the drier parts of the valley, the Kalapuya often substituted brush, mats, and bark as construction materials. Inside these lodges, the Kalapuya excavated floors of several feet in depth for hearths, drying racks, and cooking utensils. They arranged sleeping quarters along the edge of the lodge. Each lodge housed several related families and a group leader. All members worked together on tasks of hunting, gathering, and childcare. During winter occupation of villages, the Kalapuya engaged in story-telling and produced mats, baskets, and winnowing trays from tules, cattails, and beargrass while they lived off reserves stored up during the preceding seasons.[26]

In the springtime, the Kalapuya harvested camas and hunted migratory fowl. As was typical of the sexual division of labor found among other Native Americans, Kalapuya women performed all the plant collection and preservation while men hunted. In the spring, women moved out from the winter villages onto the broad floodplains of the Willamette Valley, where they dug camas with wood and bone tools. Spring proved the best time for camas collecting for a number of reasons. First, at the end of winter the plains of the valley, largely composed of clay, are saturated, and digging is much easier than it is later in the summer, when the soil dries and hardens. Second, death camas (*Zigadenus venenosus*), a poisonous plant, occasionally grows among the edible camas. By digging in spring and early summer, the blooming seasons, the Kalapuya could differentiate between the two plants' distinctive blossoms. Once the camas bulbs were collected, women preserved them by baking them in huge earthen ovens between alternating layers of hot rocks and coals, maple leaves, and soil; they then stored the bulbs in earthen pits for winter months. Meanwhile, men hunted migratory fowl, which returned to the valley at this time.[27]

In the summer, large portions of the native population retreated to the foothills. There men hunted with bow and arrow, pitfall traps, and snares, and women preserved hides and furs of captured game. They also picked and preserved ripening wild cherries (*Prunus emarginata*), elderberries (*Sambucus cerulea* and *S. rocemosa*), huckleberries (*Vaccinium parvifolium*), salmonberries (*Rubus spectabilis*), thimbleberries (*Rubus parviflorus*), hazelnuts, and bracken (*Pteridium aquilinum*), patches of which the women burned at the end of the season to ensure vigorous growth and production the following year. At sites adjacent to streams in the foothills, the Kalapuya worked oak, yew (*Taxus brevifolia*), and cedar boughs into tools. At the end of summer, they moved back down to the floor of the Willamette for annual prairie burning, acorn collecting, seed harvesting, and deer hunting. In the autumn, migratory fowl flocked through the valley once again, providing men another opportunity for hunting. As this season ended, the Kalapuya once more took up residence in their winter dwelling villages, and the cycle began anew.[28]

Within natural limits, the Kalapuya altered the environment of the valley of the long grasses. But relative stability marked the environment they and nature created, and thus their relationship to it. The Kalapuya's continuous cycle of seasonal movements among various ecosystems of the valley is one indicator of stability in the human-environmental relationship. Other evidence is seen in the fact that the Kalapuya took and stored not more than they needed to make it through the year, thus ensuring a relative balance between themselves and nature.

The stability of the environment and human-environmental association is also manifested in the Kalapuya's intellectual or spiritual relationship with the landscape and its other inhabitants. Native American novelist N. Scott Momaday has pointed out that in the native mind "nature is not something apart from him. He conceives of it, rather, as an element in which he exists." Thus, landscape to the Kalapuya was more than just individual components of weather, contour, vegetation, and wild animals that were external to themselves as people and that played roles in their survival. These ingredients of the environment shared a deep kinship with the Kalapuya people, both physically and spiritually. In the Atfalti Kalapuya's four-phase creation story, for example, Crow, Dog, Moon, Sun, and trees play various roles as progenitors to humans, who themselves become elements of the universe: stars, pebbles, and clouds.[29]

The spirit quest—the central event in the life of a Kalapuya—demonstrates best the shared bonds between these people and the environment. The spirit quest marked the passage from childhood to adulthood for boys—and in many bands, girls, too. A boy who wished to become a shaman sought his spirit power in the natural world:

> He was always swimming in the early morning. And when it would become dark at night and the moon was full, then he would go to the mountain. He would fix up that spirit power place on the mountain. He would go five nights. Always in the early morning he would be swimming. And then he would find his spirit power. While he slept he would see the dream-power, his spirit-power. That is how he did all the time.

This particular story shows the important role that inanimate fixtures of the landscape, such as water and mountains, played in the psychological quest of a young Kalapuya. In addition, the spirit powers a Kalapuya could gain during this quest all derived from the natural environment. For example, one Yamhill Kalapuya man's "spirit-power was thunder, when thunder roared, and when it rained down quantities of water. And another too of his spirit-powers, his spirit-power was deer they say." Others derived spirit power from various animals who played key roles in mythology. The coyote was a trickster, the fly a tattletale, the cougar a hero, the bobcat a heroine, the raccoon a miser, the elk a water monster, and the spider the protector of women; the eagle aided the grizzly, which was considered a villain and which crows, gray squirrels, and dogs worked together to deceive.[30]

In Kalapuya myths, furthermore, animals play central roles in the origin of landscape. One tale relates how Meadowlark and Coyote created the waterfall on the Willamette River at the northern end of the valley. They took a rope between them and stretched it tight:

> Coyote pulled hard. Meadowlark pulled with all her strength and pressed her feet against the rock she was standing on. Then Coyote called on his powers and turned the rope into a rock. The river poured over the rock. . . .

Meadowlark pressed her feet on the rock so hard that she made footprints. Her footprints stayed there for hundreds and hundreds of years.[31]

Creation stories, spirit quests, and myths reveal the Kalapuya's intellectual relationship with the natural environment. Simply, they saw humans, animals, and land interconnected.

Momaday's assertion and the intellectual evidence of the Kalapuya's
myths, combined with the ecological, biological, and anthropological
record, strongly suggest that the Willamette Valley of the Kalapuya was
a relatively stable, self-perpetuating, and therefore balanced cultural-
ecological community. Europeans and Euro-Americans began to arrive
in the Willamette region around 1800. They introduced into this environment new pathogens, new plant and animal species, a linear conception of time, and a new intellectual relationship with nature. The
cultural-ecological balance the Kalapuya had achieved was soon destroyed, releasing incredible natural energies and creating a new
cultural-ecological community of relative instability. The psychological
and biological effects of this instability on Euro-American settlement
and community are the subject of the greater portion of the remainder
of this book.

The Kalapuya, like so many other native peoples of North America,
met with a tragic demise after their contact with Europeans. Destruction
of native North American populations came in different ways. The
quickest mechanism was exposure to European diseases for which Native Americans had no immunities. Another, subtler mechanism was the
result of European disruption of native economies and cultural practices. Natives who engaged in the fur trade, for instance, easily adapted
to and became dependent on European trade goods, tools, guns, blan-
kets, and sometimes food; when a disruption, such as a depression,
occurred in the economy, natives were no longer able to acquire those
goods to which they had become accustomed. This deprivation often
resulted in starvation. Cultural practices were also thrown into disorder
when European or Euro-American settlers took important food-
gathering sites from natives or turned loose their livestock to graze and
root on those sites.[32]

All these factors played a role in the demise of the Kalapuya, but
disease had the greatest effect. The first epidemic to plague the Northwest was smallpox, which swept westward from the Midwest in 1782–
83. After ravaging the more densely populated coast and lower Columbia River, the disease moved inland and attacked the Kalapuya. Vene-

real disease spread inland from the mouth of the Columbia in the 1790s, after the first explorers' ships arrived. The Kalapuya began to gain back some of their population before the most devastating epidemic struck them between 1830 and 1833. This epidemic was classically known as "fever and ague," but it is now believed to have been malaria, which Europeans imported on their ships that visited the Hawaiian Islands before arriving in the Northwest. In the early nineteenth century, the Willamette Valley's great expanses of marshes and its few lakes, such as Labish and Wapato, ideally suited it for the breeding of malaria-infected mosquitoes. In addition, some scholars have pointed out that two cultural habits of the Kalapuya exacerbated the spread and severity of the disease. First, their food-gathering patterns and techniques brought them into mosquito-infested areas of the Willamette. Second, the Kalapuya's traditional treatment for illness—sweating in lodges followed by jumping into cold water—only quickened their demise, for pneumonia often followed.

As early white settlers recalled, the Kalapuya also used this method of therapy to treat other diseases brought by Europeans: "When the measles broke out among the Indians near the Morgan claim [on the Calapooia River] they treated the disease in their traditional manner by sweat-houses and a plunge into the cold water of the creek. That, of course, was fatal. My people tried desperately to persuade them to do differently but it was no use." This same informant added that the Kalapuya's "customs were too strong for a white man's argument to nullify. As a result a great percent of the village died."[33]

Estimates suggest that between 1830 and 1833 as many as six thousand Chinook and Kalapuya died along the lower Columbia and lower one hundred miles of the Willamette. Malaria continued to plague the valley in pockets through the early 1840s, and in the 1830s other epidemics and diseases, such as dysentery, tuberculosis, and venereal infections, spread among the natives. It must be stressed that not all deaths resulted directly from disease. Even if only a small portion of a village or band contracted an illness, the reduction in numbers could disrupt seasonal movements, burning practices, and everyday activities, leaving uninfected children and adults unable adequately to perform duties required for daily and winter survival. Often starvation resulted. Both directly and indirectly through the effects of disease, the Kalapuya's demise was nearly complete by the mid 1840s. Methodist-Episcopal missionary Daniel Lee, nephew of Jason Lee and cofounder of the Methodist Mission built in the mid Willamette Valley in 1834, remarked "there are only a few most miserable remnants left . . . and are scattered over the most part of the Walamet Valley, and will not number more than from 500 to 800." Estimates indicate that by 1841 only six hundred Kalapuya survived in the valley, and by 1844 this number had been cut in half.[34]

Evidence also suggests that disruption of the Kalapuya culture came through contact with the European/Euro-American economy and through actual settlement. These factors, however, had only a limited effect.[35] James L. Ratcliff's "What Happened to the Kalapuya?"—the only study to date on the subject—relies on evidence from the year 1838, five to six years after the worst of the malaria epidemic had already wiped out the greatest number of Kalapuya. Ratcliff claims that in that year the fourteen French families (retired employees of the Hudson's Bay Company) who had permanently settled in the Willamette Valley (the only settlement at that time other than a mission) had "reduced the camas acreage on the prairies of the valley" to the point that they had "deprived the Kalapuya of their vegetable staples." In reality, the French settlement covered a relatively small area of the very northern Willamette Valley. The settlers had enclosed 700 acres and cultivated another 550—an area of about two square miles. The settlement also had livestock, 400 hogs and 150 horses, which roamed about the local area. Although the French settlement undoubtedly had an influence on the local camas prairies, it had no impact on the great expanse of the Willamette Valley to the south.

In addition to this evidence of settlers affecting only one small locale at most, Ratcliff argues that the three gristmills on Willamette Valley's rivers and streams in 1838 significantly undercut the Kalapuya's fishing. In fact, though, the mills probably had no effect on the Kalapuya. One mill was located on Willamette Falls, which, as demonstrated above, played no vital role in their food gathering. And no mill existed at this time in the southern Willamette. In addition, the Kalapuya diet relied very little on fish. The effect of the fur trade in the Willamette is also unclear. The Willamette never produced large quantities of beaver, and trapping there was, as Ratcliff notes, conducted primarily by European trappers themselves and not the Kalapuya. Trappers undoubtedly traded with some Kalapuya, drawing them into the European economy, and trappers may have competed with Kalapuya for game, but such a small number of trappers would have had negligible impact. In minor ways, the fur trade and settlement that came at the end of the malaria epidemics undoubtedly affected the cultural practices of the few remaining Kalapuya. But evidence of debilitating diseases provides the best answer to the question of what caused the cultural disruption and death of these people.

An interesting point, however, is that the Kalapuya viewed the tragedy of their destruction as the result not of disease but of the changes in the landscape caused by European and Euro-American settlers. One of the Kalapuya tales from this time shows that they attempted to explain what happened to them as the fulfillment of a shaman's prescient dream: "Long ago the people use to say that one great shaman had seen . . . all the land black in his dream. 'This earth was all black (in my dream).' . . . Just what that was he did not know. And then (later on) the rest of the people saw the whites plough up the ground. Now then they said, 'That must have been what it was that the shaman saw long ago in his sleep.' " After the destruction, the few remaining Kalapuya looked back to the past with lamentation: "This countryside is not good now. Long, long ago it was good country (had better hunting and food gathering). They were all Indians who lived in this countryside. Everything was good. Only a man went hunting. . . . Women always used to dig camas, and they gathered tarweed seeds."[36]

Because the Kalapuya had no written tradition, we have only limited sources from their perspective on their interaction with Euro-American settlers. None relates battle with disease. Folklorists note that the stories of a people relate that which is most significant about their experience. Although the central role of disease in the demise of the Kalapuya is unquestionable, the wider implications of their experience is best captured in their own stories. It is clear that what was most significant to the Kalapuya was their loss of connection with the land, at the hands of settlers, on both the psychological and physical levels.

Though the Kalapuya had all but vanished by the commencement of extensive white settlement in the 1840s, the landscape that they and nature had created remained. Obviously, once the Kalapuya disappeared from the valley, the environment of the long grasses underwent a drastic change. But during the last days of the Kalapuya and the first days of European and Euro-American presence, the landscape of the Willamette appeared much as it had for hundreds of years. This appearance and actual physical nature captivated European and Euro-American explorers. It greatly influenced their early perceptions of and ideas about the relationship between themselves and the landscape of the valley, setting the foundations of settlement culture that influenced life and thought during the remainder of the nineteenth century.

EARLY OBSERVATIONS

The first recorded observations about the Willamette landscape and environment come from European and Euro-American fur trappers, settlement promoters, and official and unofficial explorers between 1811 and the early 1840s. The latter arrivals in this group often coincided with, and were sometimes linked to, the actual settlement of the valley. Not surprisingly, the reasons these observers had for journeying to the Willamette Valley conditioned their responses to it. All recorded descriptions of the valley can, to varying degrees, be categorized as comments on either its wilderness/primitive values or its pastoral/garden image, the two primary ways, according to Leo Marx, that early and mid nineteenth century Americans and Europeans assessed the environment.[37]

On one end of the spectrum, early observers perceived the Willamette as a wilderness and its inhabitants as uncivilized or primitive. For example, trained botanist David Douglas recognized that the Kalapuya had in some ways modified the Willamette's environment, but he nevertheless viewed them as "savages." In 1841, the American explorer Charles Wilkes, while ascertaining the strength of the British and the prospects for American settlement in the disputed Oregon Country, compared the Willamette's landscape to a domestic pastoral scene; he described the foothills of the southern Willamette as "destitute of trees, except oaks," which appeared "more like orchards of fruit trees, planted by the hand of man than groves of natural growth, and serve to relieve the eye from the yellow and scorched hue of the plains." He added, however, that no mistake could be made about the oaks' domestic state, for the groves were interspersed through great stretches of "wild prairie-ground." In this passage, Wilkes shows his failure to understand the beautiful landscape he beheld, for, although the oak groves were not exactly cultivated orchards, neither were they "natural." Wilkes, like Douglas, knew that the Kalapuya used fire on the valley floor, but he did not consider that fire both gave the oaks their orchardlike appearance and created what he described as "wild prairie."[38]

Wilkes's observations also reveal a central tension, even dichotomy, in the way European and Euro-American commentators perceived the environment of North America generally and the Willamette Valley specifically. Wilkes noted the wildness of the Willamette, but he also, often within the same passages, saw the environment in pastoral terms, as a product of the "hand of man."

Others who, like Wilkes, had political or economic stakes in the future of the Willamette Valley described it in similar terms—either as a pastoral setting in its present condition or as a landscape suitable for the cultivation of a garden. Early French-Canadian settler Francis Xavier Matthieu, for instance, compared the Willamette to a pastoral scene when he noted that the country of the French settlement was in the "condition of a park." And Wilkes's British counterparts Henry Warre and Mervyn Vavasour wrote in the 1840s that the valley offered "a field for an industrious civilized community."[39]

In *The Machine in the Garden*, Leo Marx discusses how Americans' concept of the pastoral changed over the course of the eighteenth and nineteenth centuries. By the end of the first half of the nineteenth century, when industrialization—which could be antithetical to the pastoral ideal—had definitely begun to make a mark on the landscape, Americans had broadened their definition of the pastoral to make allowance for the encroachment of "the machine" into the garden. In the Willamette Valley, evidence from the group of observers to which Wilkes, Matthieu, Warre, and Vavasour belonged demonstrates that they had accepted at least the role of industrialism in their pastoral conception by the 1840s. For instance, American immigrant promoter and settler Joel Palmer stated that the "small mountain streams" that crossed the southern portion of the valley had "valuable water privileges for such machinery as may be erected, when yankee enterprise shall have settled and improved this desirable portion of our great republic."[40]

On the other end of the pastoral-primitive spectrum from the group to which Wilkes and Palmer belonged were those who came to the Willamette Valley without economic or political stakes in its future and who thus looked on its scenery differently. David Douglas, whom the British Royal Horticultural Society sent to the Oregon Country to study and collect rare and previously undiscovered plant specimens, had no stake in the future of the Willamette. His journals commented only on the primitive beauty of the valley without reference to pastoral images. For example, he wrote, "Country undulating: soil rich, light with beautiful solitary oaks and pines interspersed through it, and must have a fine effect, but being burned and not a single blade of grass except on the margins of rivulets to be seen." Another time he remarked simply, "Country open, rich, level, and beautiful." Although economic factors motivated fur trapper Alexander Henry's sojourn in the Willamette in January of 1814, he envisioned no great transformation of the region and thus focused his attention on its primitive beauty: "The country is pleasant, thinly shaded with oak, pine, liard, alder, soft maple, ash, hazel, etc. At a short distance are ranges of grassy hills, where not a stick of wood grows; the prospect is delightful in summer, when blooming and verdant."[41]

Both Henry's and Douglas's journals reveal neither grandiose political nor economic plans for the Willamette Valley's future. These motivations, however, tempered the writings of others, such as Wilkes, Matthieu, and Palmer, and the future of the valley's environment would largely be left to people of their tradition. An interesting point is that, although these other observers noted the existing and potential pastoral nature of the Willamette, they also could not help but be drawn to its primitive beauty. Warre and Vavasour commented, "To the eye the country, particularly the left bank of the river, is very beautiful. Wide extended, undulating prairies, scattered over with magnificent oak trees, and watered by numerous tributary streams." Wilkes noted of the prairie scenery that captivated him in June 1841, "We passed in going thither, several fine prairies, both high and low. . . . The prairies are at least one-third greater in extent than the forest: they were again seen carpeted with the most luxuriant growth of flowers, of the richest tints of red, yellow and blue, extending in places a distance of fifteen to twenty miles." That same summer he remarked how the prairies, "covered with variegated flowers . . . added to the beauty as well as the novelty of the scenery." Seven years later, American settler and immigrant promoter George Atkinson prefaced his observations of the valley's pastoral image ("The oak groves on the slopes of the hills appear like orchards of the finest park scenery") with the remark, "broad prairies, forests, bands of woodland surrounding beautiful meadows . . . a vast region of prairies surrounded by hills." William A. Slacum, whom President Andrew Jackson commissioned to examine and report on Pacific coast settlements, surveyed the Willamette in 1837, showing a particular sensitivity to color:

> In ascending this beautiful river, even in midwinter, you find both sides clothed in evergreen, presenting a more beautiful prospect than the Ohio in June. For 10 to 12 miles, on the left bank, the river is low and occasionally

overflows. On the right the land rises gradually from the water's edge, covered with firs, cedar, laurel, and pine. The oak and ash is at this season covered with long moss, of a pale sage green, contrasting finely with the deeper tints of the evergreens.[42]

Some early observers of the Willamette Valley waxed more poetic in their descriptions of its primitive scenery. For instance, Gustavus Hines, who came with the Jason Lee Mission in the 1830s, noted, "Throughout these valleys [Umpqua, Klamath, and Willamette] are scattered numberless hillocks and rising grounds, from the top of some of which, scenery, as enchanting as was ever presented to the eye, delights and charms the lover of nature, who takes time to visit their conical summits."[43] Hines's description of the valley's foothills also pointed to an important aspect of the valley's landscape that could not be valued in economic terms or be captured in the pastoral image.

Writers' differing political and economic conceptions of the valley's future did temper their interpretation of the landscape's utilitarian potential, but this underlying theme of agreement about the valley's primitive or wilderness beauty gives continuity to the early exploration literature that came out of the Willamette. Overwhelmingly, however, pastoral and utilitarian conceptions seem to provide the constant counterpoint to the magnificence attributed to the primitive, natural beauty of the Willamette landscape in early writings. As a single feature of the valley's landscape, the awe-inspiring falls on the Willamette River perhaps best show this tension between the valley's undeveloped "wilderness" beauty and the economic utility it could provide as a pastoral landscape. When Alexander Henry came to the falls on 23 January 1814, he expressed his attraction to the view by simply stating that the falls had a "wild, romantic appearance." Thirty-two years later, Lieutenant Neil M. Howison, while examining affairs for the United States in the Pacific Northwest, wrote at length about the scene he witnessed at the falls on a summer day: "the sun's rays reflected from these cliffs make the temperature high, and create an unpleasant sensation of confinement, which would be insupportable but for the refreshing influence of the waterfall: this, divided by rocky islets, breaks into flash and foam, imparting a delicious brightness to this otherwise somber scenery." Hines also commented on the "beautiful cataract" but immediately brought in his ideas on development when he proclaimed, "The hydraulic privileges which it affords, and which are beginning to be extremely used, are almost boundless." And in 1841,

Charles Wilkes mentioned only utilitarian potential of the falls, which "offer the best mill-site of any place in the neighboring country. Being at the head of the navigation for sea-vessels, and near the wheat growing valley of the Willamette, it must be a place of great resort."[44]

The falls on the Willamette played an instrumental role in the environmental prehistory of the valley of the long grasses. The Kalapuya had even assigned them mythical significance. The falls also found their way into early European and Euro-American travel, exploration, and settlement literature about the Oregon Country. Europeans and Euro-Americans interpreted the falls' physical composition with relevance to their own culture. On the one hand, they remarked on the falls' primitive, natural, or wild beauty and effect on the senses. On the other hand, they easily cast the falls as an essential element of a future Euro-American pastoral landscape.

Primitivism and pastoralism in exploration literature concerning the valley of the long grasses can be refined into competing conceptions of natural beauty and industrial and agricultural utility. Those who settled in the tributary valley of the Calapooia would use these two concepts, as well as the concept of progress, as they viewed the land through the nineteenth century. These attitudes challenged the views that the Kalapuya had held. In the process of realizing these conceptions—thus replacing the Kalapuya and acting on a whole different set of cultural values—Euro-American settlers brought incredible changes to the environment of the Willamette within only a few years of settlement.

But in addition to harboring the two conceptions of utility and natural beauty as ways of looking at the landscape, settlers realized a third component in their relationship to the land that transient observers never did. As settlers and therefore insiders, they intimately interacted with it, partly changed it and partly molded their ways to it, and, most significantly, grew attached to it.

CHAPTER II

Life and Culture
on an Old Landscape:
Cis-Appalachian Antecedents

One early September day in 1847, John Courtney, who had settled on a small creek in the Calapooia Valley a year earlier, left his claim to make the seventy mile journey to Oregon City to obtain supplies. While in Oregon City he met friends, the Rinearsons, who had taken a claim nearby. They needed help in clearing their land, and Courtney was a good man to ask for assistance, since he operated a small sawmill in the Calapooia and had experience felling trees. On 12 September, Courtney and some other men used hot rocks to burn the trunks of trees targeted for removal on the Rinearson claim. That day Courtney's experience failed him, for when one particular tree began to fall, he became confused and ran in the wrong direction. "As a consequence he was struck by the falling giant of the forest and instantly killed."[1]

We do not know just how John's wife, Agnes, better known as Nancy to friends and neighbors, heard and took the news of his death. Documents do reveal, however, that she continued to reside on her and her late husband's claim in the Calapooia Valley on the creek that would later bear the Courtney name. Eventually she even obtained title to her property under the Oregon Donation Land Law.

Before coming to the Calapooia, Agnes Courtney had spent her life in the Ohio and eastern Mississippi valleys, a region referred to in this chapter as cis-Appalachia. Born 11 May 1795 in western Pennsylvania, in 1809 Agnes headed west with her parents to Ohio. In 1812, in Clarke

County, Indiana, she married her first husband, Alexander Findley. Widowed with no children in 1817, Agnes married John Courtney the following year. Their first four children were born in Indiana between 1819 and 1828. By 1836 Agnes had given birth to three more children in Illinois. In 1843 the Courtney family migrated to the Willamette Valley from their residence in Missouri.[2]

Agnes Courtney's origins, her general migratory pattern down the Ohio Valley before proceeding to the Far West and settling on the Calapooia, and thus her experiences on the cis-Appalachian landscape typify those of other early settlers of the Oregon Country. To understand the cultural-environmental baggage these pioneers brought with them to the Willamette Valley in the 1840s and 1850s, and therefore their physical and psychological responses to its environment at this time, this chapter briefly sketches and analyzes their origins in, and their experiences on, the landscape of cis-Appalachia.[3]

Of the 174 individuals who filed land claims under the federally sponsored Oregon Donation Land Law on the Calapooia between 1850 and 1855, we have birth records for 161 (table 1) and complete vital information (birth, marriage, death, and children's birth dates and places) for 65 claimants and 56 of their spouses (or a total of 121 people). Of these 121 claimants and spouses, 21 percent had birthplaces in the older eastern regions and states of New England, New York, Pennsylvania, Maryland, Virginia, North Carolina, and South Carolina. The younger cis-Appalachian states of Tennessee, Kentucky, Ohio, and Indiana were the birthplaces of a majority (55 percent) of these claimants and spouses. The still more recently settled areas of Illinois, Missouri, and Iowa supplied only 19 percent of the total number of settlers for whom we have biographical information. The other 5 percent were born in Oregon, Michigan, and foreign countries.[4]

The marriage places for the sixty-five claimant couples for whom we have information and the birthplaces of their children were farther west than were the birthplaces of the claimants and their spouses themselves. Sixty percent of these couples married in Illinois, Missouri, Iowa, and Oregon, and only 29 percent married in the older states of Tennessee, Kentucky, Indiana, and Ohio. Only two marriages took place in the eastern seaboard states. Birthplaces for the 174 children born to couples before coming to Oregon centered even farther west than their parents' marriage places. Missouri, Illinois, and Iowa were the birthplaces of

TABLE 1

CALAPOOIA DONATION LAND CLAIMANTS'
BIRTHPLACES AND DATES OF BIRTH

Place of Birth	Number	Year of Birth[a]
Pennsylvania/Maryland	14	1811
Virginia/Carolinas	20	1813
Kentucky/Tennessee	42	1818
New York/New England	17	1820
Ohio	25	1821
Indiana	17	1827
Illinois/Missouri (1 from Arkansas)	26	1829
Total	161[b]	

SOURCE: Genealogical Forum of Portland, *Genealogical Materials.*
   [a]Year of birth is the simple average for the number of claimants from a state or region.
   [b]Total number of claimants in the Calapooia study area was 174, with 13 born in foreign countries or unknown origin.

114, or 66 percent, of these children, while 39, or 22 percent, were born in Indiana, and only 16, or 9 percent, had birthplaces in Tennessee, Kentucky, and Ohio. The other 3 percent were born in other states.

In general, then, the adult population of the Calapooia during the initial stages of settlement had been born in the upper southern states of Kentucky and Tennessee, some others in Virginia, Pennsylvania, and the Carolinas, and a mere handful in New England and New York. These people grew up in Kentucky, Tennessee, Ohio, Indiana, and Illinois. They married in Indiana, Illinois, and Missouri, had their first children in the latter two states, and then moved on to Oregon and settled on the Calapooia.[5]

Although the life of Agnes Courtney fits perfectly this pattern of westward movement to the Calapooia, the rapidity with which she left a mid-Atlantic state and made her way to Oregon—during a single lifetime—was atypical. Most Calapooia settlers descended from families who took several generations to make their way across the cis-Appalachian region before coming to Oregon. For example, Nancy Shields, who settled on the Calapooia in the early 1850s, came from such a family. Her grandfather John was born in Maryland in 1755, married Mary McCollum in the 1790s, and died in Tennessee in 1833. John and Mary's son William, Nancy's father, was born in Jefferson County, Tennessee, in 1799, moved to Indiana in 1819, and there married three times. His third marriage was to Judith Bybee, who had been born in Kentucky in 1810. They had eight children in Indiana and Illinois before emigrating to the Willamette Valley in 1851. Similarly, Abraham Wigle's great-grandfather, John Wigle, came to Pennsylvania from Germany during the latter part of the eighteenth century. After residing in Pennsylvania only a short while, he "went to Kentucky when that country was a wilderness and inhabited by savage Indians." There he married Margaret Wolf. They remained in Kentucky only a few years before moving to Missouri, settling in Cape Girardeau County. In 1827 the Wigle family moved back across the Mississippi River to Adams County, Illinois. In Illinois, John and Margaret's son Jacob, who had been born in Missouri in 1807, married Nancy Hunsucker from Kentucky. It was their son Abraham who finally completed the Wigles's westward trek when he crossed the plains to Oregon and settled on the Calapooia in 1852.[6]

Settlers like Courtney, Shields, and Wigle came to the Calapooia with a culture defined in the mid-Atlantic seaboard states and tempered on the upper southern and midwestern landscape. In Kentucky, Tennessee, and especially along the eastern Ohio River, the western immigrants encountered a landscape of hardwood forests similar to what they had left behind in Pennsylvania and Virginia. These forests included oak, hickory, beech, maple, cherry, walnut, ash, and other deciduous hardwoods, whose growth indicated to settlers soil fertility. Historian Arthur K. Moore describes the forests of Kentucky as open, "not altogether treeless but with trees wide apart." Among these trees and in the open canebrakes of central Kentucky, settlers found excellent grazing; after clearing the land there, they raised corn. In Kentucky's woodlands, a cultural continuity of forest living between the eastern seaboard and cis-Appalachia remained unbroken. Historian Allan G. Bogue comments that for "generations pioneers had slashed out their farms from rolling woodlands. . . . [S]uch pioneering was the common heritage of most farm boys, well known, if not experienced on their fathers' farms." The prairies that these settlers and their descendants eventually encountered in Illinois, Iowa, and Missouri, however, tempered this forest experience before immigrants came to the Willamette Valley.[7]

Woodlands offered settlers of the eastern Midwest and upper South a

comfort in cultural continuity, but these same forests provided homes to
Native Americans who had very different ideas about Euro-American
settlement of the Ohio Valley. As land-hungry Americans poured over
the Appalachians, Native Americans met them with fierce resistance
throughout the region. In Tennessee, settlers faced an ongoing battle
with the Cherokee through the 1780s. John Mack Faragher estimates
that during the 1780s along the Ohio River, "Americans lost some
fifteen hundred men, women, and children, and over twenty thousand
horses to Algonquin guerrillas." In the early 1800s, Indianans faced
Tecumseh and his Shawnee warriors. Hostilities continued in Illinois
with the 1832 Black Hawk War. The constant battling with natives of
the Ohio Valley during some sixty-plus years of settling there led
Faragher to dub the pioneering period a "paramilitary experience."[8]
Pioneers of the Ohio Valley took with them to the Calapooia their fears
of, and learned militant behavior toward, Native Americans. But their
experience with the natives there proved quite different from what it
had been in cis-Appalachia.

In addition to their difficulties with natives who tenaciously held on
to their homelands, Ohio Valley settlers often had to vie with each other
for these same lands, primarily because of problems of speculation and
the confusing nature of the metes and bounds system of land survey
applied in parts of the early cis-Appalachian West. Coming to Kentucky
and Tennessee out of the colonial Virginia experience, the metes and
bounds system of surveying used natural features of the landscape, such
as streams, trees, ridges, and stones, for land-claim markers and boundaries. In selecting property, furthermore, the claimant could choose to
include what appeared to be the best meadows, timber, and streams
without any particular regard to regularity of shape or continuity of
claim boundaries to neighboring properties. The use of natural features
of the landscape as markers and the claiming of oddly shaped pieces of
property led to disputes.[9]

In Tennessee, but particularly in Kentucky, this relatively unsystem-
atic or nonrational survey system created serious problems. As Kentucky opened for settlement in the 1770s, Virginians and Carolinians
poured over the Appalachian Mountains. The abundance of "open"
land led to unprecedented speculation and fraud, and the survey system
permitted numerous overlapping claims. Historian Paul Gates has commented that after Kentucky joined the union, its government granted
enough land to cover the state four times over and that new settlers to

Kentucky usually found they had to deal with several different owners claiming the same parcel of land. After they had dealt with all apparent previous claimants, they often found themselves facing "ejectment proceedings wrought by persons having prior rights to their tracts." The difficulty encountered in claiming land motivated many Kentuckians to move north of the Ohio River.[10]

Settlement north of the Ohio had already begun in the 1770s, and earliest settlers there also took out claims using the traditional metes and bounds system. The Northwest Ordinance of 1785, however, initiated the rectangular land survey partly designed to alleviate some problems encountered in older states such as Kentucky. Under this newer, more "rational" system of survey, officials could easily account for, dispose of, and identify claims. Surveys began in Ohio in 1785, in Indiana in 1798, and in Illinois in 1804. Initially settlers could purchase only full sections (640 square acres). In 1800, half sections became available; in 1804, quarter sections; in 1820, half-quarter sections (eighty acres); and finally in 1832, quarter-quarter sections (forty acres). Thus, as settlement progressed across the Midwest, land claims took on smaller rectangular forms, departing greatly from more irregularly shaped claims in older parts of cis-Appalachia—Kentucky and Tennessee—and the eastern seaboard states. While land-claim shapes gradually changed, the same old desire for the best lands continued, producing a tension between the imposed system of order on the land and the settlers' aspiration to include the best features of the landscape in a claim. Cis-Appalachian emigrants took order and their desire to enjoy the bounty of nature with them to the Calapooia. There, a historical-environmental process resolved the tension between nature and order through the alteration of both humans and landscape.[11]

After leaving Kentucky and Tennessee, settlers moved into Ohio and Indiana and then into Illinois. Although forests covered most of the former two states, they each contained parcels of prairie lands, which settlers later found to be much more extensive in Illinois, Iowa, and Missouri. As settlers moved into midwestern regions of mixed woodland and prairie, they avoided the latter in preference for the former. Scholars have given a host of reasons why midwestern settlers avoided the open prairie. First, evidence shows that settlers believed winter weather too severe on the prairies to permit human habitation. Second, in summer the tall grasses of the prairie dried and became highly flammable, thus creating a great fire danger. Third, a lack of wood and water, both resources essential to daily survival, inhibited settlement on the prairies. Fourth, settlers feared wet prairies, which they believed bred diseases. Fifth, before the improved technology of steel came in the 1840s and 1850s, the midwestern prairies resisted the plow. Another popular explanation for avoidance of the prairies is that their tree-lessness indicated low soil fertility. In addition, some scholars have suggested that the open prairies did not provide, as did the forestlands, psychological security to a people who had lived among trees for two hundred years. Finally, since the earliest transportation routes—navigable waterways such as the Ohio and Mississippi—in the upper South and Midwest also happened to be surrounded by forests, it is not surprising that settlement initially concentrated there.[12]

Although the extent of open prairie or mixed prairie and woodland for each midwestern state varied, the process of settlement in the Midwest usually began in the deep forests along the mouths of waterways and then followed the banks of these streams to areas of mixed prairie and woodland. Settlement in the latter area occurred along the edges of the timber belt, with cabins built just inside the tree line, to take advantage of the availability of stream or spring water as well as wood. Fields and pastures extended out from the cabin onto the prairie. Abraham Wigle, who settled on the Calapooia in 1852, remembered an experience from his youth in the 1820s and 1830s in Adams County, Illinois, which readily depicts this pattern of settlement: cabin among the trees and fields away from the timber. Wigle reflected, "Our house was in the edge of the timber and we had a dog that frequently went out hunting by himself." One day Wigle and his mother, who were at the cabin, heard the dog "baying something" in the woods. Abraham "wanted to go see what he had treed," but because his mother was afraid, she instead sent him "to the field where Father was at work . . . that he might come and kill whatever it was. It proved to be a large wild cat."[13]

To the woodlands and prairies of Indiana, Illinois, and Missouri of Wigle's youth, the upland southerners of Kentucky and Tennessee brought a generations-old lifestyle of hunting and livestock rearing. Scholars have used these different customs of cis-Appalachian settlers as evidence to support their conclusions that these people were either back-woodsmen fleeing into the wilderness to escape other incoming settlers or materialists bent on recreating a market economy in the American wilderness. Regardless of interpretation, the fact remains that upland southerners who settled in the Midwest during the very late eighteenth and early nineteenth centuries had a predilection for both hunting and livestock raising.[14]

Settlers geared their settlement patterns to maximize an economy based on these two practices. Prairies afforded an excellent place to graze cattle in the summer, while timber offered them protection from the elements during winter. The woodland edges, with their profusion of leaves, nuts, and roots, not only attracted an abundance of wildlife but also provided a fine place to run hogs, probably the most important nonvegetable food source for settlers of the Ohio and Mississippi valleys. Faragher notes for a community he studied in Illinois that "farmers paid little or no attention to breeding, and their swine did not fatten as well as improved stock, reaching a maximum weight of only some two hundred pounds; but the most important consideration was the ability of these feisty 'razorbacks' to survive on the forest provender, with a little occasional corn in the farmyard to keep them some what connected to their owners." Faragher also found that the "carnivorous appetites" of the typical Illinois pioneer family required a herd of about a dozen swine, "although some farmers built up herds of fifty or more."[15]

Not only did swine provide a nearly ideal food source for western families who lived just above the subsistence level, but they also proved useful as currency. And since settlers had limited transportation to get products to market, livestock such as swine and cattle were a good commodity, since they could walk on their own legs. Livestock, however, also "ran at large, and in so doing caused an unusual amount of trouble" for settlers' crops and fences.[16] Settlers took this culture of swine and cattle raising, with all its headaches and benefits, to the Calapooia Valley.

The vital role that livestock played in the early culture and economy of cis-Appalachia warranted the necessity of having both timber and prairie together. This desire to have access to two ecosystems was so embedded in the midwestern settler's mind by the mid nineteenth century that it spurred concern about emigrating to the Oregon Country. A Mr. Smith of Indiana believed this necessity so great that while contemplating a move to the Willamette Valley in 1852, he wrote to his friend Thomas S. Kendall, who had taken up a land claim through which the Calapooia River flowed. Smith asked, "Is there in the timbered part of the country [where you settled] sufficiency of grass for cattle to live on?" and, "In the open or prairie part of the country is not good timber very scarce?"[17]

In addition to raising livestock, the early midwestern settlers did undertake some cultivation. Their primary crop, corn, provided winter food for cattle and hogs. Corn was, in the words of the historian George F. Parker, "from the eastern borders of Ohio to and including Missouri and Iowa . . . the foundation of industry and prosperity. . . . [It was] the means for developing and making a new country." But settlers also grew wheat and oats for family consumption. At first settlers found the prairies they encountered in the Midwest unamenable to cultivation because of the thickly intertwined root masses of native grasses. This prairie sod of the Midwest broke wooden and even cast-iron plows. Faragher relates that some people in the Illinois community he studied found the sod so impervious to the plow that they had to dig holes in it with axes and plant seeds individually by hand. Not until the 1830s with the prairie plow, and especially in the 1840s and 1850s with John Deere's steel plow, did improved technology finally permit easier cultivation of the midwestern prairie. Even at that, farmers sometimes still required several yoke of oxen to turn the prairie sod.[18]

In summary, life on the cis-Appalachian landscape was composed of the cultural experiences of plowing tough midwestern prairies; battling fierce Indians for life and land, and sometimes fellow settlers for the same parcel of property; adjusting to a new system of survey; raising hogs and other livestock; cultivating corn; and attempting to balance one's home between woodland and prairie. Pioneers carried this culture out of cis-Appalachia to the new landscape of the Willamette. A major theme in following chapters is how this culture both accommodated to, and simultaneously caused changes in, the Willamette Valley environment.

Scholars have given various reasons to explain why these pioneers left their homes on the banks of the Ohio and Mississippi and undertook a six-month, two-thousand-mile journey across sun-parched plains, deserts, dangerous rivers, and one of the highest and the most extensive mountain ranges in North America to take up new residence in the Willamette Valley. Motivations included zeal for adventure, hope for economic improvement, the lure of free land, a wish to be rid of slavery and its inherent problems, political and patriotic considerations, a frantic quest to escape natural disasters plaguing the Mississippi Valley, and a desire for better physical health.[19]

Settlers of the Calapooia have left records indicating that a variety of these reasons played a role in their decision to travel west. Abraham Wigle wrote, "Father wanted to go to Oregon that his children might secure homes and settle near him." Timothy A. Riggs, who came to the Calapooia in the late 1840s, noted:

> As to the motive for coming to the Willamette Valley at that early date I hardly know how to answer, unless it was the love of adventure, as the question of sovereignty had not been settled between the United States and England when I came here. True, the United States senate had been discussing the matter of giving each settler in Oregon six hundred and forty acres of land, and we rather expected that would be done, but we had no real assurance that such would be the case.[20]

Actual settlers of, and planned emigrants to, the Calapooia left numerous documents indicating their overriding concern with disease and health. For instance, in 1852 an Indianan wrote to Thomas Kendall asking about prospects for settling on the Calapooia; because the writer's Wabash neighborhood suffered from "miasma," which annually filled the "grave-yards with multitudes of the slain," the subject of health was the very first question that he posed. Abraham Wigle mentioned that in Missouri his father's family had suffered "considerable sickness and consequently he had a good many doctor bills to pay." On 9 August 1852, Lucy M. King of Louisville, Clay County, Illinois, wrote to her cousin James Swank of the Calapooia Valley, "The cholera has not been to our *ville* yet, though it has been within 32 miles of us." She went on to inquire as to "the description of the [Calapooia] country, whether there are any good schools there, and if you like to stay there." But she quickly added, "Let me know whether the cholera is in your region or not." Less than six months later, on 22 January 1853, William McHargue of Chariton County, Missouri, before moving to the Calapooia, wrote to his brother James McHargue, who had settled there in 1847, that Missouri "has been a very healthy place to live in this last year, but this year it has been very sickly, with much winter fever, typhoid fever and many other complaints." Jonathan Keeney and his family, who settled on the Calapooia in 1846, had suffered greatly in the Midwest, losing three brothers to tuberculosis in the five years before emigrating from Missouri.[21]

While midwesterners emigrated to the Willamette Valley of Oregon in part to escape the disease-plagued Ohio and Mississippi valleys, they unwittingly, as explained in the last chapter, sent their diseases ahead and wiped out the Willamette's native population, thus making their own settlement there that much easier. Moreover, in the process of migration, midwesterners still brought their diseases with them. However, their new home on a new landscape proved healthier than the one they had left behind.

The pioneers from cis-Appalachia brought with them to the Willamette and Calapooia valleys a preformed culture. As the following chapters argue, in the process of molding this culture to the valley of the long grasses, they found that the environmental conditions in the Willamette resembled and differed from the landscape from which they had come and therefore that some of their old practices were not always appropriate in their new home. In introducing and attempting to shape their culture to new environmental conditions, and simultaneously attempting to reshape the environment to their old cultural habits, Ohio Valley transplants developed an intimate connection with the landscape of the Willamette Valley and also altered the ecological balance of the region. One of the results of this process was the development of a settlement culture indigenous to western Oregon.

PART TWO

Living in a New Land

CHAPTER III

Material Culture:
Settling the Calapooia Foothills

When immigrants from the Midwest and the upper South came into the Oregon Country in the early 1840s, it was not an untouched wilderness. Native peoples had made it their home for millennia, shaping its environment through their cultural practices. In addition, the Oregon Country had been the scene of European and American activities for a number of years: explorers had probed its shores and interior beginning in the 1500s; trappers had exploited the fur-bearing animals by sea since the 1780s and by land since 1809; and by 1840 the British Hudson's Bay Company's properties in the Pacific Northwest included several trading posts in the western and eastern portions of the region, the Fort Vancouver headquarters, and the Puget's Sound Agricultural Company.[1]

The timing of the earliest permanent settlement in the Willamette Valley is disputable. Some evidence suggests that retired trappers may have resided there as early as the later 1810s. But the best evidence indicates a more likely date of the mid 1820s. By 1831–32, at least three permanent farms existed in the northern Willamette Valley. In October 1838 the Willamette's Euro-American population included fifty-seven adult males: twenty-three French-Canadians, eighteen American settlers, and sixteen clergy and laymen connected with Jason Lee's Methodist Mission. The first large-scale overland emigrant party to the Willamette arrived in 1842. That group consisted of between 105 and 140 new settlers. The "Great Migration" of 1843 brought between seven hundred and one thousand more to the valley. By September 1845 the

Willamette settlement population had reached five to six thousand, with French-Canadians and other British subjects totaling no more than twelve hundred.[2]

Until 1844, new settlers of the Oregon Country followed the pattern of their predecessors and located in the northern portion of the Willamette Valley. In that year, though, about a decade and a half after permanent settlement commenced in the northern valley and only one year after large-scale settlement began in the Willamette, immigrant John Packwood crossed the Santiam River, sixty miles south of the Willamette Falls, and became the first Euro-American to settle permanently in the southern Willamette Valley, in what became Linn County (map 1). A year later Isaac Hutchens became the first to settle on the Calapooia, though he did not remain. The lateness of settlement in the southern as compared to the northern part of the Willamette Valley is best revealed in the population distribution of 1850, the first year the United States government conducted a census there. In that year the three northern Willamette Valley counties, Clackamas, Yamhill, and Washington, had a population of 6,023. The two midvalley counties, Polk and Marion, provided homes to 3,800 settlers, while the two physically larger southern valley counties, Benton and Linn, at that time had a population of only 1,808.[3]

The exigencies of the local landscape, along with settlers' habits from life in the Midwest and upper South, influenced settlement patterns in, and material culture responses to, the Willamette Valley environment during initial years of occupation. During settlement, the early Willamette Valley immigrants came in contact with a new land, discovered its idiosyncrasies, and learned to accommodate themselves to it, but they also changed it in significant ways in the hopes of making it better satisfy their own needs. In this process, both the settlers and the landscape worked on each other and produced a new western Oregon culture that differed subtly from the Ohio Valley culture and that also resulted in tremendous environmental change in the Willamette Valley.

Historically, culturally, and environmentally, the small tributary Calapooia Valley is in many ways a microcosm of the Willamette. This and the following chapters use that microcosm to examine in detail the collective pioneer experience on the western Oregon landscape. These chapters demonstrate that, on the level of material culture and in the realm of the mind, the relationship between the Euro-American settler and the wilderness environment can be described only as complex.[4]

THE CALAPOOIA LANDSCAPE

The Calapooia River, little more than a stream, rises in the western Cascades and tumbles down a narrow, forested canyon in a northwesterly course for about twenty-five miles before flowing out onto the level plains of the lower Calapooia Valley. In its canyon the river winds its way around foothills that rise above the level, narrow valley—not more than a mile wide—for about six miles. One small but important stream, Brush Creek, joins the river before it cascades down a waterfall of less than ten feet in height and enters the wider—up to three miles—lower valley of the Calapooia, still surrounded by foothills reaching fifteen hundred feet in elevation. For another six miles the Calapooia hugs the foothills along the northern wall of its little canyon, and then the river finally flows out onto the floor of the Willamette Valley; trending in a north-northwesterly direction, it winds its way sluggishly through numerous oxbows for thirty-one miles to its confluence with the Willamette. Over this distance it drops only 145 feet, or roughly five feet per mile.

During the winter of 1852–53, six years after permanent settlement began in the Calapooia Valley, federally hired surveyors came to the locale to fix township, range, and section lines. Their detailed notebooks make it possible to reconstruct the early geographic and vegetative landscape of the Calapooia (map 2). The surveyor described the southern wall of the Calapooia as "high broken hills & mountains with numerous deep ravines and rocky ridges timbered principally with fir with a thick und[er]gr[owth] of hazel vine maple wild cherry fern & briars." The hills to the north of the river, with a southern exposure, he reported as drier and less densely forested. They were "covered with scattering" of oak, fir, and pine and produced "a fine quality grass."[5] At the western terminus of the small Calapooia Valley, its prairies mingle with the Willamette's. At this point, the foothills of the Cascade mountains continue to the north until broken by the South Santiam River valley. From the south side of the Calapooia Valley's mouth, foothills, now known as the Coburg Hills, stretch southward in a high, unbroken chain to the McKenzie River.

When settlers first arrived in the Calapooia Valley, its floor, from its eastern extension to its opening onto the Willamette, consisted principally of open prairie with a scattering of ash and oak trees. The ash thrived in thickets and low-lying swales while the oaks grew either as

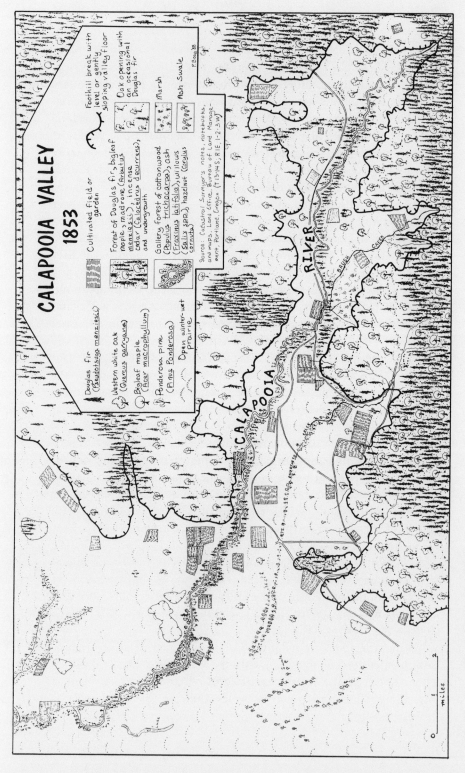

CALAPOOIA VALLEY 1853

Douglas fir
(Pseudotsuga menziesii)

Western white oak
(Quercus garryana)

Bigleaf maple
(Acer macrophyllum)

Ponderosa pine
(Pinus ponderosa)

Open winter-wet prairie

Cultivated field or garden

Forest of Douglas fir, bigleaf maple, madrone (Arbutus menziesii), incense cedar (Calocedrus decurrens), and undergrowth

Gallery forest of cottonwood (Populus trichocarpa), ash (Fraxinus latifolia), willows (Salix spp.), hazelnut (Corylus cornuta)

Foothill break with level or gently sloping valley floor

Oak opening with an occasional Douglas fir

Marsh

Ash swale

P. Boag '88

Source: Cadastral Surveyor's notes, notebooks, and maps, Land Office, Bureau of Land Management, Portland, Oregon (T13/14 S, R1 E, 1-2-3 W)

CALAPOOIA RIVER

BRUSH CREEK

Map 2. The Calapooia Valley, 1853.

solitary giants on the prairie or in the form of savanna or oak groves. The eastern portion of the Calapooia, through which Brush Creek flows, was more heavily forested with oaks than was the western portion adjoining the Willamette Valley, which the surveyor described as having a "scarcity of timber." The prairies of the Calapooia and adjoining Willamette Valley he noted as "level . . . with a rich soil of clay loam which produces an abundance of superior quality grass. The prairie being nearly level is very wet in the rainy season." Surveyors described lower Brush Creek as either marshy or simply a swamp. Courtney Creek, a slightly smaller brook in the western portion of the Calapooia, typified the valley's "several small streams that head in the mountains but sink on reaching the prairie." Along the Calapooia River, bottomland ranged from one-fourth to one-half mile in width and was "subject to inundation to the depth of 5 or 6 feet & is well timbered with fir maple ash & balm [cottonwood] undgr[owth] hazel vinemaple & briars." The river's characteristics varied from one end of the valley to the other. In the eastern portion it reached only fifty-five links (about thirty-six feet) in width and in the west one hundred links (sixty-six feet). Its current was described as rapid throughout its length in the Calapooia Valley proper.

In 1846 the first Euro-American settlers permanently located at the base of the hills and mountains on the banks of the Calapooia. They did so at a time in American history when, according to the landscape architect John R. Stilgoe, steam, iron, and a developed market economy, as well as new systems of organization inherent in the industrial revolution, were effectively changing the relationship between people and the land in some parts of the country.[6] On the Calapooia, still newly settled and relatively distant from the influences of the industrial revolution, early settlers experienced a time lag of a few years during which they had few intermediaries, such as a developed market economy and industrial systems, to distance them from the land. Rather, during the initial years of contact, settlers related directly to the land and acquired an intimate understanding of its physical configuration and idiosyncrasies as they molded a midwestern and upper southern culture to it. While settlers had to contend with natural catastrophe and components of the landscape that they never could accept, they also, through their daily activities, developed a positive relationship with their new landscape.[7]

EARLY LIFE AND CULTURE ON THE CALAPOOIA
LANDSCAPE, 1846–60

After traversing the Oregon Trail during the late spring, summer, and early fall, immigrants to the Oregon Country generally arrived in the Willamette Valley just as the wet season began. Sometimes they immediately continued south to find a new home, as did Benjamin Freeland, who came to the Calapooia in 1853–54: "We was six months in Crossing the plains and after we got in the Valle we started up the Valle and to look for a home we traveled slow we would stop and look and we traveled over one hundred mieles till we Crost the Calapooya river and on the Calapooya we found A Clame and bought it which we paid fore yoak of oxen. Claims is skerse." Other settlers wintered in the north near Oregon City and then headed south in the spring to choose a claim that they could immediately begin to work. For instance, although John Courtney's family arrived in Oregon in autumn 1845, they reached the Calapooia only the following spring.[8]

In the winter of 1852–53, after completing the first survey of the township that extends from the mouth of the Calapooia Valley out onto the Willamette's prairies, the federal surveyor wrote a brief description of the area he had just traversed. In his notes he captured the essence of the Calapooia's early settlement pattern: "township contains about 20 settlers principally along the hills on the Eastern side and on the Calapooia on the Northern side. . . . The prairie part of the township is principally vacant owing to the scarcity of timber and the wet state of the land in the winter."[9]

Examples abound of settlers' determination to avoid the Willamette's winter-wet plains in preference for the foothills that bordered smaller valleys such as the Calapooia. Before resorting to the better-drained hills of the Calapooia, John Wigle's family attempted to make a go of it on the open prairies of the Willamette. But they soon gave up that notion when, within a few days of their arrival in the winter of 1852, they experienced, in the words of Wigle, "an Oregon rain with [a] continuous blow for three days and nights." In no time their "little log house" and "the low ground" nearby "was flooded and we were anything but jubilant." John Grath Bramwell remarked in later years that "before drainage ditches were opened the whole valley was like a swamp. The streams, many of them, had no definite channels but spread out over the floor of the valley, wandering here and there all over the land."[10]

Settlers were concerned not only by standing water, but also by the full-fledged floods that regularly inundated the prairies. When John McCoy looked to settle on the plains between the Willamette and Calapooia rivers, he examined first a "beautiful claim" before choosing another, for during one of his "several trips of investigation" he discovered "signs of driftwood . . . upon one of its highest point[s]." He became convinced that "at some time past, high water from the river overflowed the entire claim." Fifteen years later he began to think that at first he had been misled, but "in December 1861 a flood of the Wallamet river came that swept over the ground to a depth of several feet." The threat of high water forced Americus Savage, who claimed land along the Calapooia out on the floor of the Willamette River in the 1850s, to build his home on the top of a low butte whose summit stood almost forty feet above his prairie claim. Dissatisfied with this inconvenient location, during the great flood of 1861 he "resolved that it was time to see just where in the neighborhood it was safe to build . . . [and] he therefore took a boat and rowed across the [flooding] river inspecting the country."[11]

In the near-subsistence agricultural community that developed on the Calapooia during the early years of settlement, settlers had neither adequate technology nor a large enough labor force to check floods and drain the prairies for cultivation. Lack of drainage simply made it impossible to put in essential crops until very late in the season. But by settling along the lower slopes of the foothills, the earliest pioneers on the Calapooia and the southern Willamette Valley found well-drained soils ready for the plow. The soil there, commented Wilson Blain in 1851, "is a deep loose, black loam, resting on a substratum of rock or blue clay. This land is adapted, in eminent degree, to all the productions of the farm."[12]

The environmental consequences of Kalapuya burning practices also influenced settlement patterns during initial years of contact. First, settlers needed wood for construction, heating, and cooking purposes, but the 1852 surveyor noted that the open prairies had a "scarcity of timber." The absence of trees on the prairie caused another problem: persistent rains waterlogged the Willamette prairies in winter and spring, but because burning had left them essentially treeless, during the warm summer months the flow of spring's and small streams decreased or completely vanished, leaving the plains without water. Settlers looked instead to the unburned forests and stands of timber along the well-drained foothills, which provided all the necessary resources. There they had access to timber, and the cooler, moister conditions of the forest environment, according to Thomas Kendall, also provided along "the base of the buttes and hills . . . small collection[s] of water, which after running slowly the distance of a few rods [onto the prairies], entirely disappear." Therefore, as Kendall noted in 1852, "What are now called the best claims, that is those seized upon primarily by the settlers, as combining the three great elements of convenience, good land, timber, and water, are principally held by claimants under the present law." Finally, in choosing to settle along the edge rather than in the deep forest, settlers still had access to the open prairies needed for the grazing of livestock. In later years, Calapooia resident Archie Frum recalled, "All of the first settlers to this valley chose their homes on the foot-hills of the Cascades or about the various buttes. The reason was that good springs and plentiful wood was found there and they could live conveniently and still pasture their stock all over the open valley."[13]

Natural exigencies of the landscape, such as drainage, and Kalapuya-caused changes in the environment, such as the absence or presence of prairie, trees, and springs, influenced Euro-American settlement patterns in the southern Willamette Valley. Because the Kalapuya could move seasonally between different valley ecosystems, they could obtain the variety of resources they depended on for food, clothing, tools, and housing. By contrast, Euro-American settlers' culture of private land-holding resulted in a relatively sedentary life-style, necessitating access to a great variety of resources on their individual claims. The earliest settlers, aware of the benefits and drawbacks that the single ecosystem of prairie could provide them on the open, flat plains of the southern Willamette Valley, reconciled themselves to the natural facts and headed instead for the forest-prairie edge along the foothill periphery. In balancing themselves with the Calapooia terrain, early settlers understood their natural setting and adjusted their lives accordingly.[14]

Map 3 shows the progression of land claiming in the Calapooia Valley between the years 1846 and 1855. To 1851, settlers claimed the vast majority of the periphery of the Calapooia where wooded foothill met open prairie. A few early settlers took land on the Willamette

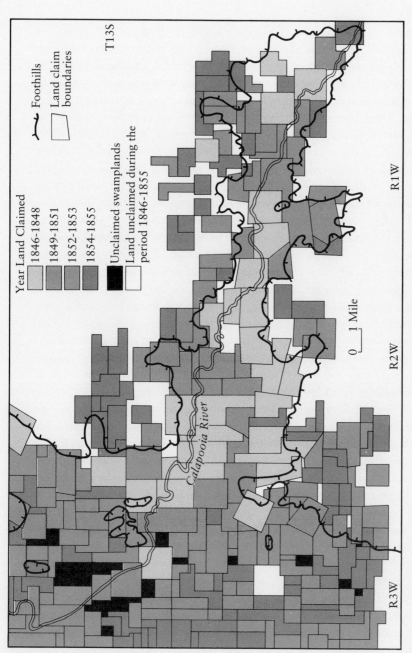

Map 3. Land claiming in the Calapooia Valley and on the adjacent Willamette Valley Plains, 1846–55. The area represented in the map is larger than the study area and thus includes more land claims than have been used for statistical purposes in this study.

SOURCES: Genealogical Forum of Portland, *Genealogical Materials*; surveyors' maps and Donation Land Claim maps, Land Office, Bureau of Land Management, Portland; *Linn County, Oregon*; Manuscript Population Census Returns, Linn County, 1850.

prairie right along the banks of the Calapooia, for there, too, in addition to available fresh water, they also found the special features of the edge: timber growing in thickets along the riverbanks, plus open prairie extending beyond this narrow wooded band. These prairies close to the river, in fact, included what later proved to be some of the best agricultural lands, being fertile and well drained because they rested atop cobble. But claimants during the early years never ventured far from the foothills or the river. Early settlement throughout the southern Willamette Valley followed a similar pattern (map 4). Most settlers located claims at the base of the foothills, while a few settled in the gallery forests of larger streams. No settlers centered their claims in the midst of the valley's wide, open prairie. Only later, between 1851 and 1855, when the best claims were gone, did settlers begin to take up the initially less desirable land on the open, winter-wet, summer-dry, and timberless prairie, as well as on less desirable lands higher in the rugged foothills.

However, it is important to note that although early settlers consciously avoided the prairies, as they initially had in the Midwest, they viewed them positively in futuristic, pastoral terms. Thomas Kendall commented in 1852 that "the best land, the most sightly locations, in the very heart of the grazing portions, and what will one day be the great agricultural spots, I mean the central portions of the prairies, are yet as the Creator left them, uncultivated, unclaimed."[15]

The settlement pattern along the Calapooia valley demonstrates the influence that nature, cis-Appalachian precedent, and the Kalapuya had on Euro-Americans. It also shows that Euro-American settlers had an intimate understanding and closeness to the natural world—prairies, trees, hills, and plains—on which they depended. Settlers' intimacy with the Calapooia landscape also developed through the actual laying out of the boundaries of individual claims.

During the years 1846 to 1851, before federal surveyors imposed the cadastral survey on the Calapooia wilderness and before new methods and technology made it easier to mitigate certain features of its terrain, the natural landscape guided the laying out of land-claim boundaries, just as it had in the early cis-Appalachian West. However, the Oregon Donation Land Law, which went into effect on 1 December 1850, called for the imposition of the rectilinear cadastral survey on the valley and required that new claims adhere to these north-south, east-west survey lines. From 1843 to December 1850, only the basic laws of the provisional and

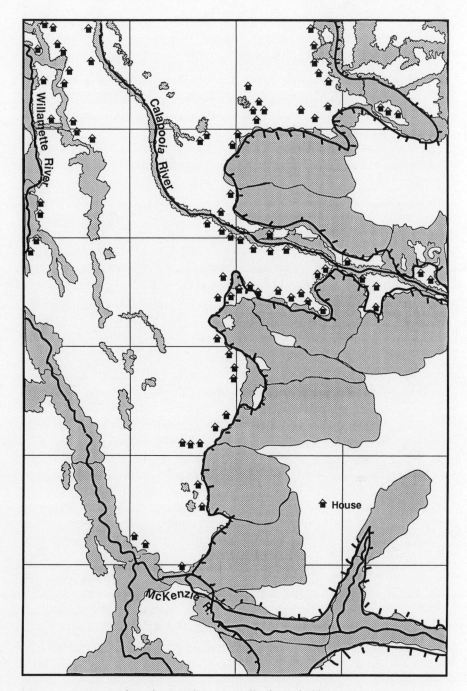

Map 4. Location of southern Willamette Valley households, 1850.

SOURCE: William A. Bowen, "Mapping an American Frontier: Oregon in 1850."

territorial governments guided the settlers' land claiming as they attempted to balance themselves, their cis-Appalachian culture, and the need for natural resources with what the landscape afforded.[16]

The provisional and territorial governments stipulated no pattern for land claiming according to cardinal points of the compass, as did the later federal Donation Land Law. The geographer Harlow Zinser Head has concluded from this circumstance that "the objective of the federal land policy . . . was to halt further settlement in the haphazard manner" of years prior to 1851.[17] In fact, the territorial and provisional governments did not necessarily encourage a "haphazard manner" of land claiming in the Willamette Valley, for certain rules did force a minimal regularity to land claim boundaries. On 5 July 1843, for instance, the Oregon provisional government enacted its first land law. Article 1 required that a person "holding or hereafter wishing to establish a claim to land . . . shall designate the extent of his claim by natural boundaries, or by marks at the corners, and on the lines of such claim, and have the extent and boundaries of said claim recorded in the office of territorial recorder." Article 3 stipulated that a claimant could take no more than 640 acres (one square mile). It also required that claimants take land "in a square or oblong form" but granted an exception to what "the natural situation of premises" afforded. A new comprehensive land law, passed a year later (25 June 1844), slightly revised requirements for taking out land claims. Section 2 ordered that all claims made after that date "shall be in a square form, if the nature of the ground shall permit; and in case the situation will not permit, shall be in oblong form." Section 3 excepted claims already made: where lines had already been agreed on, claims did not have to be "in a square or oblong form."[18] Thus, the early Oregon governments at least attempted to bring regularity to the landscape and prevent the sort of problems that had arisen in the east, particularly in Kentucky.

Theoretically, then, up to June 1844 the provisional government allowed settlers to take their claims in any form they desired. Between 1844 and 1850, laws still allowed settlers to orient square or rectangular claims according to what the local landscape afforded. Calapooia settlers between 1846 and 1850 took advantage of this allowance, and although most did use cardinal points of the compass to lay out their rectangular claims, some did not. A study of the early land claims reveals that settlers used both regular and, not surprisingly, irregular claims to take advantage of the variety of lands available along the prairie-forest edge. Those who had "regular" boundaries placed large claims in areas where they could take advantage of as many resources as possible. Since they were the earliest and first settlers, they could readily do so.

Though Jared Michael's 1847 claim (map 5) and Thomas Ward's 1850 claim (map 6) were both perfectly square claims of roughly 640 acres each, they also stretched the limit of the law that required imposing rectangular lines on a landscape that had no semblance to "rational" order. Both claims tilted away from the cardinal points of the compass in order to take into account local geographic features and the exigencies of landscape that nature and the Kalapuya had shaped. Michael's took advantage of both water that collected from springs at the base of a foothill on his claim and of timber at the top of the slope. The gently fanning prairie that made up two-thirds of his claim was readily cultivable and in fact made up the entirety of his farmland when the surveyor sketched his claim in 1852–53. Ward's claim had an even more unusual configuration. By the time Ward made his claim, earlier settlers had already taken most of the best land along the foothills. So Ward took a claim on the plains, but this claim completely surrounded a steep, conical butte that rises almost six hundred feet above the valley floor. In essence, Ward's claim is an isolated microcosm of land-claiming patterns along the foothills. Settlers like Michael and Ward worked within early land-claiming laws and still positioned their claims to take advantage of the natural topography and environmental conditions.

The Michael and Ward claims exemplify the general pattern of land claiming in the Calapooia and southern Willamette Valley as a whole: the claiming of land where the lower flanks of the foothills gently fan out onto the prairie. Calapooia settlers preferred to claim land at the base of the foothills and occasionally on the Calapooia River itself (map 2); many of these early claims, especially those tucked alongside the foothills, had "irregular" forms (map 3).

Although provisional and territorial laws proved plastic enough for settlers to mold them—through the boundaries of an actual land claim—to the special nature of the land they governed, these laws also encouraged the claimant to gain knowledge of his or her local landscape. Claim laws stipulated the claimant's responsibility for surveying his or her own property "by natural boundaries, or by marks at the corner." This process of defining land according to landscape features, and then recording it by the use of natural markers (essentially the old

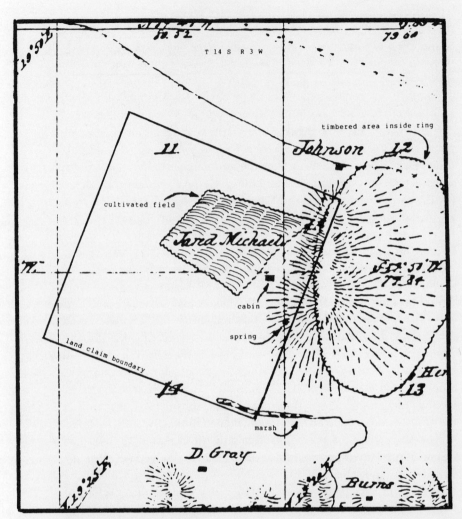

Map 5.   Jared Michael's land claim.

SOURCES: Surveyors' maps and notes and Donation Land Claim maps, Land Office, Bureau of Land Management, Portland; U.S. Geological Survey, topographic maps, Halsey quadrangle.

metes and bounds system from colonial and early cis-Appalachian settlement days), forced the early Calapooia settlers to gain intimate knowledge of—and therefore connection with—the landscape. For instance, on 15 July 1848 William Robnett claimed 640 acres situated "on the Calapooia river about 2 1/4 miles above Finley[']s mill . . . and bounded

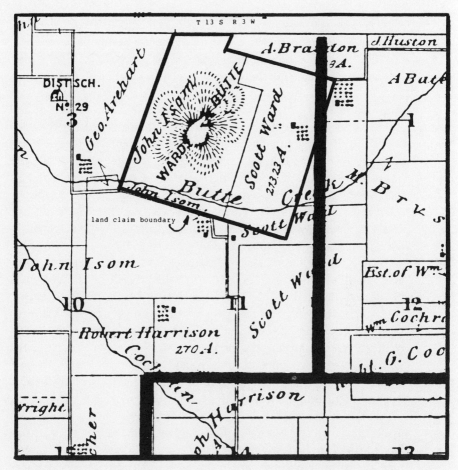

Map 6. Thomas Ward's land claim.

SOURCE: *Illustrated Historical Atlas Map.*

as follows To Wit Commencing at the SW corner an Ash tree marked on the S side of the river—Thence running N crossing the Calapooia river one mile to a stake—Thence E one mile to a stake—thence S one mile recrossing the river to a stake thence W one mile to the place of beginning." Jonathan Keeney's 640-acre claim of 26 April 1847 had an even more primitive definition, requiring great knowledge of the local landscape. The claim was located "about 5 miles above the Calapooiah river on the first branch near the foot of the mountain. Beginning at the NE corner a stake on the prairie about 100 yards W of a bunch of Ash trees, joined at the roots, standing on the N side of the branch, marked thence running W one mile, thence S one mile crossing said branch, thence E one mile, thence N one mile to the place of beginning." Other landscape features in early claim descriptions included "a stake on a hill," "an ash swale," "a fir on the mountain," "a white oak tree," and "the falls of the Calapoiah."[19] By relying on such features, the earliest Euro-American settlers appropriated into their minds and activities fixtures of landscape the Kalapuya had incorporated into myths and legends explaining creation and their own connection with the land. Though the new "Calapooians" had very different emphases and reasons than had their predecessors, these fixtures of landscape still played significant roles in settlement culture. This chapter examines the role these landscape features played in everyday activities, the next analyzes them on the level of the settlers' imagination.

During the early years on the Calapooia, 1846–51, settlers took up land through a process requiring an intimate knowledge and understanding of their new landscape. They used natural features when surveying claims, and they had great leeway (of which they readily took advantage) in positioning claims in a manner that suited their own tastes, their past experience, and the configuration of the Calapooia landscape. Essentially, the special configuration of the Calapooia and southern Willamette valleys redefined and gave new meaning to the subsistence-oriented agricultural life-style that early settlers brought with them. Virtually forced to live among the hills, settlers developed an intimate association with this fixture of the landscape at the same time that they looked onto the plains with desire. The tension between foothills and plains is essential to the cultural meaning of pioneering in the Calapooia Valley.

The cis-Appalachian experience did, in a small way, influence settlement patterns and land claiming in the Willamette. In addition, it influenced other aspects of Willamette Valley settlement culture, in particular the style of houses constructed on the new landscape. After deciding on a suitable site, immigrants constructed homes from resources the land provided—timber, clay, moss, and rocks—and thus they came into intimate contact with the Calapooia landscape; however, they fashioned these natural resources into traditional architectural styles. First homes tended to be log cabins—a form that pioneers had carried across successive American frontiers from the colonial period. When Timothy Riggs and Asa Moore settled on Brush Creek in the fall of 1847, their first duty was to "cut logs for our cabin." In building more elaborate structures, Calapooia immigrants used traditional styles brought with them from the Midwest and upper South. John Wigle's first residence, though crude, relied on a midwestern architectural style. "Our dwelling house consisted of one room, a round log house very similar to our school house in Illinois." He described his bedroom as a "pole pen about ten feet square." John McCoy, who settled not far from the Calapooia in the late 1840s, built a house typical of the log cabins that these settlers had previously built on other American frontiers. The McCoys built their home

> after the style of the usual pioneer cabin, of logs laid up in a square, notched on the corners, to make them lay properly, faced down with a broad-axe inside and out after being laid up; cracks chinked and daubed—sometimes with clay and sometimes with moss from the trees—to keep the cold out. A fireplace, the jambs and back made of baked clay with chimney, built with split stick daubed inside and out with clay. A puncheon floor, and the roof covered with clapboards held down by weight-poles to keep from blowing off, nails being out of the question at that early date. Door with wooden hinges, opened by a latch string always hung out.

Later, McCoy built a similar cabin "nine or ten feet away in line with the first" and eventually "the space between the two was enclosed." Hugh Brown of Tennessee settled in the Calapooia in 1846 and built a similar abode of two cabins connected with a breezeway. Settlers carried this particular style, a typical double-pen log house, with them in their cultural baggage from the upper South and Midwest. Settlers naturally incorporated local materials into their homes.[20]

After selecting an appropriate claim and building their homes, settlers prepared their property for cultivation. In the process, they found that the Calapooia landscape influenced their cis-Appalachian agricultural practices. After settling on the Calapooia, Thomas Kendall wrote to an Indiana friend who had concerns about cultivation in the Willamette Valley. On the "most heavily timbered parts," Kendall confided, clearing land was

> much less difficult . . . than on the heavily timbered bottoms of Ohio and Indiana. . . . A large portion . . . of the timbered country consists of open woods, with little and often no undergrowth of shrubbery, sometimes several acres bearing only a few large trees, and those not so very difficult to remove: chop or bore with an auger through the bark, and the white wood, which is not deep, then apply fire, and with little attention they will burn down.[21]

Calapooia and Willamette settlers generally found the valley soils of
their new home much easier to plow than the prairies of the Midwest,
which are thousands of years older than the Willamette Valley's. Also,
the Willamette's mild, wet winters cause vegetative matter to decom-
pose relatively quickly. Thus, whereas Midwestern sod consists of years'
accumulation of undecomposed, tough grass roots reaching several feet
deep, the sod of the Willamette is relatively thin. Settlers commented on
the ease of plowing in the Willamette and Calapooia. In 1849 Gustavus
Hines suggested that Willamette prairies were "unlike those of any
other country. They are naturally mellow, and appear . . . as though it
had been but a year or two since they were cultivated." Hines also noted
that the Willamette soils were not "swarded over with a thick strong
turf, as in Western States" and that they could be "easily ploughed with
one good span of horses the first time." George Atkinson found in 1848
that "a man can live with half the labor [in the Willamette] done in the
States. . . . An immigrant will come during the autumn, put himself up a
log house . . . [and] break eight or ten or twenty acres of prarie." In
1846 Neil M. Howison found the Willamette prairies "free from the
encumbrance of trees or other heavy obstacles to the plough, stretch
along, ready for the hand of the cultivator." Although settlers could
cultivate midwestern prairies successfully only with steel plows, settlers
in Linn County and the Calapooia Valley often found wooden plows
adequate. With a plow constructed simply out of a "twisty pice oak,"
Robert Earl's family plowed twenty acres their first season of residence
in Linn County. The Wigle family settled just south of the Calapooia
Valley's mouth in 1852 and "got along with a wooden toothed harrow
and brush drag," even though John Wigle admitted "those were poor
tools with which to work sod ground." And John McCoy's first plow in
1847 was simply a "wooden mold-board, carved by himself out of a
pice of oak wood" with a "steel lay and land-bar" and "stocked with
wheels sawn from a tree." Although he needed three yoke of oxen, he
did plow thirty-eight acres that spring alone.[22]

Settlers also found that certain crops grew poorly in the soil of the
Calapooia. Though corn was central to the development of the Midwest, settlers could not successfully cultivate it in western Oregon because of the cool summer nights. One late nineteenth-century traveler in
the Willamette summed up the problem: "For this plant the nights are
too cold. That refreshing coolness following quickly upon the retreat of
the sun, hastening down from the mountains to close our eyes in well-

blanketed and undisturbed sleep, is fatal to Indian corn, which glories in the blaze of the midsummer heat, and waxes fat and succulent through the damp and sultry midnights." Of the twenty-nine farms in the Calapooia reporting cultivated land in the 1850 agricultural census, none harvested corn, while eighteen farmers produced 2,265 bushels of wheat and 70 pounds of oats. Inhabitants produced only 573 bushels of corn in the entire Willamette Valley that year, while wheat production totaled 199,558 bushels, and oats 54,524 bushels.[23]

Although settlers could not successfully transplant corn, the key animal fodder in the Midwest, to the landscape of the Calapooia, they still had a predilection for raising livestock during the early years. As had been the case in the cis-Appalachian region, the exigencies of economy and transportation in large degree determined the hog and cattle culture of settlers on the Calapooia, but it was especially the unique configuration of the Calapooia and southern Willamette that encouraged age-old husbandry practices. The nature of the local prairies and prairie-forest edges made the southern Willamette and Calapooia valleys an excellent place to run both cattle and swine. Calapooia settlers chose claims along edges in order to have access to the prairies as well as the forests, as they had in the Midwest. They could then simply turn their livestock out onto the unclaimed, unfenced, open prairies during early years. Thomas Bird Sprenger remarked that each "farmer had a few acres broke up and some fenced to protect the crops from ranging cattle. . . . Stock raising was a most important part of our work. Cattle ran at large everywhere." In 1850 Wilson Blain wrote, "Here cattle roam at large, summer and winter, asking nothing from the care of man, and are always in the finest condition. One portion of the country is known as the land of Bashan." Swine also ranged about the countryside, feeding on oak mast and various roots growing on the prairie-woodland edges of the valley. One of the primary foods for hogs proved to be the bulb of the camas plant, the staple of the Kalapuya diet. John Minto noted that swine "lived on the grasses and oak mast . . . [and] the roots which were the chief foods of the natives." In the summer of 1846, Thomas Kendall "procured one full grown sow and two others about half grown." Because of the abundant provender, especially the camas, which when in bloom gave the valley the appearance of "a big blue lake . . . at least a thousand acres of it," by just turning his three hogs out onto the prairie "without any feeding . . . except a handful of something now and again, . . . to keep them domesticated," Kendall had in "nine months . . . more than 50 head."[24]

Because of mild conditions and the only recently ceased Kalapuya burning, livestock found adequate forage in the valley year-round, something different from experience in the Midwest. In an 1856 petition to the territorial government to force cattle owners to confine animals running at large and ravaging the petitioners' own "grass claims," citizens of Linn County even regarded the "grass claim of each settler as being to *him here* what his *Corn-Crib* was in the States." Kendall summed it up best:

> For rearing cattle and horses, I have no doubt that Oregon is one of the best countries in the world. During the crop season you labour hard to lay up [corn and hay] for your stock in the winter. Amid its storms your cattle and horses look to you for food and shelter, ours, "like the wild deer and wolf," look to the wide canopy of heaven as their stall, and to the vast fields which God of nature has spread before them, for their food. Through the wet season through dry, they never call at your barn for a meal.[25]

Southern Willamette settlers depended on livestock raising in early years. The 1850 census reveals that in the Calapooia community, twenty-four people owned 247 cattle, with Hugh Fields having 75, Isaac Hutchens 40, and William Cochran 57. In addition, the census taker found 153 milk cows and 122 oxen on the Calapooia. Thirty people owned a total of 709 hogs. William R. Kirk alone maintained a herd of 100, Hugh Fields claimed 60, and three others owned 50 apiece. The 1852 tax assessment rolls show Calapooia residents owning 972 cattle, while Linn County as a whole had 5,784. The number of hogs equaled 900 for the Calapooia, and 4,970 for the county. Calapooian Jonathan Keeney alone owned a herd of 224 swine.[26]

The interplay between nature and the Kalapuya created a landscape in the Willamette that proved in many ways beneficent to the subsistence agricultural community that developed on the Calapooia during the first few years of settlement. Foothill slopes, grasslands, trees, prairie-forest edges, springs, and camas meadows provided for the needs of Euro-American settlers and their livestock. This same landscape also supported an abundance of wild game that proved to be a blessed addition to the diet. Albert Waggoner recalled that other than livestock, what his family "could bring in with their guns was their living for a number of years."[27]

The natural and Kalapuya-created landscape influenced the quantity of deer and other types of game and animals inhabiting the valley.

Deer—especially white-tailed, which are attracted to grasslands rather than forests—abounded year-round in the southern Willamette. Silas V. Barr recalled that deer ran "freely over all of these hills, especially in winter. There were some black-tailed deer but perhaps more white-tails. The black-tails would come down from the mountains in winter. The white-tails were permanent residents here." Redman Pearl recalled, "The white-tailed deer were then common all through the valley." A. J. Shank remembered that "deer could be seen daily, grazing in the pastures with the cows," on his father's land claim. Although undoubtedly an exaggeration, during the first year John McCoy lived in the southern Willamette Valley, 1846–47, he reportedly "killed one hundred and sixty two deer without drawing the blood on one that he did not get." Lewis Tycer stated simply, "The hills were full of deer . . . and it was never any trouble to get plenty of meat."[28]

The grasslands of the southern Willamette Valley, which innumerable ponds and marshes inundated during winter months, also provided perfect feeding ground and habitat for wintering and migrating geese, ducks, swans, cranes, and other fowl. The annual number of geese alone flocking through the Willamette was so great that a Linn County newspaper humorously reported in 1876, "The number of wild geese that have passed . . . going northward, during the past two weeks, is placed at 3,713,811." Extant diaries and memoirs indicate that early settlers spent much of their time during the fall and winter months hunting fowl. For instance, in November 1866 Jasper Cranfill went goose hunting almost every day; by the twenty-sixth of that month, he could muster only enough energy to confide to his journal, "Remained at Home tired of Hunting etc." Calapooian Andrew Kirk remembered that one year he shot four hundred ducks just for family use, once getting thirteen in a single shot.[29]

Geese also caused serious problems for Calapooia and other Willamette Valley farmers. As soon as grain crops like wheat began to grow, flocks of geese invaded the fields. According to one Calapooian, they would "clean two or three acres off in a single night" so that a field that looked "green and thrifty one day" might the next morning "look as bare and black as though it had never been sown." Some farmers spent nights walking up and down their fields shooting guns to scare birds, while others hired boys to do the patrolling or even resorted to "twining." As Redman Pearl recalled:

[Twining] a field was done by driving stakes, perhaps twelve or fifteen feet tall, in rows all across the field. These rows of stakes were in squares or "checks," perhaps one hundred feet, or one hundred and fifty feet apart each way. Across the tops of these stakes twine was stretched. When the birds attempted to alight on the grain fields their wings would strike the stretched twine and it would scare them away. . . . [Or] it was very likely to become twisted in the cord and hang helpless and trapped.

This practice also made it easy for settlers to gather even more fowl for the table.[30]

Settlers had mixed reactions to wildfowl, but they roundly condemned wolves, bear, and cougar. Linn County resident Robert Earl reminisced about his brother William, who one night in the late 1840s heard hogs squealing near their house. William jumped out of bed and ran to the scene, but with neither pants nor gun. "[When] he got there he found a cogar hold of a hog he scared him loose [The cougar] acted like [it] wanted a man for super [William] started home there was another man had got up and Started down ther to See what was the mater and he meet William coming with his Shirt tail standing out Strait."[31]

Grizzly bears, though not as numerous as cougars, proved just as troublesome. Although they naturally ate camas bulbs, tubers, roots, berries, acorns, fish, and carrion, they occasionally attacked settlers' livestock. In the 1840s a grizzly took a swipe at one of John McCoy's calves, nipping its tail. But the lost "tail was the only damage done. . . . The steer was ever after known as Bob." Albert Waggoner, probably exaggerating a bit, recalled the extermination of the last grizzly in Linn County, which had been marauding the settlement.

[Father] took an old musket and loaded it heavily . . . [and] tied it to a big crooked rail in the fence near his home and set a bait nearby so that taking the bait would discharge the gun. That night the grizzly came and took the bait. The recoil of the gun broke the big rail, and the charge blew a hole in the grizzly's side and lungs large enough so that my father could run his arm into it up to the elbow, nevertheless that grizzly walked for a full mile before he dropped.[32]

Although accounts of wolves in the Calapooia are few—Kendall briefly mentioned them in an 1852 letter—they inhabited the Willamette Valley in large numbers at the time of settlement. In 1846 Neil M. Howison reported, "Wolves are numerous, and prey upon other animals, so that the plains are entirely in their possession." When Charles

Wilkes traversed the valley in 1841, he reported that "bands of wolves were met with, and heard throughout the night in various parts of the valley." Wolves did cause serious depredation. In response, northern Willamette Valley settlers called the first "wolf meeting" in early 1843 to work out some type of defense against wolves and other fearsome wildlife. At subsequent wolf meetings, settlers considered other problems the youthful Willamette settlement faced. Eventually, these meetings developed into the provisional government. The first resolution of the wolf meeting held in March 1843 was for the community "to take immediate measure for the destruction of all wolves, bears and panthers, and such other animals as are known to be destructive to cattle, horses, sheep, and hogs." Bounties of $3 for large wolves, $.50 for small wolves, $5 for "panthers," $2 for bears, and $1.50 for lynx were approved. Over the next decade and a half the provisional and territorial governments would continually revise bounties paid for "noxious" animals. Linn County itself provided bounties on wolves, bear, and cougars during the nineteenth century.[33]

Euro-American settlers responded to the wild animals of the Willamette paradoxically. On the one hand, they appreciated the bounty of game; on the other hand, they feared the grizzly, cougar, and wolf. Euro-American settlers also encountered other inhabitants of the landscape: a few surviving Kalapuya. The settlers held racist attitudes toward their predecessors. Linn County resident Mrs. James Miller wrote in 1852, "They are dying here as elsewhere, where they are in contact with civilization. . . . I used to be sorry that there was so much prospect of their annihilation. . . . Now I do not think it is to be much regretted. If they all die, their place will be occupied by a superior race." Part of this racist attitude can be explained by the fact that the Kalapuya, as Miller noted in her letter, had just undergone demographic collapse. Their culture was in a shambles, their villages destroyed, and communal food-gathering activities no longer existent. To Euro-Americans, these starving people must have appeared as little more than, as Miller wrote, "heathens."[34]

The half-starved Kalapuya, never posing a real threat to those who replaced them, only looked to the settlers for food. One evening soon after settling on the Calapooia, Clarissa Brown "had just a little flour and decided to make . . . bread to surprise" her husband, Hugh. As she was baking in her Dutch oven before the fire,

a shadow fell across the open door and looking up a big buck Indian was
seen advancing into the room and muttering something she could not understand, whatever he may have been saying . . . he meant to have the bread.
[Clarissa, who] never weighed over 100 pounds, was just as determined that
he should not have the bread intended for the Brown family. She grabbed the
tea kettle of boiling water . . . and started for the Indian. This was a foot
race . . . but he beat. . . . He never came again.

Folklorists will note that this tale is strikingly similar to other tales told
on other frontiers. It relates important information about the settler-
Native American relationship in the West as the former replaced the
latter, but it is also rooted in factual basis. Documents reveal that numerous similar incidents actually occurred on the Calapooia. In the fall of
1847, for example, Calapooia settler Timothy Riggs occasionally fed a
Kalapuya who showed up at mealtime. Soon a number of Kalapuya
began consistently to show up for supper. Fearing he "would run out of
provisions before spring," Riggs was obliged to "quit feeding them." In
another instance, shortly after Richard Finley settled on the Calapooia
in 1847, Kalapuya "stole" one of his oxen. Finley and neighbor Riggs
tracked the "thieves" to the Santiam River, where they found them
"camped and . . . drying the beef." In retaliation, Finley opened fire and
wounded one of the Kalapuya. When Timothy Riggs and Asa Moore
began building a cabin on Brush Creek in the autumn of 1847, "Indians
appeared on the scene and inquired what [they] were doing there."
After Riggs told them that he and Moore were settling, the Kalapuya
demanded payment. Riggs and Moore "made a bargain with them agree-
ing to pay them wheat and pease after the next harvest."[35]

Although a few remaining Kalapuya caused occasional consternation
among the new Euro-American residents, the only serious threat they
posed to settlers was in the settlers' minds, made fertile by experiences
in cis-Appalachia. For example, after the Keeney family arrived in the
region, local Kalapuya entered their living quarters: "The children, having heard so many stories of Indian scalping parties, thought they were
doomed." Also, Finley's shooting of one of the Kalapuya who had
stolen his ox "caused quite an excitement in the settlement." Many
settlers feared that it would "cause an outbreak among the Indians."
And finally, in the 1850s reports of rampaging tribes in other parts of
the West and Northwest brought tensions to a high point in the Willamette and Calapooia valleys. Wilson Blain noted in a letter dated 30
October 1855 that "the panic was universal, and such another time of

alarm and excitement, I have no wish ever to witness. One might have supposed on last Thursday, that the Willamette Valley was full of bristling, and savage warriors." Blain went on to point out that in fact "there was not a hostile Indian in the whole valley."[36]

In retrospect, it is easy to see that the settler-Kalapuya relationship was a painful moment in history. The Kalapuya and Euro-American civilizations converged for a few years in the Willamette Valley. This period of overlap occurred at the worst time for the possibility of humane settler-native relations. The few remaining Kalapuya, having suffered the loss of tradition, wandered about the land in a starving, dying condition, while the Euro-Americans, fresh from cis-Appalachia, harbored militant attitudes toward all Native Americans. A treaty of 4 January 1855 forced the remnant Kalapuya officially to cede the Willamette Valley to the United States.[37]

When the Euro-Americans replaced the Kalapuya, new attitudes toward landscape and environment invaded the Willamette. Chapter 1 presented two passages from the Kalapuya's perspective concerning their loss of the Willamette to the Euro-Americans. One passage referred to a shaman who long ago had seen the earth all black in his dream. Later on, the Kalapuya saw the dream come true as the whites plowed up the land. The other passage went further and noted that "this countryside is not good now. Long, long ago it was good country (had better hunting and food gathering)." These and the following few excerpts from the Euro-American perspective highlight the differences in the conception of land and property between the Kalapuya and the settlers, and thus offer much for understanding the environmental change the Euro-American's wrought in the Willamette during the nineteenth century. As an example, for the payment of land to the Kalapuya, Timothy Riggs resorted to "wheat and pease," fruits of Euro-American cultivation from the very land he was taking from the Indians. Interestingly, he believed that the natives demanded payment for the land he claimed as his own, when in fact natives had no concept of private property. And Richard Finley bore arms to recover the private property (in the form of an ox) that natives "stole" from him. By contrast, the natives told no tales of begging and "stealing" from whites for food. The Kalapuya's view of their interaction with the white settlers at this time directly concerned their altering relationship with the landscape. The whites "plough[ed] up the ground," and thus the Kalapuya's own relationship with it. The plowing rendered the environment "not good."

The land was good only when Kalapuya occupied it and men hunted and women gathered. The Kalapuya viewed themselves as living in symbiosis with nature, a symbiosis destroyed by the arrival of Euro-Americans. The Euro-Americans viewed the settlement process, in part, as one of the advancement of their environmental conception, which included private property and deriving money from the land. As the next chapter demonstrates, however, Euro-Americans did not necessarily see themselves totally separated from the land.

Early settlers looked at the few remaining Native Americans with a combination of skepticism, fear, and occasional regret. They viewed the wildlife and climate of the Calapooia with mixed emotions, too. Settlers could at least defend against the worst of the marauding wolves, cougar, and bear and the perceived threats from their human predecessors. However, the weather and climate of the Willamette posed greater problems. Winters caused great concern, primarily because of persistent rains and flooding. When Charles Wilkes visited the northern Willamette settlement in 1841, he interviewed a Mr. Walker, who had come to the country with his family the previous year. According to Wilkes, Walker "did not like the country, and wished to go to California by the first opportunity. His principal objection was to the climate, which was too wet for business." Wilkes's British counterparts Henry J. Warre and Mervyn Vavasour found in 1845–46 that "notwithstanding the advantages to be found in this valley, many of the American emigrants become dissatisfied, and remove to California, where the climate is more salubrious." During the winter of 1852–53, Wilson Blain remarked in a letter, "Heavy rains, deep snows, high waters—perfect floods, great destruction of property along streams, a considerable amount of live stock perished, poor homeless emigrants badly discouraged, these and some other matters of a like nature were 'wafted' on 'Chill November's surly blasts.' "[38]

Rainfall in winter months usually resulted in flooding and high water. Lewis Tycer recalled that the school term at the McHargue school "usually lasted only a few months in the spring when the rivers and creeks had gone down enough to make it safe for the children to cross." On 18 January 1866, Jasper Cranfill dramatically stated that "Muddy [Creek] nearly as high as yesterday. Sharp cold wind blowing—all communications with the outside world cut off by high water. About four hundred yards of fence gone." Three days later he recorded that "over one hundred & sixty of J.L. Coons sheep—were drowned by high water" and that he had found "a fish in the Prairie some six inches long in the Puddles." But the weather in 1866 was not particularly atypical. In 1861, though, the largest flood in postsettlement history occurred in the Willamette Valley. During November of that year, precipitation fell in amounts more than twice the normal for the Willamette basin. The heaviest rainfall occurred between 30 November and 2 December. Added to this precipitation was heavy snowfall in the mountains; moderating temperatures at the end of November resulted in snowmelt, which compounded the problem. Settler Michael Plaster kept a weather log at his home on Diamond Creek, just south of the Calapooia. In it he noted that from 15 November to 9 December rain fell every day, and on "December the 1 the big fresh on Calapooya all the bridges & Rigg's mill went off." The flood also destroyed Richard Finley's gristmill on the Calapooia, and settlers soon ran out of flour and were forced to use cornmeal. Two other major floods, one in January 1881 and the other in February 1890, occurred in the Willamette Valley before the end of the nineteenth century.[39]

Flooding and poor drainage, most apparent in winter, influenced settlement patterns and movements on the land and also determined where settlers developed roads. The earliest route to the Calapooia, which twisted and turned along the base of the eastern Willamette Valley foothills, was formed through wagon use, the drivers desiring to stay off the winter-wet prairie. In 1848 the territorial government commissioned a survey of this path, officially designating it the east-side Territorial Road and appointing Calapooia settler Alexander Kirk as commissioner of the survey. After viewing the route, Kirk described it in a passage full of natural features of the landscape: the road touched "a point of timber," went "through a field" and "to an ash tree," and was often "meandering along the hills"; and it ended simply by "crossing the Calapooa."[40]

Settlers developed other roads through the valley proper in much the same fashion that they had developed the Territorial Road. Thomas Bird Sprenger, who grew up along the Calapooia, recalled in later years, "When we wished to start for town . . . we just headed off across the country in the general direction . . . avoiding low places in winter as best we could." Early settlers also developed a road, actually a succession of interconnected farm lanes, that followed the base of the foothills on the south side of the Calapooia Valley (map 7). The road began on the west at Wilson Blain's claim and continued east several miles to Richard Finley's claim on the Calapooia.

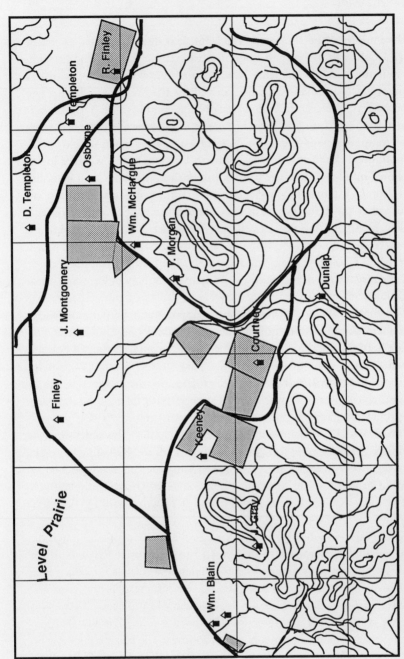

Level Prairie

Finley

D. Templeton

Templeton

Osborne

R. Finley

J. Montgomery

Wm. McHargue

J. Morgan

Wm. Blain

J. Gray

Keeney

Courtney

Dunlap

Map 7.   Early roads in the Calapooia Valley.

SOURCE: Surveyors' map, Land Office, Bureau of Land Management, Portland.

Despite attempts to locate roads in well-drained areas, routes remained notoriously bad throughout the nineteenth century. When the Oregon and California Stage Company tried to raise rates to fifteen cents a mile on the Territorial Road in the early 1860s, a local newspaper chided, "We suppose the advance [in rates] is caused by bad roads. The more the passengers have to walk and the harder they work to pry the vehicles of that company out of the mud, the more they are charged for the privilege." In later years, residents of the Calapooia Valley desired a connection with the railroad, remarking that it was "impossible to make a wagon road that is passable over six months of the year." Sarah Jane (Savage) Cornett recorded in her diary on Sunday, 7 January 1883, a trip to visit nearby friends: "we come back around the lane whew it was muddy the water was pretty high today." Three weeks later, on 29 January, after her husband had returned home from a local funeral, Cornett noted that the weather that day was "foggy heavy mist and rain most all day" and "the roads were terrible terrible." Two and a half months later, Cornett noted a common occurrence when she wrote that her son "got stuck in the mud" while hauling wood.[41]

The rains and floods of winter months influenced settlement patterns and road construction in the Willamette and the Calapooia valleys. They also destroyed homes and livestock herds. But while winter months often provided stormy, rainy, and unpleasant weather, they also proved generally mild, something that pleased settlers. On 16 January 1865, for instance, Jasper Cranfill noted in his diary that the day was a "cloudy gloomy day characteristic of the Oregon winters." A year later, he commented, "As Oregonians may expect continuers rain for about two weeks then fine weather." And in February 1853, Wilson Blain remarked, "The sun is bright—the grass is green—the birds are singing gaily, and all hands are vigorously prosecuting their agricultural and horticultural operations."[42]

If harsh weather occasionally occurred in the winter, summer months were "sufficiently delightful to counter balance all this," according to Gustavus Hines. In the Willamette Valley during the summer, "the howl of the storm and roar of the southern winds" of winter "are hushed to silence" by the gently fanning "western zephyr." Inhabitants described the occasional summer showers as "angels' visits, few and far between." Although summer evenings required "two quilts and a flannel blanket" to keep warm, temperatures during the day ranged from "sixty-five to eighty degrees at noon."[43]

Though these descriptions tended to put the best face on the situation, settlers genuinely noted an agreeable difference between summers in the Willamette Valley and the Ohio and Mississippi valleys. As a late nineteenth-century Linn County Immigration Agent declared, "When the thermometer here marks 90 degrees, the heat is not so oppressive as the same degree in the Mississippi Valley." He further commented that in "the east, when in summer the thermometer gets to 80, people seek the shade—in this state they seek the sunshine from choice; there is a tonic in it at this temperature." Blain noted in 1851, "Those sweating and sweltering nights you suffer in the [cis-Appalachian] West are to us forgotten, or remembered only as unpleasant dreams of the past." It is true that the Willamette Valley experiences markedly less humidity in the summer than do the Mississippi and Ohio valleys, but it still occasionally gets quite warm. Thus, one Linn County resident frankly described one summer day as "hot enough to make a fellow throw stones at his grandmother."[44]

Early residents and travelers in the Willamette and Calapooia also noted the lack of thunderstorms there as compared to the midwestern states. Kendall remarked in 1852, "Thunder and lightning are of rare occurance." One 1846 observer declared this a "consoling circumstance to our countrywomen, who had been previously subject to its terrifying effects, on the banks of the Illinois and Mississippi."[45]

Thus, although settlers of the Calapooia and Willamette valleys sometimes grumbled over the persistent winter rains, they also appreciated some of the ways in which the climate of the Willamette Valley differed from that of the Midwest and upper South. In comparing the negative and positive aspects, settlers in the Willamette and Calapooia were essentially coming to terms with a new land. Nineteenth-century Calapooia residents even went so far as to suggest that the climate and configuration of the Calapooia landscape actually resulted in a healthier atmosphere than that of the Midwest. Kendall commented to a correspondent in Indiana:

> You can no doubt trace on your rich Wabash bottoms the elements which impregnate your atmosphere with the miasma from which pestilence and death are shot through society. . . . Apply the same principles to the land of my adoption. During the rainy season our winds and rains are directly from off the Pacific . . . in passing over the vast expanse of water, the miasma, containing elements of disease and death have principally at least been absorbed. . . . Through the dry season, though from another direction, we still

have the pure ocean breeze. Neither have we the extremes of heat and cold to which the Atlantic countries are subjected.

Kendall argued further that vegetation decomposes slowly in the Willamette Valley, keeping the air purer: "From this source [i.e., rotting vegetation], therefore, our atmosphere cannot be vitiated."[46] In fact, in western Oregon organic matter actually decomposes very rapidly, and although the relation to illness in this case is questionable, Kendall obviously felt that this difference explained why the Calapooia landscape was healthier than the Midwest.

Kendall and other residents of the Calapooia and the Willamette also noted the relationship between the landscape—such as "pure water dashing from the mountains" in brooks, creeks, and rivers—and health. Blain remarked that "where pure water prevails, we have one of the best guarantees of healthfulness." Blain also recognized that the valley's standing waters and swamps sometimes "engender even ague in Oregon," but this illness was limited—at least among the Euro-American population. In fact, settlers' draining of land and confining of rivers and streams to narrower channels eliminated malaria from the Willamette Valley by the end of the nineteenth century.[47]

Whether referring to atmospheric conditions, decomposition of organic material, or pure water, Calapooia settlers attempted to understand, through environmental explanations, why the Willamette, according to Blain, had "restorative power for all kinds of invalids." Sick and "broken-down" miners coming in from California, for instance, "soon experience the bracing and healthfulness of our climate, and are restored to health." The thousands of persons in the Midwest states "whose constitutions are worn out with the various forms of bilious disease," Blain further noted, "would in a few months be restored to health by a residence in Oregon." After emigrating to the Calapooia from the Midwest, Fielding Lewis wrote home in 1853, "I am in better health than I have bin in fifteen years."[48]

Sickness on the Calapooia frontier was not unknown. Blain occasionally commented on "ague" or malaria. He further declared that "a man knowing that he *lives in a world of sin*, would simply be insane to suppose that he would never be sick here." A diphtheria epidemic ravaged the banks of the Calapooia in 1876–77, and the same disease continued to crop up throughout the nineteenth century. In 1885, Herman Gragg wrote to his sister from the Calapooia town of Brownsville about diphtheria. And, scarlet fever, smallpox, cholera, and other diseases commonly occurred in Oregon in the nineteenth century. During the earlier years, however, with a small population on the Calapooia, illness seemed to be limited. Blain commented in 1854 that "only some four adult persons have died in the bounds of my congregation since we came here four years since." W. B. Mealey, doctor in Linn County, had stated in 1852 that "most physicians are complaining of the want of business [and] are obliged to go at some other business for a lively-hood."[49]

Although the evidence is subjective, and therefore only suggestive at best, a number of Calapooia settlers did believe that the climate, weather, and configuration of the Willamette landscape rendered Ohio and Mississippi valley diseases less potent. This belief is one example of how living in a new land differed significantly from living on the older landscape of the Ohio and Mississippi valleys.

Settlers' experiences in the western Oregon environment, as this and the next chapter suggest, shed light on the ways in which the frontier both affirmed and challenged cis-Appalachian culture as it was brought West. As settlers attempted to replicate that culture in the Willamette environment, they had to impose it on an unfamiliar landscape, one whose central components were foothills and plains. This landscape made the settlement culture on the Pacific Northwest frontier of the Willamette and Calapooia slightly different from the culture of cis-Appalachia.

Living in a new land included shaping old habits to new environmental conditions, often with agreeable results. Settlers continued the age-old practice of plowing the soil, though they found it an easier task in the Willamette. They continued to plant most of the crops that they had before, though because of lack of humidity and cooler weather (something they found most agreeable), they grew more wheat than corn. They continued to build the same style of houses, but with new materials. And they continued to favor the raising of livestock, though the mild climate of the Willamette allowed a greater reliance on nature than had been possible on the Ohio. Kalapuya burning presented settlers with unparalleled livestock forage, the grasses and camas of the Willamette supplanting midwestern corncribs. Nature and the Kalapuya had rendered in the Willamette a landscape filled with an abundance of wild animals, which both had benefits and drawbacks. Wolves, cougar, and bear created numerous problems and Native Americans were feared, though without real reason; nevertheless, settlers on the Calapooia appreciated the abundance of game the landscape of the Willamette provided.

The Willamette landscape that Euro-American settlers came on was not simply "natural," though nature had played a role in its definition. The Kalapuya had also helped create the landscape. Natives needed various ecosystems from which to gather plants and hunt game. To ensure these commodities, they consciously manipulated the environment and moved from place to place. By contrast, Euro-American culture prized private property and a sedentary existence. Under such a system, to gain access to as many resources as possible, settlers had to choose carefully from a large geographic area a single piece of property that could offer them various necessities for daily living. Euro-American settlers needed wood and water, which they obtained from the forests of the valley. They also needed land for grazing, which they obtained from the extensive prairies. In addition, settlers sought out well-drained lands for early planting. Wood, water, grasslands, and well-drained soil influenced settlement in the Willamette as they had in the Midwest. All these qualities of landscape, the variety of ecosystems necessary for comfort in a new land, came together along the base of the foothills, where the Kalapuya-created forest-prairie edges also existed. There the earliest arrivals took the first claims. In choosing carefully, earliest settlers showed an understanding of the unique exigencies of the southern Willamette landscape. Through land-claiming procedures, furthermore, settlers came into intimate contact with contour and vegetation. This intimacy is demonstrated in their land-claim descriptions and in contemporary maps showing painstaking positioning of claims. In daily activities, then, earliest settlers developed an intimate connection with the foothills, though they also looked to the plains as the future.

Material evidence from the early settlements on the Calapooia shows that the westering process can be described only as complex. It was not a story of settlers simply desiring to and then actively forcing an objective will on the land. The landscape, partly natural and partly artificial, influenced settlers, too. And settlers' responses to the land also included a large degree of the positive. In the process of coming to terms with the new physical circumstances of the Willamette, settlers attempted to define a harmonious relationship with the environment, which is seen most effectively—at least on the level of material culture—in the way they physically placed themselves on and in that landscape. With limited technology to permit a change in the natural exigencies of the environment, settlers related to it, especially to the terrain of the valley, in an intimate way. Intimacy formed the linchpin of settlers' relationship to the wilderness.

CHAPTER IV

Aesthetics: Responding to the Calapooia Landscape

John McLoughlin, chief factor of the Hudson's Bay Company's Columbia River Department from 1824 to 1846, resided during these years at
Fort Vancouver on the north side of the Columbia River, just across
from the mouth of the Willamette Valley. During this period he observed rapid change in the Oregon Country and especially in the Willamette Valley, where all but a few of the early migrants to Oregon settled.
On 20 November 1840, McLoughlin wrote to the governor of the
company:

> If there was more Prairie Land at the Cowelitz it would be possible to
> encourage emigration to that place but the Puget Sound Association requires
> all there is and though the soil is equally as good as that of the Wallamatte
> the larger extent of the Prairies of the Wallamette and the abundance of Deer
> on them and their more beautiful Scenery causes them to be preferred to the
> Cowelitz and Settlers will never settle on it till the Wallamatte is settled or till
> the wood at the Cowelitz comes in demand.[1]

In this passage, McLoughlin relates his belief that the Willamette
Valley enticed more immigrants than did the Cowlitz Valley, north of
the Columbia River, at least partly because of the former's "more beautiful Scenery." He also suggested, however, that in time the economic
factor would outweigh the aesthetic as a consideration for settlement,
noting that one day the Cowlitz Valley's wood would be "in demand."
Early Oregon Country settlers did not initially participate in a market
economy, instead depending primarily on near-subsistence patterns—

hence their concern for "an abundance of Deer." Given their independence, they could afford to include natural beauty as a criterion in their selection of a place to live. Settlers' concern for the aesthetic is only one type of evidence suggesting that western pioneers had a positive and complex relationship with the environment.

McLoughlin, though a longtime resident of Oregon, was not an actual settler. Thus, his appraisal of settlers' motivations is that of an outsider. What then of the actual settler? A careful reading of early documents, coupled with evidence from material culture offered in the last chapter, demonstrates that Willamette Valley settlers had an appreciation of, and intimate relationship with, the environment: an experience strikingly different from the older historical interpretation, which pits the ax-wielding pioneer against the forbidding wilderness.[2] History does show that Euro-American settlers wished to alter the environment, and their actions consequently destroyed the wilderness. But the concept of pioneers versus wilderness, on the levels of both the real and the imaginary, fails to account for the complexities and subtleties of the relationship between settler and environment in the Willamette specifically and the West generally. Like the explorers before them, early Calapooia setters conceived of their environment in terms of the positive, romantic conventions of primitivism and pastoralism. Unlike the earlier transient observers, however, settlers came to stay and therefore developed a more intimate and multifaceted relationship with the land based not only on pastoral and primitive conventions but also on the exigencies of the environment, changing ecology, aesthetics, utilitarian potential, fear, and praise.

PRIMITIVE AESTHETICS AND INTIMACY

One Calapooia settler, the Reverend Wilson Blain, noted at length both the aesthetic appeal of, and his emotional attachment to, the valley's primitive landscape during his early years of residence. Born in 1813 in Ross County, Ohio, Blain was living in Indiana in 1847 when the General Synod of the West of the Associated Reformed (Presbyterian) Church appointed him missionary to the Oregon settlement. Blain and his family migrated to Oregon, arriving in 1848. First they settled at Linn City, across the falls of the Willamette from Oregon City, where Blain edited the *Oregon Spectator* from October 1849 to September 1850. He also served on the first territorial legislature at this time.[3]

After ministering to members of his church up and down the Willamette, including for the first time the Calapooia settlement on 18 June 1849, "and after carefully and prayerfully considering the whole subject," in 1850 Blain relocated his home to the juncture of foothill and prairie at "the western extremity of the Diamond Hills, and just where the valley of the Calapooya loses itself in the extended prairies of the Willamette." There he built a church—the first United Presbyterian church—an academy, and a small village he named Union Point. Blain glowingly wrote that his location "is in the midst of one of the most beautiful neighborhoods in the valley."[4]

The primitive beauty of the Calapooia, as well as the whole of the southern Willamette Valley, greatly affected Blain. He devoted extensive passages in his letters to his developing relationship with this landscape. For instance, he wrote to a friend residing in Pennsylvania about a particularly memorable experience on the landscape he had in the winter of 1851. In noting that "all the circumstances surrounding . . . serve to lend a strange enchantment to the scene," Blain reveals that his experience was multisensual. In his letter he first leads his correspondent "to the summit of yonder green hill," for it is only from this eminent vantage that his own experience is possible to comprehend. To further help recreate the scene, Blain invokes imaginary olfactory and tactile sensations, urging his correspondent to "imagine now that you are breathing the air of the first week of February" and that "a soft balmy breeze [is] fanning your brow." Then, commanding his reader to "cast your eye abroad on the landscape," Blain commences to describe the vista imprinted in his own memory: "The prairies broad and smooth, in all directions and generally the south sides of the hills, are covered with a rich verdant sward of green and *clover*. The forest trees—the pine, fir, cedar, yew, laurel, etc., are all clothed with the foliage of perpetual verdure. With this fresh green world around, the deep azure of a cloudless sky above, . . . tell me is not this beautiful, glorious winter?" Once he has created a general panorama of splendor, Blain then defines specific textural features of the landscape:

> Looking eastward, the eye rests on the western slope of the Cascades, penetrated at frequent intervals by sweet little valleys. To the westward and far to the north and south, lies the valley of the Willamette, interspersed with lines and clumps of timber. And in the distance beyond, reared aloft, are the undulating summits of the Coast Mountains. All around this scene of ver-

dure, and marking a brilliant and lofty line between earth and heaven, the snow rests on the mountain's brow.[5]

In both the above letter and in one of 1851, the valley's buttes and foothills play a central role in Blain's intimate, even ecstatic, experience with the landscape of the Calapooia and southern Willamette valleys.[6] In the second letter, Blain wrote that one day, "while out on pastoral duty," his way led him "over a smooth, grassy ridge, whose summit was, perhaps, some two hundred feet above the level of the Williamette prairies." On reaching the top of this rise, Blain "was permitted to contemplate a singularly beautiful combination of natural grandeur." He vividly described this startling vision. First he commented on his immediate surroundings: the "surface of the ground on which I stood was covered with a species of small yellow flowers." On the "higher slope of the mountain" above "waved a luxuriant growth of flowers of unsullied whiteness; above these the dark forest frowned; higher yet . . . the mountain's brow was wrapped in chilling snows."

Although he was taken with the scenery of the foothill on whose lower flank he perched, it was, significantly, "in the opposite direction," down to the valley, that Blain's vision was pulled, for there the true "beauty of the scene was exhibited." "Almost on a level with the point of which I stood hung a cloud, which formed a dark blue canopy over the entire country. It seemed like a vast awning stretched from the Cascades to the Coast Mountains." This "awning" provided a protected place under which, according to Blain, "the whole valley of the Willamette . . . reposed calmly in verdure and bloom. . . . On the upper surface of the cloud the sun shed its mild radiance. And around the further edge of the cloud the Coast Mountains reared their snowy crests, and glittering in the light of noon-day sun a waving margin of dazzling brilliance." What particularly struck Blain about this unique, "magnificent picture" was the ability of the southern Willamette landscape to afford a beautiful arrangement of a variety of seasons at one time, including stark opposites: "The warm sun and balmy breeze of summer, the verdure and bloom of spring, and the snows of winter."

Blain's letters reveal an intimate and complex connection with the primitive landscape of the Willamette. In the first he explained an experience of communion with the Calapooia and southern Willamette environment. Through multiple sensations—the "soft balmy breezes fanning" his brow, "breathing the air of the first week of February," and viewing the great expanse of the open valley—Blain actually blended into and became part of the landscape. In the second letter Blain successively described "frowning forests," a valley that could "repose," flowers that "waved," and a mountain whose "brow" was wrapped in chilling snows. The physical landscape, through the prism of Blain's mind, took on animate qualities.

It is important to reiterate the key role of the valley's foothills in the bond Blain had with the landscape. Although the hills had a beauty of their own, they were not the focus of Blain's attention, for he continually describes the character of plains below him. In fact, at one point he notes specifically that "it was in the opposite direction," away from the foothills and toward the valley, "that the beauty of the scene was exhibited." However, it was only from the vantage of the foothills and buttes that these visions of the landscape and experiences with the local environment became possible for Blain. As the last chapter demonstrated, foothills played a key role in the physical reality of early settlement history of the southern Willamette Valley. The tension between foothills and plains also found its way into the settlers' psychological and emotional connection to landscape.

Granted, as a missionary settler of the Calapooia, Blain's tasks included encouraging others of his faith to go West and settle, and he undoubtedly wrote with that intention. But it is significant that he often chose the primitive over the pastoral landscape to inspire others to journey west. He also meant what he said. He had a strong attachment to the environment as it was. Once other settlers did begin to arrive, he felt equivocal about their encroachment on the landscape he so loved. He particularly questioned the exclusive attitudes he perceived them as harboring toward the environment. In his letters of 5 March and 1 April 1851, he commented that while his reports on the countryside resulted in only "feeble attempts to describe . . . [his] object of admiring observation," this world was "after all, not a paradise," for it "is truly a portion of the world of labor, sin and trouble." "Our attachment to Oregon," he wrote, "does not all arise from the charm of its scenery or its climate. With the people of this utilitarian age these things would have little influence. It is a country of vast resources, which are easily developed."[7]

The primitive landscape held special meaning for Blain, and he wanted others to come West and settle it; however, he also felt uncertain about how they would relate to it and thus what the consequences for the landscape would be. In a way, Blain proved an important observer of the settlement process, a process he viewed paradoxically. Although he proved correct in his assertion that the new residents of the Calapooia did harbor utilitarian designs on their new landscape, he nevertheless failed to gauge the depth of their appreciation for the same primitive landscape that he enjoyed. Though perhaps not as eloquently as Blain, they also expressed their admiration for the "charm of its scenery," as had the explorers and travelers who had preceded settlement. Thomas Kendall, for instance, remarked in an 1852 letter that "the plains on either side of it [the Calapooia River], presenting as handsome and good and pleasant locations as any country. . . . In the quality of their soil, in the grass with which they are covered, in the kamas with which they abound, and in their healthfulness, I venture to say, they are unsurpassed in almost any country." Even settler Benjamin Freeland, less proficient in written expression than his neighbors Blain and Kendall, could not help but appreciate the beauty of his primitive surroundings on the Calapooia when he wrote to his brother on arrival in early 1854:

> We have a good piraier [prairie] Clame. I dont beleave it Can be beat in oregon or in any Other Country for production and for beauty the prere [prairie] or butts [buttes] and parts of the mountains are coverd over with grass as fine in quality and in goodness as your blew grass in the states . . . and the ballance of the Cuntry are Covered with timber as good as ainy timber . . . it are one of the hamsomest site in the World you can see the prairie all covered with green grass and look a round you and you can see the mountains all covered with green trees at all seasons of the year.

Other Calapooians felt similarly about the landscape. George Waggoner proclaimed the Calapooia "a beautiful place of gently rolling grassy lands, a great mountain peak above, and the broad beautiful valley in full view below." Another settler simply remarked in later years: "You can not imagine the beauty of this country when we first came here."[8] Though perhaps neither as poetic nor emotionally expressive as Blain, who "gazed with rapture" on "many delightful scenes," Kendall, Freeland, Waggoner, and other early settlers of the Calapooia appreciated the primitive beauty of the land they came to settle.

SENTIMENT

Analysis of settlers' admiration of the primitive landscape is one way to ascertain their connection to the western wilderness environment. For

instance, Blain's very thick descriptions also reveal his emotional attachment to the land. Other observers, such as Kendall and Freeland, tended
to be terse in their evaluations, and so we can only speculate how
landscape may have moved them.

Another way to illuminate the elusive feelings of connection that
early Calapooia settlers had with the environment is through an evaluation of their activities on the land and the words they chose to describe
them. Fleeting yet telling moments of intimacy with landscape come
from the words and activities of settlers Amelia Spalding and John
Wigle. The Henry Harmon Spalding family settled in the Calapooia
Valley in 1848, a year after the gruesome Whitman Massacre (in which
Henry and Eliza Spalding's companion missionaries, Marcus and Nar-
cissa Whitman, were murdered by Native Americans at the Waiilatpu
Mission). One informant reported that when Henry Spalding considered making a will, he had two parcels of property. He initially wanted
to bequeath the "old home place" to his daughter Amelia. But Amelia,
realizing that her sister Eliza had "always wanted the old place," wished
not to create animosity between herself and her sister. So she forsook
her domestic residence and responded to her father, "Give me the hill
farm and it will be all right with me. I love that hill place. I always liked
the woods and running brooks and I would be so happy there." John
Wigle reflected on a similar experience in his reminiscences: "Now let
me stop my narrative and indulge in a little meditation as I sometimes
did while out by myself with nothing to disturb my thoughts, only the
level valley and occasionally a coyote." For Wigle and Spalding, natural
elements such as woods, brooks, the open valley, and coyotes either
evoked sentiments or provided psychological or physical refuge.[9]

Social geographers have noted that people construct mental maps
that conform to the spatial environment surrounding them. In the process of constructing mental maps, people eliminate unnecessary detail,
retaining only those physical features most significant to their lives in
that environment.[10] In the Calapooia and southern Willamette valley, in
reality and imagination, foothills and buttes played a prominent role in
the relationship between settler and the physical world. For example,
when Catherine McHargue described the death and subsequent burial
of her sister on 7 December 1852, she noted that her father "looked
about the place to make a grave. He went up on the hill near the house
and started to dig." Because of the heavy autumn rains, water "immediately began to rise in the hole. Unable to complete the grave, father went

still further back from the house and tried again." But again the same thing happened. "He then went far back on the place, nearly to the southwest corner of the claim and at the summit of a bench-like rise. Here the soil was more open and the drainage more perfect and the grave was completed and my sister buried." Catharine constructs in these few sentences her mental image of her family's spatial relationship with the land and the special role foothills played. Catharine refers to the foothills, the "bench-like rise," as actually being behind the cabin and not in front of it. Metaphorically, the ridge acted as a barrier or shelter, something to which she could turn her back in safety. At the same time, she also implies that the positioning of her home on the landscape allowed the front to face down the slope, with a view onto the open plains below. More explicitly, George Waggoner, whose family settled in the Calapooia area in 1852, commented, "So much water was encountered in the valley that we took to the hills . . . a beautiful place of gently rolling grassy lands, a great mountain peak above, and the broad beautiful valley in full view below." Waggoner actually tells us what McHargue only intimates: that his view was pulled down the foothills to the "beautiful valley in full view below."[11]

Forced to live in the foothills to avoid high water and to ensure survival in the wilderness, McHargue and Waggoner used words such as *above*, *up*, *far back*, and *below* to place themselves and their homes in the landscape. Words such as *up*, *down*, *below*, and *above* are obvious ways to refer to mountains and valleys. But when seen in light of sentiment, settlement patterns, early movements on the landscape, and the lack of intermediaries separating humans from the environment, mundane words such as these took on vital significance in local thought during early years of Calapooia settlement.

The geographer Yi-Fu Tuan has noted the symbolic value of landscapes to westering Americans. He has argued that settlers of the American West had a proclivity to travel through and make their homes in valleys, rather than on open plains, because "enclosed space signifies the cozy security of the womb, privacy, darkness."[12] The landscape of the Calapooia Valley, in many ways, both molded locals' thought patterns and acted as a womb within which these earliest settlers of the southern Willamette Valley found a protected place to live. As discussed elsewhere in this volume, a number of practical considerations encouraged immigrants to settle on the periphery of the southern Willamette environment, especially in small valleys such as the Calapooia. But what of the symbolic value of locating in small valleys rather than on the open plains of the Willamette? In this regard, the story of Calapooia settler Tennessee (née Lewis) Tycer, which has been passed on through oral tradition, suggests a more complex psychological relationship with landscape than even Wilson Blain's.[13]

Tennessee Tycer's family followed the general pattern of settlement in the southern Willamette Valley. Rather than taking a claim on the prairies of the valley proper, they chose to take up residence along the periphery, tucked in among the bordering hills. Informants described Tycer as a "very nervous and excitable" woman. One "wild and stormy night" something startled her, and she cried out " 'Indians! Indians! Indians!' Her panic was contagious and everyone in the house ran out." Others joined in the flight, "and so the panic spread from neighbor to neighbor and from house to house." The Tycer family and other settlers took "refuge among thick brush in a deep canyon." Later that night, trembling in horror, they "heard the dogs back in the settlement begin to bark, and they said to each other, 'Now the Indians are at the cabins. They will . . . burn the houses.' " When morning arrived, however, the settlers found "their houses still standing and not a thing touched."

The settlers could not reproach Tennessee for the panic, for they recognized their own complicity in creating the hubbub. Instead, they constructed an elaborate yet convincing explanation to account for their collective actions: "It was finally decided that the cause of the panic was the low flight of an immense flock of wild geese, which confused in storm and fog had dropped very low and frightened a band of horses. These horses, stampeding through the night, had been mistaken for wildly riding Indians." Since objects in the Willamette environment created the situation to which Tennessee reacted, they also made it possible to explain her actions. Never mind that Tennessee was "nervous and excitable": neither she nor the other settlers could be blamed for the fright. Rather, the environment caused the trouble.

The significance of this story is manifold. First, the settlement community explained its fears concerning the wilderness and its Native American inhabitants as largely imaginary. Second, once settlers realized the lack of basis to their fear, they attempted to explain their fright with a series of unlikely events linking together knowable and innocuous elements of the environment: geese, horses, and a storm. Third, on the level of the commonplace, settlers simply ran for cover. In their action, however, they demonstrated that the environment did not merely induce fear; it could also provide cover—security and sanctuary—from fear. This example shows a complex relationship and interdependence between the environment and the settlers on both the mundane and symbolic levels; it also demonstrates that the concept of "settler versus wilderness" is rather useless as an analytical tool.

The variety of evidence that the Tycer and Spalding stories provide, as well as information gathered from settlers and other early westerners such as McHargue, Waggoner, Blain, McLoughlin, Wigle, Kendall, and Freeland, suggest that the environment—not only of the Willamette but of other frontiers as well—was not inert during the settlement process. As the next two chapters illustrate, and as other environmental historians have shown, the environment actively reacts to ecological changes that humans initiate. Moreover, evidence from this chapter demonstrates that the environment, especially fixtures of landscape, also actively shaped settlers' attitudes and interpretations. In the realm of the mind, and as well as in daily, material activities—for instance land claiming, field plowing, and road building, as noted in the last chapter—the western settlement process was multifaceted and in some important ways a positive interaction between the people and the environment.

NATIVE AMERICANS AND THE LANDSCAPE

Formerly, cultural historians argued that westering Europeans and Euro-Americans feared the wilderness because they saw it as a moral vacuum, as the "savage" nature of its native inhabitants made clear. Once the settlers were turned loose in the wilderness, with its absence of social strictures, nothing would rein in deeply rooted human passions, and the settlers, too, would be reduced to savagery. This traditional cultural explanation of European settlement in North America set off wilderness and the Native American as the antipodes of civilization and the settler. This interpretation perpetrated the no longer acceptable myth that westward expansion across the North American continent was a story in which civilization and settlers triumphantly replaced wilderness and savages.[14]

The evidence from the Calapooia settlement suggests that the pioneer-wilderness relationship was rather complex. Undeniably, however, one of the greatest fears Euro-Americans harbored toward the western environment concerned its native inhabitants. From the beginning of colonization, Native Americans—whose intentions were not always clear—seemed persistently to lurk about the outskirts of the settlements. As discussed in the preceding two chapters, years spent fighting natives across the continent preconditioned the responses of Calapooia settlers to the natives of their newly acquired home.

At the time of Euro-American settlement in the Calapooia and the southern Willamette valleys, there survived only a remnant of the Kalapuya people, but they made up as significant a component of the environment as did geese, trees, rivers, creeks, and hills. In many ways, the Kalapuya had shaped and created this environment. For settlers, learning to live with them was also a lesson in learning to live on the new landscape of the Calapooia. Settlers' responses to the actual physical presence of local Native Americans differed greatly. Stories of how two contemporary pioneer women reacted to the Kalapuya have come down to us. These stories, which show markedly contrasting perceptions of and reactions to Native Americans as part of the environment, are important metaphors for responding to a new land.[15]

During 1847–48, Richard C. Finley constructed a flour mill on the falls of the Calapooia. Many locals aided him in his work. Andrew Kirk recalled that his father, William Riley Kirk (known locally as Riley Kirk), helped in the construction. Because Riley had no horse and "oxen were too slow to use, . . . he walked to work." About seven miles separated Kirk's residence and the falls of the Calapooia, so he routinely left his home on Monday morning and worked for the entire week before returning; he thus left "Mother [Julia] and the children . . . alone all the time with the Indians all about." According to son Andrew,

> Whiskey was the Indian's worst failing. One old Indian who came to my mother's door begging for whiskey was cured effectively. Mother, growing tired of his begging, finally poured for him a big cup of pepper sauce. He drank it at a gulp, and then left the cabin in great haste, running for the banks of the river to quench the "fire." Just as he went, father chanced to return home. The Indian never stopped to greet him, but went down the river bank in great jumps, exclaiming "Whoosh! whoosh! whoosh!" at every leap. He never came back to beg for whiskey.

The experience of Sarah McHargue, during the time her husband, James, worked on the Finley mill, differed significantly from Julia Kirk's. As Sarah's daughter Catharine Louise recalled, "All during the winter, father worked on that mill. He would leave home long before daylight and work long until after dark besides walking the several miles each day. . . . Mother was so afraid of the Indians that as soon as father was gone she would shut and barricade the cabin door and taking her child, my oldest sister Ellen, would crawl under the bed and hide there until father returned at night."

Because of their respective distances from the Finley mill, Riley Kirk and James McHargue spent different amounts of time away from their homes and wives. In Riley's absence, Julia felt very comfortable in the Calapooia environment. As she went about her daily duties, the ever-present Kalapuya caused no greater problem than just an annoyance. In fact, when the Kalapuya became demanding, Julia quickly took the upper hand, thus effectively extending control over this component of the environment. So afraid was Sarah McHargue, however, that she barricaded her cabin door and hid under the bed the entire day. By limiting her activities and declining each day into a horrified stupor, Sarah permitted herself to be ruled by the Calapooia environment, specifically the Kalapuya themselves.

Many factors should be considered when trying to explain Sarah's and Julia's different responses to the Kalapuya; two factors in particular can enlighten our understanding. First, because of the extensive absences of her husband, Julia Kirk had to become familiar with the Kalapuya, for she could not hide under her bed for five days at a time. By contrast, Sarah McHargue did not have to accommodate herself to the environment; she could simply make do for a few hours, as her own daughter claimed, until her husband "returned at night." Second, in the Kirk tale Kalapuya are in fact present. In the McHargue story they are present only in Sarah's mind. This is a crucial difference between the stories of these two women's experiences. Julia Kirk actually knew the Kalapuya; she eventually adopted a Kalapuya boy as her son. Her ease with the Kalapuya might also have been in part due to the fact that her husband had "made a reputation for himself by thoroughly thrashing any Indian who became troublesome. . . . [and] the Indians came to understand and respected him accordingly." Sarah McHargue knew no Kalapuya, and thus the meaning they had for her was quite different from that which they had for Julia Kirk.

The stories of Sarah McHargue and Julia Kirk and their relationships with the local Kalapuya provided lessons in learning to live on the Calapooia landscape. They are metaphorical for a number of relationships: the settlers and the Native Americans, the settlers and the wilderness, and imagination and realization. Accepting the presence of and interacting with the Kalapuya, Kirk, even though she took a measure of mastery over them—through both her husband's example and her own action of adopting a native boy—eventually balanced herself with the Calapooia environment. By contrast, McHargue was unable even here to accept the environment on its own terms and therefore failed to balance her life with it; indeed, she even allowed it to govern her activities. These two examples of the ways settlers reacted to natives on the western frontier show that beyond the sociological matters of racism and ignorance, settlers harbored multifarious attitudes toward wilderness and its native inhabitants.

Another case from the Calapooia reveals that on the level of the imagination, the symbolic meaning of the western Native American was not necessarily negative. In an 1854 letter, for instance, Blain described a journey from his congregation in the Calapooia Valley to the settlement in the next valley to the south, the Mohawk. Blain and his companion, Brother David Thompson, found this twelve-mile journey "a wild and rugged way." Of the end of the trip Blain noted, "we were wearied with clambering over hill and hollow, and at the close of day were glad to avail ourselves of refreshment and repose under the hospitable roof of our Christian brother, Wm. C. Baird, . . . the outside frontier man at the head of the Mohawk valley." Blain described the road that they followed through the dense forests of the Willamette's periphery as "nothing but an Indian trail." In the process of following this trail into the wilderness, Blain lost his identity and became, in his words, "Indianlike." For Blain, a Presbyterian minister, this was not a frightening experience. Although he was "glad" to "repose" in the domestic environment of a Christian brother at the furthest extension of civilization at the close of the day, he also declared his appreciation for the "wild, beautiful, and from some points sublime" vistas of the Calapooia and Mohawk that he saw that day, as well as for the captivating botanical life he encountered along the way.[16]

Various levels of intimacy with landscape and the meaning of the Native American are apparent in Blain's experience. First, he had no difficulty entering the "wilderness." As already indicated in his 1851 letters, Blain felt a particular affinity with the valley's primitive nature. Second, his ambivalence over settlement is also apparent in this passage. He enjoyed his sojourn in the "wilderness" and at the same time felt glad at the end of the day to return to the hospitality of civilization. Third, the experience in the "wilderness" that this expedition afforded proved particularly compelling. By 1854, Blain must have felt himself surrounded by the settlement about which he felt increasing uncertainty. The arrival of more settlers in the Calapooia and southern Willamette valleys made his trip into the still unsettled and wild expanse between the Calapooia and Mohawk that much more intensely two-sided. On the one hand, he invoked the romantic cultural convention of the sublime to clarify the impact of the wild scenery on his mind. On the other hand, and in a way opposed to civilization, he invoked the identity of the "Indian" that he might even more fully participate in the wonders of the nature he extolled.

Blain's walk through the tongue of the southern Willamette wilderness that stretched between the newly settled Calapooia and Mohawk valleys compares with the trampings through the eastern woodlands of his contemporary Henry David Thoreau—journeys elaborated on in Thoreau's well-known essay "Walking." Certainly, Blain's experiences are as significant for understanding attitudes of actual western settlers as Thoreau's are for understanding the intellectual climate of the East with regard to the wilderness and the Native American.

PRAIRIE PLAINS:
GARDEN IMAGE, DOMESTICITY, UTILITY

As mentioned in the last chapter, the foothills on the periphery of the southern Willamette Valley provided the material wants for the near-subsistence-level community that early settled the Calapooia; thus, settlers avoided the open prairies. Scholars of the westering process have noted the desire of pioneers to seek out valleys and forests rather than plains and prairies for protection, and evidence from the Calapooia supports the conclusion that this desire played a motivating role in early settlement there, too. Evidence does not reveal, however, that these settlers either feared or were hostile to the open prairies. In fact, just the opposite appears true.[17]

For example, this chapter began with McLoughlin's contention that the Willamette's open prairies actually enticed settlers there. Kendall wrote in 1852, "the best land, the most sightly locations, . . . what will one day be the great agricultural spots . . . [are] the central portions of the prairies." Freeland remarked two years later, "we have a good piraier [prairie] Clame. . . . it are one of the hamsomest site in the World you can see the prairie all covered with green grass." Writing in 1851 while settlement still remained confined to the southern foothills, Blain commented positively about the lure of the open, unsettled prairies:

> Not a few persons have . . . come into Oregon by the Columbia river, and never ascended the Williamette more than twenty-five miles; and, of course, have seen nothing but rough and craggy hills, clothed with dark forests. Yet these are the persons whose reports are to be taken as correct delineations of the character of the territory. Believe them not. They have not seen our green fields and extended plains, and magnificent natural scenery.

On 15 July 1848, several miles north of the Calapooia in the middle stretches of the Willamette Valley, the Reverend George Atkinson ascended a hill. From the summit of the rise, he looked over "broad prairies, forests, bands of woodland surrounding beautiful meadows. It seemed to be a vast region of prairies surrounded by hills. These were in part barren of trees, others were spotted with oaks. All could be cultivated." Aesthetically pleasing descriptions of prairies such as Kendall's, Freeland's, Blain's, and Atkinson's demonstrate that settlers did not fear the open prairie. They viewed the prairies as their future and often spoke of them in positive, pastoral terms that were conventional in the nineteenth century. As Atkinson declared, the prairies would one day become "like a garden."[18]

Settlers' writings from the early Calapooia show a concern with this image of the "garden," which historian Henry Nash Smith has described as the dominant paradigm in western settlement during the nineteenth century. In his classic study on the West as symbol and myth, Smith argues that the idea of the West as garden included a series of metaphors—"fecundity, growth, increase, and blissful labor in the earth"—centered on the image of man as an "idealized frontier farmer armed with that supreme agrarian weapon, the sacred plow."[19]

Central to westward expansion during the nineteenth century, the garden image was fully developed in the literature of the Calapooia Valley. Metaphors implicit in the garden image, especially fertility of soil, appear in early documents from the Calapooia. Freeland wrote of his claim, "I dont beleave it Can be beat in oregon or in any Other Country for production." Blain commented on and even exaggerated the fecundity of the soil:

> I also witnessed some remarkable evidences of the productiveness of the soil. I measured a beet (the common red kind) which was thirty-two inches, and it

was still growing. White turnips weighing from twenty to thirty pounds are not unusual in all parts of the valley. Peaches, wherever cultivated, commence bearing the third year, and produce fruit abundantly. There can be no doubt that this valley possesses productiveness enough to be capable of sustaining as heavy a population as any country of equal extent on the globe.

Kendall commented on both the fertility of the soil and the role of the idealized farmer: "Good cultivation I doubt not would ensure an average yield of from 25 to 30 bushels per acre. . . . A neighbor of mine last fall gathered 39 bushels of onions from a spot of ground not more, I think, than 3 rods square. . . . I had a fine garden last year, . . . after planting it never received a stroke from either plough or hoe; every thing flourished and produced finely."[20]

The central role of the farmer in this scheme is even more apparent in another of Blain's comments: "The soil is various, requiring variety of culture in order to ensure a crop. . . . Here indeed, is found one of the charms which this country has in the eye of an agriculturist." Blain further remarked of the landscape and its potential for the farmer, "It is supposed to possess more land adapted either to the plow or to grass than any other country." Thomas Kendall buttressed this point when he declared, "I don't believe that there are ten acres of poor land, and unfit for agricultural purposes, in the whole valley." The notion of increase is also apparent in the vision of these men. As Blain stated, "The question is frequently asked, Is the country sufficiently large to admit of an extensive settlement? I reply its full settlement is only just commenced."[21]

When Calapooia settlers looked onto the open prairie as a place to plant their garden, they also viewed it as the refuge for a domestic ideal, one that both men and women worked together to achieve. Historians have long noted that, unlike the rough-and-tumble male frontier of gold-rush California, the Willamette agricultural frontier was settled primarily by families. From the outset, the domesticating influence of women and family was part of the settlement culture in the Willamette. The Calapooia settlement demonstrates the point. In 1850, for instance, the census taker enumerated thirty-seven households in the Calapooia, of which thirty-six included families consisting of one or two parents and at least one child (by far, two-parent households with several children dominated). The other domicile contained a single male, but he lived next to the household in which his parents resided. In addition, religious meetings, revivals, and churches promoted ethics that strongly influenced early settlers. A Congregational Church appeared in 1848;

the Associated Reformed Presbyterian Church organized in 1849; Blain formed the first United Presbyterian Church and a religious academy on his claim between 1850 and 1852; in the late 1840s, the Methodists already had a circuit that included the Calapooia Valley, and communicants finally built a Methodist Episcopal Church sometime between 1848 and 1852; the Pleasant Butte Baptist Church formed in November 1853; and religious camp meetings took place on the early Calapooia as well.[22]

Domestic ideals influenced the Calapooia population as a whole, and thus their interpretation of the garden to be planted on their valley's landscape. Some telling documents from women during the early period of the Calapooia indicate their concern about landscape. As previously pointed out, landscape played a central role in Catharine McHargue's vision of daily activities, centering around her family's home. She placed the back of her family's home against the protective foothills, while the front faced the open valley below. In Catharine's mind, the special configuration of the Calapooia landscape gave domesticity a protected place to repose. In another instance, Benjamin Freeland, who settled on the open prairies in 1854, noted at length that he and his family were "well please with the Country with the Exception of the old woman [i.e, wife] and I think she would be well please if she had her children here." Perhaps the open plains on which the Freeland family settled remained barren of domestic meaning for Mary Ann Freeland because her children no longer resided with her. Documents also reveal that Elizabeth Blain planted sweetbrier (a type of rose) around her and Wilson's claim and that the Courtney family, presumably Agnes herself, went about their cabin planting garden flowers and currants, the blooms of which must have added domestic tranquility to a claim Agnes was left to manage herself. Finally, Mrs. James Miller noted of the prairies in 1852, "There are still claims to be taken, four or five miles from here, mostly in the prairie, without timber." The prairie near her home was, she wrote, "about twelve miles wide . . . covered with grass, and dotted over with fat cows and horses, which gives the country a much older appearance than about Oregon City."[23]

Primary sources from the Calapooia reveal not only how women felt about domesticity and landscape but also how the men felt. In particular, we see a quest for a domesticated and morally governed landscape in Blain's description of the progress of settlement on the Calapooia at the time of his arrival in 1850–51: "The point selected for my future operation is in the midst of one of the most beautiful neighborhoods in this valley. It is a choice agricultural district, where some 20 or 30 families could yet locate the best of farms on the public domain. The whole neighborhood is under moral and religious influence, and at present it is much the heaviest settlement in the country." Blain envisioned this domesticated society one day spreading onto the nearby open plains: "Fifty families could locate advantageously in our neighborhood on delightful prairies." He commented further, "We most heartily wish our people in the States could only see the beautiful lands in this vicinity to be had simply for the taking," and "we cherish the hope that our cause will be greatly strengthened by immigration." A morally upright population inhabiting the prairies was also the desire of Thomas Kendall, who commented on his pleasure with a "small congregation in my neighbourhood" and stated, "There is yet an abundance of good land in our neighbourhood unclaimed."[24]

On the early agricultural frontier of the Calapooia, men and women held a vision of the community they wished to plant in a domesticated landscape. By the end of the nineteenth century the garden image would in many ways be realized. But the garden image—embracing the metaphors of fecundity, growth, domesticity, and the idealized farmer cultivating the earth—was largely an artifice, something formulated completely within the human mind. In fact, though, the environment was itself active and independent, as the settlers themselves recognized. The history of the Calapooia shows that Euro-Americans did not simply force their objective will onto the land. Rather, the pioneering process was an exchange between landscape and people. In the Calapooia specifically, the garden necessarily included the landscape's physical and aesthetic qualities, as Wilson Blain, Elizabeth Blain, Mrs. James Miller, John Wigle, Thomas Kendall, Benjamin Freeland, Catharine McHargue, Tennessee Tycer, Amelia Spalding, John McLoughlin, George Waggoner, Jared Michael, and Thomas Ward, to name only a few of their generation, suggest in written and material evidence. Along the Calapooia, settlers would necessarily plant the garden—germinated in eighteenth- and nineteenth-century thought—in the valley's primitive landscape, which they already considered beautiful: the "most sightly location"; a "beautiful specimen" of timbered and open prairie land, whose "plains on either side of it [the Calapooia River], present[ed] as handsome and good and pleasant locations as any country"; "a beautiful place of gently rolling grassy lands . . . and the broad beautiful valley"; "one of the hamsomest site in the World"; "a beautiful elevation"; in "this land of Beulah"; a natural "scene of enchanting beauty"; and "a beautiful landscape almost literally covered with a variegated bloom" of wildflowers.[25]

More simply put, in the Calapooia the human-formulated image of the garden would necessarily be planted in a landscape whose appearance, preceding white settlement, was already considered beautiful in its own right. In fact, in the Calapooia country, the landscape's quality of primitive or "natural" beauty helped to both hold the garden image together and to preserve it through the end of the nineteenth century. But in quest of a garden, Euro-Americans would necessarily alter and transform the ecology and symbolic value of the Willamette environment and wilderness, creating a whole new set of physical and psychological dilemmas.

Settlement on the Calapooia occurred at a place and time still relatively untouched by the industrial revolution and other factors of "modernization." Living on the new, undeveloped frontier of the Pacific Northwest, Calapooians experienced a brief time lag that allowed them a few years to develop an intimate and in many ways positive relationship with their environment. The beauty of their new landscape reinforced this intimacy.

But this was a short-lived period. The garden image itself had an inherent contradiction in its metaphors of increase and growth. At the same time that increase and growth could be applied to blissful labor in the earth and a growing population—forces themselves that could be destructive to an intimacy with the landscape—they also geared the settlers to take advantage of the valley's utilitarian potential at this critical point in history, as Blain already feared in 1851. Soon, intermediaries of the modernizing world would disassociate settlers from this landscape.

Significantly, from the commencement of settlement on the Calapooia, locals did proclaim their valley's utilitarian qualities: its natural resources as well as its potential for industrial and agricultural increase and growth. In the early 1850s Kendall commented on the availability of timber "which will be converted into use"; likewise, in 1852–53 a surveyor wrote that the foothills "are well timbered . . . and in many places . . . acceptable for teams and will become valuable to the settlers." Benjamin Freeland commented on the abundance of nearby timber for home use: "We can cut eleven rails off one tree. . . . The balm of

Gilliad is first rate to split and to make rails and to last." Kendall also commented on topics as diverse as the prospects for livestock raising, the availability of water, and the health of the region, as did the surveyor: the Calapooia, he said, "affords several fine locality for mills," and the prairies were "well calculated for grazing." And Linn County petitioners in 1856 remarked that "the Grazing facilities of our Country are one of her Chief sources of wealth and prosperity"; with proper attention, the "Great natural Meadows with which our whole Country abounds, might, and would continue to be a source of incalcuble advantage to her Citizens."[26]

Blain, who expressed concern over what he perceived as the exclusively utilitarian attitudes of his age, could not help but comment on the valley's utilitarian prospects. In one letter he commented successively on timber, prairies, convenience of prairie and timber, native grasses, productiveness, markets, health, and the climate. In other letters he remarked that "the Calapooya is a bold, rapid mountain river, affording fine hydraulic privileges" and that "it is a great country for an industrious man, for in no other place in the world are industry and economy more speedily rewarded with affluence."[27]

This recognition of the landscape's beauty and utility both reinforced and was reinforced by the garden image. In the late nineteenth century, "modernizing" forces, which included, among others, rail transportation and a widening market economy, helped residents attain a domesticated or pastoral landscape.[28] Attainment of the garden image in the Calapooia Valley, however, was in part the attainment of an artifice. To build this type of community, the settlers had to pay the price of the loss of a close, intimate connection with the Calapooia's natural or primitive landscape that developed during the early settling years.

Settlers at first related to the landscape on a number of levels: the emotional, the aesthetic, and the utilitarian. As these people went about planting their garden—both domesticating the landscape and realizing its utility—they actually lost the intimacy that they had initially enjoyed with the primitive landscape. This loss was not readily recognizable, since intimacy with the land was an inner and emotional experience, difficult to understand and appraise. At the end of the nineteenth century, however, when the Calapooians and other Willamette Valley inhabitants sat back in their domesticated landscape, they did finally recognize this loss.

PART THREE

New Meaning for a New Land

CHAPTER V

Early Economic, Attitudinal, and Environmental Change on the Calapooia

The nineteenth-century history of the Willamette Valley is the story of the region coming under the influence of an expanding European and Euro-American economic and biological system. The settlers themselves were invaders. Furthermore, their reactions to the Willamette landscape—though partly, and importantly, modified by contact with this new land—were conditioned by cultural conventions that had originated outside the region. One way they viewed the environment was with a desire for personal gain. This attitude invited into the Willamette Valley new plants, animals, and methods of altering the land, and especially the influence of expanding regional, national, and world markets—markets that demanded agricultural and natural resources. As Willamette residents participated in these markets, the Willamette environment experienced increasing and intensified change.

Other histories have dealt extensively with the interrelated social, economic, and environmental consequences that the expanding European and Euro-American economic and biological system had on particular localities and native peoples in North America.[1] But what were the consequences for the local Euro-American population's cultural relationship with the land?

The earliest Euro-American settlers interacted with the Calapooia Valley environment on a variety of levels and in complex ways. They did not harbor the simple desire to rush off to the western wilderness to avoid the onslaught of civilization, nor did they wish to "tame the wilderness" or even to destroy the primitive landscape. Although it is true that certain components of the landscape—for instance, wildlife and Native Americans—caused problems and could be and were controlled and even eliminated, the settling process on the Calapooia was one in which the earliest Euro-American arrivals, left to fend for themselves in a new landscape, recognized the independence of the environment and actually attempted in a number of psychological and physical ways to balance themselves with it. As a result of this balancing process settlers developed an intimate and in many ways positive relationship with the landscape.

At the same time, settlers also envisioned creating a pastoral community out of the primitive landscape of the Calapooia. But in their minds, the pastoral would not simply replace the primitive. Certainly, to the early settlers, the landscape's primitive aesthetic qualities were to play a central role in the building of their community, as would the utility that they could draw out of the land. The question they faced was one to which Wilson Blain alluded early on: could feelings for the charms of the scenery—indeed, a complex and intimate connection with the land—be reconciled with the utilitarian attitudes that his generation also harbored?

This and the following chapter assess community building in the Calapooia and ways in which the Calapooia and Willamette settlers and environment increasing became tied into broader, outside markets during the late nineteenth century. These chapters also outline some of the concomitant and subtle ways in which certain aspects of settlers' and their descendants' perceptions of the Willamette Valley landscape intensified and other aspects diminished in importance during this process. History reveals that as these people worked toward the type of community they had envisioned and were drawn into wider economic markets, their activities altered not only the original landscape but also their relationship with the land. In fact, this process led to an estrangement between themselves and the land. The course of events leading to an estrangement of the late nineteenth-century residents of the valley from the landscape did not occur in a continuous progression. But ultimately, gradually, subtly, and quietly—indeed, unbeknownst to the Calapooians—forces originating both inside and outside the valley effectively separated them from the land. Chapter 7 reveals that by the end of the nineteenth century the Calapooians had achieved a version of the pastoral community they had initially desired to create, but the victory came with a price both they and the environment paid.

RICHARD FINLEY'S GRISTMILL:
LANDSCAPE AND COMMUNITY VALUES

From the very commencement of settlement on the banks of the Calapooia River there existed forces within the valley itself that ultimately led to the psychological separation of Calapooia residents from the landscape. The incidents depicting this process are numerous, but the story of the construction of Richard Finley's gristmill on the falls of the Calapooia perhaps best shows these agents at work at a very early date. In this story, landscape plays a key role.

After arriving in the Oregon Country in the fall of 1845, John and Agnes Courtney wintered in the lower Willamette Valley. The following spring they traveled south and settled on the southern side of the Calapooia Valley on a small stream that now bears their name. With them came an entourage of immediate and extended family members, including their son John R. Courtney, who subsequently took up a claim of his own, just a few miles northeast of his parents. When John R. recorded his claim with the Oregon provisional government on 15 August 1846, he gave the following description: "640 acres of land in Champoeg County, situated on the Calapooigah river, above the Santyam, Commencing at an oak tree at the N.E. corner, thence running S. one mile to a stake, thence W. one mile to a stake, thence N. one mile to an oak tree marker, thence to the place of beginning. *Said includes the falls of the Calapoiah and is held in personal occupancy.*"[2]

For reasons that are not known, Courtney temporarily left his claim without making further improvements to it, even though the letter of the law required that a settler, to retain title to property, had "either personally [to] reside upon his claim himself, or to occupy the same by the personal residence of his tenant." Courtney did neither. But he also did not intentionally yield his rights to his land when he walked away from it. He had every reason to expect that the frontier custom of the "tomahawk claim" or "tomahawk law," long practiced in cis-Appalachia, protected his land from intruders.[3]

Because of the settlement nature of the early cis-Appalachian frontier, new arrivals there had for years abided by the tomahawk law, a

commonly recognized convention that flouted the letter of the law requiring occupation and improvement of claims. Under the tomahawk
law, a settler, in order to hold his claim, had only to mark its boundaries
by girdling a few trees. This practice allowed him freedom to move on
to see if some other claim might suit him better. If he found no better
site, he could always return to the earlier claim.[4]

Settlers carried the tomahawk law to Oregon. Men often left their
families in the lower Willamette, sometimes even back in the Midwest,
while they went ahead to find a suitable claim in western Oregon. Elias
Keeney, for example, settled by himself on the Calapooia in 1847,
headed to the gold-mining region of California in 1848, returned to his
Calapooia claim in 1849, and then, in 1850, went to Missouri. When he
returned to his land in the Calapooia, he brought a new family with
him.[5]

On returning to their tomahawk claims, however, Willamette settlers
sometimes found their lands occupied by people whom they considered
"claimjumpers," but who in fact had every legal right to take up the
technically abandoned land. Claim-jumping in the Willamette Valley
frequently occurred during early years of settlement, particularly in the
more heavily populated northern regions where poor land surveys, land
frauds, dubious land sales, and speculation ran rampant. But in areas
where effective government control did not exist, the community—
particularly families, but also organized protective associations—
generally rallied to support the first settler, as they had in cis-
Appalachia.[6] A similar event, though with different results because of
perceptions of the landscape's utility, occurred on Courtney's claim at
the falls of the Calapooia in the late 1840s.

At about the time Courtney walked away from his claim on the falls
of the Calapooia, two separate groups of families—who had become
acquainted with each other during the migration of 1846—entered the
northern Willamette Valley. The first group included James and Sarah
Blakely of Tennessee and their five children and James's uncle Hugh and
aunt Clarissa Brown, also from Tennessee, and at least five of their
children. The other group comprised Alexander and Sarah Kirk with
four children, their son William Riley Kirk and his wife and one son,
and Alexander and Sarah's daughter Mary "Polly" (Kirk) Finley and
her husband, Richard Chism Finley, and their two children, all from
Tennessee, Indiana, and Missouri.[7]

On entering the Willamette Valley, the Blakely and Kirk parties headed south. The Finleys stopped on the Marys River on the west side of the Willamette, while the others went on until they reached the Calapooia. The morning after arriving, they surveyed the valley as far east as the falls on the Calapooia River (i.e., John R. Courtney's tomahawk claim) and decided that the little valley afforded them a suitable home. They proceeded to take up four contiguous claims near where the Calapooia River flows out onto the open Willamette prairies.[8]

James Blakely and Alexander Kirk found Isaac Courtney, brother of John R. Courtney, occupying the particular parcel of land they desired. Kirk had a special interest in the eastern portion of Isaac's claim because it straddled the Calapooia River at a ford where the developing pioneer wagon trail along the eastern foothills of the valley would probably lead farther into the southern Willamette and eventually to California. In acquiring such a claim, Kirk knew he could "control both banks of the river" where he would soon construct a toll ferry. Blakely later recounted that, "Mr. Kirk and I traded a yoak of oxen for . . . the parcel of land" Isaac held.[9] These apparently amicable relations with the Courtneys, however, soon soured.

With the Browns, the Blakelys, and William Riley Kirk entrenched in their claims, Alexander Kirk hired Isaac Hutchens to reside on his land while he returned with his family to the Marys River, where the Finleys had remained. It is likely that the Kirks, on reaching the Marys, related to their son-in-law Richard Finley—a miller by trade—the encouraging news about the falls they had found on the Calapooia, which locals described as "the best spot," "a fine site," and even "the only available spot" to build a gristmill.[10]

The Kirks and Finleys wintered on the Marys, but the following spring they headed for the Calapooia. At the time Finley entered the Calapooia, settlers in the southern and mid Willamette Valley had to travel as far north as the Hudson's Bay Company's mills at Oregon City to have their wheat ground into flour, a trip requiring about ten days. James Blakely later recalled that some spent as many as seventeen days taking wheat to the mill at Fort Vancouver, on the north side of the Columbia. For the ostensible reason that such travel was an inconvenience, a group of settlers headed by Blakely and Brown encouraged Finley to build a mill at the falls of the Calapooia on the site of John R. Courtney's claim.[11] Disregarding the tomahawk claim, they noted that

Courtney had gone away "without making any improvements [and] had no right to hold it," and they promised to "back Finley up in his claim at any cost." Finley wasted no time: on 22 April 1847 he was in Oregon City to have the claim legally recorded in his name with the provisional government.[12]

Finley returned to the Calapooia to begin to improve his claim. Just as he felled a tree for a footbridge across the river, John R. Courtney suddenly reappeared. Some versions of the story suggest that Courtney made threatening advances toward Finley, ordering him off his land. But Finley, ax in hand, was not to be trifled with. Courtney retreated to get reinforcements from his family, and Finley sent word to those settlers who had encouraged him to take the claim. Soon, two armed bands gathered at the disputed site. Finley's supporters included Blakely, Brown, Alexander Kirk, and possibly William Riley Kirk. The Courtney contingent comprised John B. Courtney, John R. Courtney, John Dunlap (Agnes Courtney's first husband's brother-in-law), and possibly Isaac Courtney.[13]

The traditional story holds that the Courtney clan did not want to sacrifice human life and so finally backed down. But it is very likely that the Courtneys realized that, although frontier tradition affirmed their superior moral position, they were legally in the wrong. Equally important in the Courtneys' decision to back down was their realization that the valley actually needed a gristmill. John Dunlap, in fact, calmed John B. Courtney, "who was very angry about the whole affair and was going to kill Finley," by assuring him that "Finley is all right and he will build a mill here long before you ever could." And Finley did (figure 3).[14]

Finley and his supporters saw the utilitarian significance of the landscape in this parcel of the Calapooia, and they were ready to take advantage of it. In this instance, utilitarian concern outweighed a vision of the land based on moral principles. As Finley's own daughter, Eliza, later pointed out, this event opened a social wound in the Calapooia community that took years to heal. But probably neither Eliza nor other Calapooia residents detected that this single instance of struggle between traditional morals of land claiming and the benefits of economic development—something that had occurred and would continue to occur on other parts of the western frontier—also opened a wound that slowly festered in the settler-landscape relationship on the Calapooia.[15]

Figure 3.   Richard Chism Finley's gristmill, ca. 1940. The flood of 1861 destroyed Finley's first mill, built 1847–48. On the same site, the falls of the Calapooia River, Finley immediately constructed this second mill, which the McKercher family purchased about 1890. Courtesy of the Oregon Historical Society, Portland (negative number ORHI 0029-P317).

GOLD RUSH, LIVESTOCK, AND ENVIRONMENT

The influence of the California gold rush on the economic development of the Calapooia illustrates that forces that affected the settlers' relationship to the landscape also originated outside the valley. The gold rush also had a profound impact on the ecological balance of the valley. When Euro-Americans came to the Calapooia in 1846, the residents of the middle and northern Willamette Valley, with a longer settlement tradition there, had already developed a very limited market economy, though agriculture remained at or barely above the subsistence level. These settlers depended on the Hudson's Bay Company for some consumer goods and marketing outlets until the late 1840s. Limited access to outside markets and to hard currency kept the Willamette Valley economy in a state of virtual depression until the stimulus of the California gold rush in 1849. In response to the depressed economy, in 1845 the provisional government even made wheat legal tender, though valley residents had been paying debts in kind—wheat and shingles—for several years. The worst of the depression came in 1847–48, when a surplus of wheat brought low prices.[16]

Although the older settlement in the northern Willamette Valley marketed some wheat through the Hudson's Bay Company—in the early 1830s the company already had a grain receiving station near Willamette Falls—settlers of the Calapooia had little opportunity to participate in the fledgling market economy for two principal reasons. First, the Calapooia in the late 1840s was a young settlement, and pioneers just arriving there occupied themselves primarily with building homes and clearing land. Second, the southern Willamette Valley simply lacked adequate transportation to the few outlets that existed. Therefore, the agricultural production that southern Willamette Valley settlers engaged in remained at subsistence levels. Thomas Kendall, who observed the settling process from his claim on the Calapooia, noted in 1852, "Our emigrants often hurry in a crop after they arrive, with as little preparation as possible, in order to bread them the following year; others attempt nothing more than to raise a sufficiency for their own use—and the very facility with which grain is produced leads to habits of careless cultivation." The 1850 census lends statistical support to Kendall's observation. Of the thirty-four Calapooia farms in the census, eighteen produced a total of only 2,265 bushels of wheat, and two farms produced seventy pounds of oats. Most people subsisted on potatoes, swine, and wild game.[17]

Because there was no developed market economy, hard currency remained scarce in the Calapooia. The plight of James McHargue is a case in point. He settled on the Calapooia with his family in 1847, paying his last twenty-dollar gold piece for squatters' rights to a land claim. Now poverty stricken, the McHargues could only borrow flour from their neighbor Jonathan Keeney, who, after sizing up McHargue as "an impecunious young man from whom he could never hope to collect the loan," gave his new neighbor some of the poorest flour that he had. McHargue sowed about twenty acres of wheat that year and, according to an admiring descendant, surprised Keeney by paying him back in wheat twice that which he had borrowed. On another occasion, Clarissa Brown tailored a buckskin suit for McHargue, who paid for it with a pig.[18]

Some cash- and possession-poor arrivals like James McHargue found employment at Finley's gristmill. Of course, some of the settlers had either a more direct stake in the valley's economic prosperity or familial connections to the Finleys, or both, and thus donated their time and energy to mill construction. James Blakely, for instance, "hewed the timber free" for the mill, and Riley Kirk resided with his sister and brother-in-law for days at a time while he worked on the mill. But others in the valley, like the newly arrived McHargue, needed paying employment, and some received it from Finley. Unable to pay his workers in hard currency at first, however, Finley probably partially compensated them in kind, though he also ran up quite a debt.[19]

Just as Finley completed his mill in 1848, news of the gold strike in California came to the Willamette Valley. Being "so much in debt in building the mill" and wishing "to find a quick way to repay what he owed," the very day he ground the first flour, "he got on a horse and rode away to the California mines." From California, he sent gold to his wife, who "never kept the dust in her possession a moment longer than was necessary. Whenever she received a shipment . . . she would notify all the people about to come and present their bills. Upon the stated day, she would portion out the dust in equable portions as long as it lasted." Other locals also went to California and brought back gold with them. For instance, Elias Keeney went to California in 1849 and reportedly came back with fifteen thousand dollars in gold. But it was through the gristmill that settlers first exchanged gold in the fledgling local economy.[20]

Although the Calapooia community as a whole occupied itself with subsistence crop cultivation, a few other early settlers moved to establish local industrial and commercial enterprises. At the opposite end of the valley from son-in-law Finley, Alexander Kirk built a winter ferry across the Calapooia in 1846–47. Kirk located his ferry at the strategic spot where the river flows out of the foothills and onto the open plains of the Willamette. Because the floor of Willamette Valley was watersoaked through much the year, early travelers stayed along the base of the well-drained foothills bordering the valley. With his strategic position on the Calapooia, right where the road descends the foothills to ford the river, Kirk captured the profitable business provided by traffic moving into the southern Willamette Valley, and even on to California, as well as that coming to the Calapooia to deal at Finley's gristmill. By 1853 the Linn County court was allowing Kirk to charge "for wagon &

span of horses or yoke of cattle fifty cents, for each additional span of horses or yoke of cattle 12 1/2, man & horse 25 cents footman 10 cents lumber 100 ft 8 cents horse with packs 12 1/2 cents." Kirk probably had no real worry about losing his monopoly on traffic, but in 1848 he made sure to have himself appointed one of the two viewers for the official "Territorial Road," which he subsequently surveyed from Oregon City "to the crossing of the Calapooa at A. Kirks." With the Kirk-Finley economic axis firmly established, development continued in the valley. Kirk built an inn on his claim, and in 1850 Hugh Brown and James Blakely built a store on the road that traversed Blakely's claim between Kirk's and Finley's enterprises. In addition, small sawmills in the Calapooia flourished as increasing numbers of new settlers came to the southern Willamette. John Courtney built a mill on Courtney Creek soon after claiming land there in 1846; William T. Templeton built a sawmill on the Calapooia in 1850; Richard Finley built one in 1852; and Philemon Vawter Crawford did likewise in 1854.[21]

The stimulus of the California gold rush ended the depression in the Willamette and settlers' dependence on the Hudson's Bay Company for markets. For these reasons, historians have viewed the gold rush as a crucial turning point in the economic development of the Pacific Northwest. But while the gold rush called for greater production, stimulating trade, sawmills, and gristmills in some parts of the Willamette Valley, it limited development in the south. As Wilson Blain, whose house sat along the road leading south out of the Calapooia, noted, "Men bound to the gold mines are passing our door almost hourly for some weeks past; so that I should suppose the male population below this place must be pretty much gone to the far famed gold fields." Estimates indicate that two-thirds of the Willamette Valley's able-bodied men went to California, leaving not only unharvested wheat in the fields but also the limited labor of wives and children to look after farms. Because settlers arrived on the Calapooia precisely as the gold rush began, they had time only to claim land, make a few improvements, and perhaps sow a few acres to wheat before heading off to California. Thus, the more labor-intensive endeavor of large-scale agricultural production did not occur in the Calapooia at this early date.[22]

Other differences between development in the northern and southern Willamette Valley that the gold rush engendered are accounted for by the fact that in the north, with access to the confluence of the Willamette and Columbia rivers, settlers could more readily ship lumber to

California. Also, because of longer settlement history in the north, agriculture was more advanced there by the time of the gold rush. Those who remained in the northern valley reaped benefits as California markets demanded produce and timber. By contrast, in the southern Willamette, which had few roads and faced seasonally waterlogged prairies, lumber production remained local, and most other goods could not be shipped.[23]

In the southern Willamette Valley, then, still newly settled, far from markets, and suffering transportation deficiencies, the gold rush limited development, especially agricultural. Instead, remaining male settlers, or women and children left behind, found it easier to raise livestock, particularly cattle but also swine, which could walk themselves to the markets the gold rush generated. By the late 1850s, valley residents were herding up to twenty thousand cattle a year to California. In Linn County in 1850, the census taker counted 4,619 cattle, or almost five head per settler. Of the abundance of cattle, Benjamin Freeland commented that it looked like there "are as maney cattel in origen as . . . in the states but it owen to the hevery Emmegration and the deamand in the gold reigon and the heavy demand in Califo[rnia] for all kinds of produce."[24]

Thus, the southern Willamette Valley did slowly begin to participate in the expanding markets that accompanied the gold rush; however, because of the southern valley's poor transportation, limited labor supply, and recent settlement, the gold rush kept the region's agricultural practices at a subsistence level. In the Calapooia Valley in 1850, 219 people lived on thirty-four farms. They herded 522 cattle (more than fifteen per farm) but produced only 2,265 bushels of wheat, which works out to roughly two bushels of flour per person for the entire year. Fifteen farms produced no wheat, five farms had not a single acre of improved land, and the average amount of improved land (which the census took to include grazing and fallow lands) per farm was about twenty-six acres.[25] These statistics show that subsistence (perhaps even below subsistence) agricultural conditions dominated the economy of the Calapooia in 1850 at the peak of the gold rush.

The gold rushes and conditions of transportation, then, impeded large-scale commercial agricultural production in the southern Willamette Valley, but they also led to the growth of an enormous cattle industry. Increasing numbers of settlers spurred the growth of fledgling manufactories. The cattle industry and local sawmills and gristmills broke the Calapooia settlement's ties to complete economic self-sufficiency. Yet this new market economy remained not yet fully developed. Freeland noted that "all kinds of produce" were in demand in California, and neighbor Fielding Lewis commented that "times is good and brisk here," but neither suggested that a market economy was fully developed. In fact, at about the same time Blain noted in a letter that "though the natural facilities are good, and merchandize of every description is abundant in consequence of money occasioned by our vicinity to the gold mines, markets, in the sense of exchanging agricultural products for merchandize, have almost no existence."[26] In other words, while Calapooians could sell produce more readily during the gold rush years, in the early 1850s they still did not benefit from a fully developed market economy.

Only in the late 1850s did wheat production pick up and allow for the expansion of gristmills on the Calapooia and elsewhere in the southern Willamette Valley. At that time, Richard Finley and Philemon Crawford, more readily able to conduct business with the influx of hard currency, built the Boston Flour Mill on the lower Calapooia. John A. Crawford, who had an interest in the mill, carried on a trade beyond the valley itself, for he shipped flour to the California gold mines by pack trains, each trip netting him one thousand dollars.[27] Thus, in the late 1850s, demand for lumber, distant (albeit limited) demand for flour, and the influx of California gold all induced the growth of a fledgling market economy in the southern Willamette Valley.

The livestock trade, particularly in cattle, gave the Calapooians and other southern Willamette Valley settlers their greatest access to the California markets during early years. As noted in chapter 3, the Willamette Valley's environment suited it ideally to the raising of both cattle and swine. The great demand for livestock in the gold regions, their ability to walk to market on their own, and the relatively little care they needed in the valley environment made them a good item of trade, particularly for the Calapooia and southern Willamette Valleys, where large numbers of cattle were herded (table 2).

The livestock trade dominated the local economy and at the same time changed the ecology of the Willamette and intensified certain aspects of the Calapooian's attitude to the landscape. Livestock seriously affected the "natural history" of the Calapooia and Willamette grasslands. Shrub invasion of the prairies largely resulted from the cessation of burning (discussed in greater detail in chapter 6) as white settlement commenced and the Kalapuya disappeared, but cattle also destroyed

TABLE 2

NUMBER OF CATTLE,[a] 1850–80

	Calapooia		Linn County		Willamette Valley	
1850	522 (2.4)[b]		4,619 (4.6)		32,794 (2.8)	
1852	972	(+86%)[c]	5,784	(+25%)	—[d]	
1860	—[e]		20,121 (3.0)	(+248%)	93,094 (2.7)	(+85%)
1870	1,069 (1.0)	(+10%)	8,810 (1.0)	(−56%)	45,692 (0.9)	(−51%)
1880	2,055 (0.9)	(+92%)	12,754 (1.0)	(+45%)	73,970 (1.0)	(+62%)

SOURCES: Manuscript Census Returns for Agriculture and Population of Linn County for 1850, 1870, and 1880; *Linn County, Oregon: Early 1850 Records;* U.S. Department of Commerce, Bureau of the Census, *Seventh Census,* 1006–007; *Agriculture of the United States in 1860 . . . Eighth Census,* 120–21; *Statistics of the Wealth and Industry of the United States . . . Ninth Census* (1872) 3:231; *Report on the Productions of Agriculture . . . Tenth Census,* 167; *Ninth Census of the United States, Statistics of Population* (1872), 57; *Statistics of the Population of the United States . . . Tenth Census* (1884), 1:405.

[a]Includes beef cattle, work oxen, and milk cows.
[b]Per capita, rounded to nearest one-tenth.
[c]Percent change, i.e., the change over preceding *available* figures, rounded to the nearest percent.
[d]1852 records are not available for the Willamette Valley.
[e]Linn County Manuscript Agricultural Census, 1860, is missing.

tempting native grasses, such as *Festuca idahoensis,* which has a low resistance to grazing, and left alone unpalatable shrubs, both native and newly introduced. The plant ecologists William Moir and Peter Mika have argued that the complete story of grazing effects on the Willamette prairies remains unknown and probably unanswerable. But they also note that a combination of grazing and agriculture did have serious consequences for native vegetation. By 1919 perhaps as much as 52 percent of the 106 species of grass in one study area had been introduced in the sixty years after settlement. As early as 1872, one viewer of the southern Willamette Valley commented on the stock owners' "indiscriminate pasturing" of large cattle herds on the prairies during the gold rush and stated that it "injured the grasses and reduced them to shorter growth." Just twenty years earlier a Calapooia settler had noted the "nutritive qualities" of the prairie grass as "unsurpassed by any species of grass throughout the world."[28]

Cattle and swine disturbed the natural environment of the Calapooia and Willamette, and they also influenced the settlers' view of the landscape. Although utilitarian concerns for the Calapooia landscape had always been present, they had also been intertwined with the valley's aesthetic qualities, but this attitude soon began to change. During the 1850s and early 1860s, both Calapooians and other Willamette Valley settlers raced to exploit the prairies, grazing tens of thousands of cattle on them. Profit far outweighed any aesthetic or symbolic value of the prairies as valley residents realized the utility of the landscape and the profit to be had by participating in regional markets. In a series of petitions, settlers from Linn and Lane counties, the two southern Willamette Valley counties with the largest open prairie lands, voiced a new concern for the landscape when they complained about problems associated with cattle grazing during the mid 1850s. The inhabitants of both counties expressed annoyance with "wealthy men resident Among us ... [and] wealthy men who reside on other localities" who leave "their cattle & other stock to run at large on the grass land of others" who had no livestock and lacked the resources to fence their claims. Petitioners complained of these cattle's "viscious & wild habits" because they attacked and wounded citizens and in some instances prevented children from attending school, but the heart of their message dealt with economic concerns. Linn County residents stated specifically that "the Grazing facilities of our Country are one of her Chief sources of wealth and prosperity, and that if proper care were observed the Great natural Meadows ... would continue to be a source of incalculable advantage to her Citizens." To southern Willamette Valley inhabitants it appeared that the problem resulted from "the *rich*" taking advantage of "the *poor*." As a solution, they asked that a law be passed apportioning the "number of Animals that may be allowed to run at large to a given number of acres."[29]

Marauding swine proved no less a problem to the environment and amicable social relations than did hordes of loose cattle. Hogs plundered the valley's great expanse of camas. Early Willamette settler John Minto wrote, "Swine ... were the chief destroyers of the roots which were the chief foods of the natives." Swine caused social tensions as well. In 1856–57 more than seventy-five Linn County residents, many of them Calapooia settlers, petitioned the territorial government "to enact some law to prevent swine from running at large and that all persons keeping swine be compelled to keep the same upon their own land." One of these petitioners was Robert W. Elder, whose claim lay along the lower Calapooia. At the same time that this petition was circulating, thirty-two other settlers drew up a counterplea stating that "a Law passed at the present time compelling people to keep up their hogs would be a great damage to many citizens." When Americus Savage, whose land claim bordered Elder's immediately to the north, became the first signer of this counterpetition, the stage was formally set for a personal quarrel.[30]

In retaliation for Savage's hogs constantly invading his gardens, one evening Elder marched over to Savage's home, which sat atop a small butte, and angrily knocked on the door. When Savage answered, Elder temporarily stunned him with a slingshot whose projectile was made of lead formed in the shape of an S. Whether the S stood for "Savage" or "swine" or both, we can only guess. But gathering his senses, Savage made his way to a pile of fir poles near his house. Grabbing one, he beat Elder all the way down the side of the butte. Because of the proximity of the small town of Boston, locals later referred to this fight as the "Battle of Bunker Hill."[31] Probably none realized at the time how the underlying causes of this battle fit into the ecological revolution then occurring on the banks of the Calapooia.

Once residents began to realize the utility of the prairies whose primitive and pastoral beauty they had at one time praised so gloriously, the meaning of these grasslands changed. Rather than a vision of beauty, or even an idyllic natural garden where prosperity and a pastoral community could be attained, the southern Willamette and Calapooia prairies became a battlefield on which the settlers waged economic warfare.

To combat unruly livestock, settlers had to enclose their land, especially since the provisional and territorial government laws left the legal burden on those who wanted to protect their property. The provisional government early on wrote into law meticulous specifications for building fences: "strong worm fence . . . locked at each joint, five feet in height, . . . or a hedge two feet high, or a sod fence three feet high, with a ditch on each side three feet wide and three feet deep, or a stone fence four feet high."[32]

By the mid 1850s, settlers had enclosed much of the Calapooia landscape. R. S. Williamson, railroad surveyor for the United States, traversed the base of the Calapooia foothills on 5 October 1855, remarking in his journal, "The road today was excellent, but greatly interrupted by fences." The open plains of the valley became so broken up with land-claim fences already built during the early years that James Ayers commented, "If a man wished to cross the valley, there was no way to go except through the farms, opening gates as he came to each line fence." And, of course, fencing continued in the Calapooia for decades. Thus, when Calapooia resident William Templeton related the following in 1879 about the activities of his sons, he outlined some of the most important forces at work on the valley's landscape. He wrote that his sons "have got all their fence posts Drove they are going to make fence between them and Hugh Fields and Galbraith and on this side of the lane down from the orchard."[33]

The open-range cattle industry in the Willamette Valley declined during the 1860s, largely because of fencing and the diminution of demand from California as the gold strike played out there and other sources of cattle became available. In addition, the new mining strikes that occurred in eastern Oregon and Idaho in the same decade drew the Pacific Northwest cattle industry east of the Cascade Mountains, to the arid and semiarid Columbia Valley and Great Basin. There, cattlemen had access to wide-open ranges where their herds could roam at large. Despite this important shift in economy for western Oregon, the number of cattle—beef, milk, and work oxen—in the Willamette fluctuated greatly through the end of the nineteenth century: from 93,094 in 1860 to 45,692 in 1870, and back up to 73,970 in 1890.[34]

The relative economic importance of cattle declined, however, as the basis of the Willamette Valley agricultural economy changed. By 1870 wheat had finally become the single most important crop in the Willamette (though oats were important as well), and it remained so through the end of the nineteenth century.[35] The following chapter details this later shift in the economy, other commercial developments, and the accompanying environmental and perceptual changes of landscape in the Calapooia and Willamette for the remainder of the nineteenth century.

CHAPTER VI

Changes in Landscape, Changes in Meaning: Settling the Calapooia Plains

During the late 1840s and early 1850s, the few commodities that southern Willamette Valley settlers had for sale were vended locally, herded to trade centers, or, in some few cases, carried in wagons to the navigable Willamette River and drifted downstream in flatboats and canoes to market. In the late 1840s, for instance, John McCoy in west Linn County built a dugout canoe to carry up to two thousand pounds of bacon from his farm to Oregon City, one hundred or so miles down the Willamette River.[1]

More advanced forms of transportation soon provided southern Willamette Valley settlers greater access to markets. In the early 1850s steamboats began running on the Willamette River. In 1856 the *James Clinton* became the first steamer to navigate the Willamette all the way from Oregon City to Eugene, and boats such as the *Multnomah* carried up to fifteen hundred bushels of wheat down the river at a time. Steamboat traffic on the upper Willamette River reached its peak in the 1860s and 1870s.[2]

The Calapooia's small size, and the fact that debris cluttered it, made it inaccessible to steamers, flatboats, and even canoes. But residents who lived along the foothills of the valley—distant from the Willamette River—did not completely have to fend for themselves. The Linn County government, for instance, aided Calapooians when it commissioned the construction of roads to them from the Willamette River. On 9 April 1852 the County Court "ordered that the Road from

Albany [on the Willamette] to Finley Mill be established, recorded and opened."[3]

Coinciding with the extension of improved roads and the steamboat into the southern Willamette Valley, farmers increased agricultural production, especially wheat. In 1868, when the first direct shipment of wheat from Portland to Europe occurred, Linn County produced 388,336 bushels. The production of oats (used primarily for farm animal feed) outstripped wheat, with 596,790 bushels produced during the same year. A year later Linn County production of wheat increased to 479,294 bushels, while the oat harvest dropped slightly to 519,694 bushels.[4]

When the railroad finally arrived in the southern Willamette Valley in 1870, it provided quicker and easier connections to national and international markets and had a number of ramifications for Linn County. Steamboat transportation on the Willamette declined in importance to the point of abandonment, and pioneer farming finally gave way to commercial agriculture. Within five years of the railroad's entrance into Linn County in 1870–71, wheat production had risen to 998,626 bushels, an increase of over 250 percent in seven years (table 3).[5]

During this time, southern Willamette residents realized the potential of the formerly avoided open prairies of the valley floor. The valley floor became the principal producer of agricultural crops for expanding markets. For reasons of convenience, the earliest settlers located their claims along the foothill periphery—for instance, the Calapooia—of the southern Willamette Valley and used the open prairies primarily for livestock grazing. Later arrivals, finding the best lands taken, had to claim land on the floor of the valley. Map 3 depicts the gradual movement of claims from the foothills out onto the Willamette Valley floor adjacent to the Calapooia Valley, and table 4 shows the increased area of farmland in the Calapooia, Linn County, and the Willamette for the period 1870–90.

Improved transportation, technology, and commerce reversed the economic importance of foothills and plains. In the process, these factors, as well as a whole set of related factors that allowed new settlers to make the plains profitable, also caused environmental changes in the Willamette Valley and encouraged the loss of the early, intimate relationship with the landscape that earliest settlers originally experienced. Part of the estrangement of people from the land came through new ways of

TABLE 3
WHEAT PRODUCTION, 1850–90

	Calapooia	Linn County	Willamette
1850	2,265 bu.	21,893 bu.	199,558 bu.
1860	—	145,273 bu.	660,081 bu.
1870	23,881 bu.	479,294 bu.	2,086,826 bu.
1880[a]	103,301 bu.	911,411 bu.	5,365,117 bu.
	9,019 ac.	75,310 ac.	349,285 ac.
	(11.45 bu./acre)	(12.1 bu./acre)	(15.36 bu./acre)
1890	—	1,116,074 bu.	5,779,509 bu.
		55,373 ac.	266,286 ac.
		(20.16 bu./acre)	(21.7 bu./acre)

SOURCES: Agricultural Manuscript Census for Linn County, 1850, 1870, 1880; U.S. Department of Commerce, Bureau of the Census, *Seventh Census, 1007; Agriculture of the United States in 1860* (1864), 121; *Statistics of Wealth and Industry of the United States . . . Ninth Census* (1872), 231; *Report on the Production of Agriculture . . . Tenth Census* (1883), 202; *Reports on the Statistics of Agriculture . . . Eleventh Census* vol. 50, pt. 10 (1896), 381.

[a]In 1880, wheat production was down because of rust, a fungus.

TABLE 4
FARMS AND FARM SIZES, 1870–90

	Number of Farms	Average Size (in Acres)
1870		
Calapooia[a]	58	455
Linn County	747	343
Willamette Valley	4,592	324
1880		
Calapooia[a]	209	286
Linn County	1,528	271
Willamette Valley	8,971	256
1890		
Calapooia	—	—
Linn County	1,711	244
Willamette Valley	11,536	212

SOURCES: Agricultural Manuscript Census Returns for Linn County, 1870 and 1880; U.S. Department of Commerce, Bureau of the Census, *Statistics of the Wealth and Industry of the United States . . . Ninth Census* (1872), 230, 360–61; *Report on the Production of Agriculture . . . Tenth Census* (1883), 82; *Reports on the Statistics of Agriculture . . . Eleventh Census: 1890,* vol. 50, pt. 1 (1896), 224.

[a]Figures for the Calapooia in 1870 and 1880 are not the total number of farms but the number of farms listed in the manuscript agricultural census.

claiming the land provided in the United States Donation Land Claim Act, which guided the settlement of the plains.

DONATION LAND LAW AND THE FEDERAL SURVEY: CLAIMING THE PRAIRIE PLAINS

The federal Donation Land Law, more popularly known as the Donation Land Claim Act (DLCA) provided land for males who (1) were white or half white and half Native American, (2) were at least eighteen years of age by 1 December 1850, (3) were either residents of the territory or to become such by 1 December 1850, (4) had cultivated their claims and lived on them for four years, and (5) were either United States citizens or to become such by 1 December 1851. If a settler met these qualifications, he could claim 320 acres (a half section) if single, and 640 acres (a full section) if married. The additional 320 acres were to be held in the wife's name, which made the DLCA the first federal land law granting title to women, albeit only through their relationship to men. The DLCA also allowed widows to take out claims if their husbands would have met the requirements for a claim if they had lived. For example, Elizabeth Ritchey, who settled on the Calapooia on 11 October 1853, benefited from this allowance. Her husband died in Iowa just as he was preparing to move to Oregon. He had even "obtained several waggons and teams for the purpose of going to Oregon that Season." After his death, Elizabeth determined to journey to Oregon anyway. On arrival, she received a land claim in her own name near the Calapooia River. Furthermore, the DLCA granted to male settlers who arrived after 1 December 1850 but before 1 December 1853, 160 acres if single and 320 if married. The act also required these later arrivals to live on the land and cultivate it for four years before receiving official title. In 1853 and 1854 Congress passed amendments to the DLCA. These amendments (1) commuted residency requirements on the land to two years if the claimants paid $1.25 per acre for their land, (2) allowed claimants to sell their rights to the land before receiving patents, and (3) extended the DLCA to 1 December 1855.[6]

This federal land act also provided for a surveyor general's office. The surveyor general's tasks included administering the DLCA, settling land disputes, and, most important for our discussion, establishing the township-range, thirty-six-section cadastral system in the Willamette Valley and making sure that new claims adhered to it. Section 6 of the act delineated how land claims would be taken in reference to the cadastral survey:

> In all cases it shall be a compact form; and where it is practicable so to do, the land so claimed shall be taken as nearly as practicable by legal subdivisions; but where that cannot be done, it shall be the duty of the said surveyor general to survey and mark each claim with the boundaries as claimed. . . . *Provided*, that after the first of December next [1850], all claims shall be bounded by lines running east and west, and north and south: *And provided further*, That after the survey is made, all claims shall be made in conformity to the same, and in compact form.[7]

The United States government adopted the DLCA and the federal survey at the very time that land claiming along the southern Willamette Valley foothills had pretty much ended and settlement of the plains was just beginning. Subtle but important differences existed, then, between claiming the plains and claiming the foothills. As previously discussed, earlier Oregon provisional and territorial laws governing the claiming of land allowed a certain flexibility when it came to accommodating the configuration of the landscape. The earlier method of survey—the use of natural markers—encouraged an intimacy between the settler and the landscape. Although settlers had to take claims, after June 1844, in square or oblong form, provisional government laws did not bind them to the cardinal points of the compass when positioning their claims on the idiosyncratic landscape. This older process, as explained in chapter 3, governed the claiming of the Calapooia foothills.

Based on the rational survey system initiated in the Northwest Ordinances of the 1780s, the Oregon Donation Land Law laid the groundwork not only for the way land claims would be taken out in the Oregon Territory after 1 December 1850 (and thus largely on the plains of the southern Willamette) but also prescribed abstract principles for claiming a landscape that quite naturally had little semblance to rational order. The taking of land in square form and in legal subdivisions, bounded by lines perpendicular and parallel to the (far distant) magnetic north, effectively terminated the older land-claiming process in which humans worked directly with topography. Settlers thereafter no longer had the choice of how and where to lay out a claim with reference to the idiosyncrasies of the local landscape. The imposition of the Donation Land Law and survey culminated a process, initiated by provisional government laws requiring claims to be in rectangular form, that assisted in estranging post-1850 Calapooia settlers and other Willamette Valley inhabitants from the land—particularly the land on the plains.

The government no longer accepted ash trees entwined at the roots, swales, creeks, and blazes on oaks as sufficient markers for land-claim boundaries. Rather, abstract numbers that had no relation to the landscape defined a claim's dimensions. Thomas Wilcox, who took a claim on the plains bordering the Calapooia on 10 November 1853, now knew his land as the southeast quarter of section 15, township 13 south, range 3 west; the south half of the northeast quarter of section 15, township 13 south, range 3 west; and the south half of the northwest quarter of section 15, township 13 south, range 3 west. And Wilcox and others like him had no leeway to arrange their claims on the land in the way they wanted.[8]

The new land law also affected older residents of the Calapooia. The government did allow the earlier claims to remain in their original configuration, though they had to be resurveyed and defined accordingly. Thus, the boundaries of Agnes Courtney's claim, which she originally knew as a "creek," several "white oaks," a "white fir," and "a fir on the mountain," now became a jumble of numbers that had little to do with the nature of the land that she and her husband originally settled: "Beginning 18.25 chains west of the southeast corner of the southwest quarter of section sixteen in township fourteen south range two west. Thence south 8 degrees, 15 feet west, 18.06 chains; south 81 degrees, 45 feet east, 41.27 chains; north 8 degrees, 15' east, 8.26 chains, south 81 degrees, 45 feet east, 39.03 chains."[9]

Imposing a geometric survey on an earlier system that had both complied with the local landscape and used natural features as markers ultimately led to innumerable disputes among the settlers. Henry H. Spalding's Donation Land Claim file reveals that after the surveyor completed his task in the Calapooia Valley, Spalding contested boundaries with James Blakely, John Findley, William R. Kirk, and William Glass—all but one of whom had taken land before the completion of the survey. The problem was resolved only when Spalding relinquished all disputed land to the men who claimed it.[10]

The survey left land in dispute throughout the Willamette Valley. James Andrews in Polk County, for instance, disputed with several neighbors, especially a Mr. Goff. Andrews alerted the surveyor general to Goff's claim and warned that if Goff tried to prove up on it, he was going to "have a mery time of it." Confusion engendered by the survey in the Willamette went beyond neighborhood quarrels. In some cases the entire land-claiming process simply broke down. In the French Prairie region of the northern Willamette Valley, for instance, where the early French-Canadians claimed land in odd patterns reminiscent of the manorial system, settler S. D. Snowden in 1853 had difficulty applying straight lines to the claim he wanted to take in the same vicinity. He complained that the French-Canadians seldom used "a straight line between the corners" of their claims and thus he was "at a loss how to comply with the instructions by running a line straight from the corner stake to corner stake." But Calapooian Joseph L. Evans best summed up the problem with the survey when he wrote to Surveyor General John B. Preston, "There is something going on in our County that I Doe not understand."[11]

Even as late as 1895, the survey caused problems. When Fannie Adams Cooper's parents took up a homestead on some unclaimed land in the upper Calapooia next to Frank Malone's presurvey Donation Land Claim, they made the usual improvements to their homestead, building a home and barn and planting a garden. After Malone died and his estate was settled, officials discovered that all boundary lines in the vicinity were incorrect. Not only did the Adams family find that their garden and barn were now on a neighbor's property, but they eventually lost their entire claim.[12]

In the transition from an intimate system of land claiming to an abstract system of laws to guide human activities on the landscape, both individual families, like the Coopers, and clusters of neighbors, like Spalding, Kirk, Blakely, and Glass, all encountered difficulties. At the same time, Calapooia residents began to lose their initially close relationship with the landscape. People like Calapooia settler Agnes Courtney, for example, no longer dealt with their parcels of the landscape purely in terms of its features. Rather, they now spoke of the landscape in terms of numbers, chains, links, degrees, townships, ranges, and sections. More important, rather than the exigencies of the landscape, township, range, and section lines on a governmental surveyor's map determined new claim boundaries. Changing attitudes toward the land that the DLCA and cadastral survey encouraged are exemplified in the experience of Jared Fox in the northern Willamette Valley in 1853. Fox had recently immigrated from Wisconsin, a state whose settlement the cadastral survey directed and which had thus conditioned his interpretation of the landscape. On 14 March he viewed the Tualatin plains, settled long before the cadastral survey, and asserted that they appeared "in some respects the most like live of any I have seen, good faced, well fenced & a few tolerable buildings but too many sloughs, too much clay, & they have taken their claims in any possible shape so as to take a nook of timber or prairie, which spoiled the looks of the whole."[13]

Although the DLCA and the cadastral survey helped sunder an older, more intimate relationship between humans and the land in the Willamette Valley, the former also, in a few key ways, inhibited change in the Calapooia and Willamette Valleys. Because the parcels of land the DLCA granted were so large—up to a square mile to a husband and wife—claimants found it difficult to "improve" and cultivate their entire property. At the same time, the DLCA prohibited a claimant from selling off smaller parcels to other potential cultivators for several years until the claim had been "proved-up."[14] Thus, the DLCA preserved vast expanses of the valley in a nearly natural state. Table 5 shows the amount of farmland in an unimproved state in the Calapooia, Linn County, and the Willamette Valley between 1860 and 1890.

According to historians Dorothy O. Johansen and Charles M. Gates, the huge size of the land grants, in addition to leaving a large percentage of the valley in an unimproved state, impeded the growth of towns and the diversification of occupation, industry, and crops. Nineteenth-century critics roundly denounced the DLCA for its generosity with land and thus the negative effects it had on the valley economy. As late as 1874, L. B. Judson outlined in a letter to the editor of *Willamette Farmer* the multifaceted problem that large land holdings created. He first blamed the large land holdings for the lack of population growth and economic development in the Willamette Valley. He especially chided large landholders who lived "in towns and cities enjoying the advantages of city schools and city privileges . . . while they leave the country in which their land lies, in a state of wilderness." Because of the limited economic diversity in the Willamette Valley, Judson noted that farmers who did live on their land and were forced to "make mixed husbandry a means of support, cannot . . . afford to divide their land and sell off a part and confine themselves to small places; in fact under the present state of affairs . . . [this] farmer feels the need of room."[15]

Proposed theories explaining slow development of the economy and its relationship to large land claims in the Willamette Valley varied. E. Ingersoll, writing in 1882 for *Harper's New Monthly Magazine*, suggested that the problem lay with the character of the DLCA claimants.

TABLE 5

FARM ACREAGE, 1860–90

Year/Area	Total Farm Acreage	Percent Unimproved[a]
1860[b]		
Linn County	355,441	38.2
Willamette Valley	1,605,914	52.6
1870		
Calapooia	26,435	21.7
Linn County	256,058	27.6
Willamette Valley	1,580,839	48.9
1880		
Calapooia	59,864	42.5
Linn County	413,983	38.2
Willamette Valley	2,259,284	45.6
1890[b]		
Linn County	416,827	38.4
Willamette Valley	2,382,486	49.5

SOURCES: Agricultural Manuscript Census Returns for Linn County, 1870 and 1880; U.S. Department of Commerce, Bureau of the Census, *Agriculture of the United States in 1860 . . . Eighth Census* (1864), 120; *Statistics of the Wealth and Industry of the United States . . . Ninth Census* (1872), 230, 360–61; *Report on the Production of Agriculture . . . Tenth Census* (1883), 130; *Reports on the Statistics of Agriculture . . . Eleventh Census: 1890*, vol. 50, pt. 1 (1896), 224–25.

[a]The definition of unimproved land varied; although it always included woodland and forest, it sometimes included other uncultivated land as well.

[b]The 1860 and 1890 manuscript agricultural censuses for the Calapooia are missing.

Although Ingersoll noted the beneficial effects of the DLCA—for example, promoting initial migration to the Willamette Valley—the problem remained that those who migrated and took up land were, in Ingersoll's mind, predominantly "vagabond farmers" from the upper South. "They were poor, also, in the sense of having little money, and this helplessness, added to their thriftless habits, made their possession of the land a misfortune to the State." Ingersoll expressed a prejudiced view, for though he was thankful that these "loungers" had declined in influence, he was equally happy that their children, who had taken over farming the Willamette and were apparently a "better class," had also "lost their drawl of speech and action."[16]

Opinions such as Ingersoll's about the character of the upper South pioneer, whether right or wrong, had dogged these people across the American frontier all the way to the Pacific Northwest. But regardless of the character of those who settled in the Willamette Valley, the large land claims of the DLCA and their legacy for development were facts of nineteenth-century life in the Willamette. Claim sizes, indicated by the change in farm size, decreased very slowly through the end of the nineteenth century on the Calapooia, in Linn County, and in the Willamette Valley in general. The original 174 claims taken on the Calapooia averaged 352 acres. The 58 farms enumerated in the 1870 agricultural census averaged 455 acres apiece. By 1880, the 209 farms listed in the agricultural census had dropped to an average of 286 acres each. Table 4 more clearly shows the trend in farm sizes through the latter part of the nineteenth century. Therefore, as already discussed and as table 5 demonstrates, large areas of the valley remained uncultivated.

ENVIRONMENTAL CHANGE

The DLCA had a paradoxical effect on the valley. On the one hand, it led to apparent economic stagnation, which troubled many residents. On the other hand, it preserved large amounts of land in what a casual observer might call "a state of wilderness," leaving the valley with an aesthetic appeal that defied economic valuation. Thus, when Frances Fuller Victor examined the Willamette Valley in 1872, she wrote: "Although most of the open or prairie land in Western Oregon is owned by donation claimants, locators, and others, comparatively little of it is cultivated. The uncultivated prairie lands, together with the half-wooded bench lands of the foot-hills, make a large extent of country still in its primeval condition." Victor declared that such a scene left her with a feeling of "romantic freedom."[17]

Both the process of claiming the prairie and leaving parts of it "untouched" had effects not as environmentally benign as might have appeared to Victor. First, to settle on and cultivate the level prairie lands, new settlers had to drain them. Albert Waggoner, who grew up on the Calapooia, remembered, "This valley was too wet for much farming just at first. Later, when drains had been opened up and the sloughs drained wheat farming became all important." Commenting on drainage techniques of Calapooia farmers on the flat plains of the Willamette in 1877, a correspondent for *Willamette Farmer* wrote: "the country is flat, but the farmers have an easy-going way of ditching. . . . They plow a few furrows in the center of the sloughs, and by just waiting the winter rains do the balance. I saw a few drains made in this way that were seven or eight feet wide and three feet deep, which were used as main drains into which were run one or two furrows at right angles, and this slow draining has enhanced the value of the land very much."[18]

Nineteenth-century Willamette Valley inhabitants recognized that although such ditching might not necessarily be the best way to drain lands, it did remain the most popular, for the more effective underground tiling system proved too expensive and labor-intensive. Thus, when Calapooian William T. Templeton reported the progress his sons had made in ditching during the winter of 1878–79, he related the more typical story: "The boys have been Ditching a good eale this winter but are pretty near through they have Diched down the slough back of the barn and change the water from rinning by the old Tobacco house it is all Down flat." Sarah Cornett, who lived on the level plains of the Willamette along the lower Calapooia in the 1880s, also made notes about the progress her son "J" and husband John made in ditching. For five consecutive days at the end of March 1883, for instance, Cornett noted that "J ditched today," "J ditched some," "J ditched all day," "John ditched this eveening," "J ditched," and "J ditched." Sunday, a day of rest, intervened, but on Monday, 2 April, "J ditched in afternoon."[19]

The drainage of prairie lands had a deleterious effect on the environment. George Van Winkle staked his land claim on a series of sloughs that stretched along the Calapooia River on the plains of the Willamette, where concentrated a multitude of ducks, geese, cranes, snipes, and aquatic mammals. He and other nearby farmers opened furrows between these sloughs, and "the running water cut deeper until the sloughs and lakes became a connected stream" and drained away. Once the habitat vanished, so did the animals. At least one early resident made the connection between these two events: "The draining of the lakes and swamps have all had much to do with their [birds and animals] disappearance." Another Calapooia resident noted in later years, "The geese and ducks are almost gone from the valley. . . . It has not all been from shooting, however. The draining of the lakes and swamps have had much to do with their disappearance." And early settler John Minto noted the effect of land drainage on the Willamette, which "has largely ceased to be the home of the crane, curlew, gray plover, and even the snipe, as well as the beaver, muskrat and wild duck. These damp-land and water fowls and animals, which once found here their breeding places, have gone forever, unless farmers in the near future construct artificial fish ponds, and reservoirs for irrigation when needed."[20]

Although the uncultivated lands might signify a wilderness condition to some, as they did to Francis Fuller Victor, or a stagnation in the economy to others, such as L. B. Judson, the natural history of these lands continued to change. The forces of environmental succession naturally converted the untouched Willamette grasslands into forests. With cessation of Kalapuya burning, the effects of livestock grazing, and parts of the prairie lying idle, shrubs and trees quickly colonized the uncultivated lands. In some instances, shrubs and seedlings appeared very quickly after the demise of the Kalapuya and the onset of European-style agriculture. Already in the early 1840s Charles Wilkes had noted "that since the whites have had possession of the country, the undergrowth is coming up rapidly in places."[21]

In the later nineteenth century, Willamette Valley inhabitants came to recognize the relationships among Euro-American settlement, livestock grazing and rooting, the problems that confronted the farmer who desired to cultivate the valley, and the role of the Kalapuya. One resident noted, "Since the advent of the whites the Indians have ceased to burn over the country every fall. . . . The fires burnt, and kept down, all young growth of every kind of timber in the Willamette." He went on to note that some groves of timber and shrubs, especially on the moist north sides of buttes, as well as large oaks, had escaped firing. Then he commented that livestock "have eaten out the native grasses, the turf or roots have died, leaving the earth mellow and in a fine condition for the reception of . . . seed" from the Douglas fir and oaks in the valley. This forestation caused difficulties for valley inhabitants, for shrubs and small trees invaded much land that was becoming more valuable for cultivation as the agricultural market expanded. The lamentable result for farmers, noted one valley inhabitant, was that "few have the time, will, strength, or means, to grub vast tracts of land, often so thick with brush that you can hardly 'stick a butcher-knife through it.' " But the value derived from productive land, assessed at $40 per acre, was well worth the estimated $22.50 per acre cost of slashing down the brush in June, burning it the following autumn, putting goats on it to eat for a year, and then plowing it twice.[22]

Cutting and burning shrubs—what residents called brush—occupied much of the time of late nineteenth-century Calapooia farmers. A typi-

cal notation in Sarah Cornett's diary from the 1880s about daily activities on her family's farm was "John cut and burnt brush." One scholar
of nineteenth-century Willamette Valley civilization found that white
day laborers tended to refuse the arduous task of brush grubbing, so
typically the head of a household had either to do the work himself or
hire Chinese labor.[23]

Willamette Valley farmers waged an ongoing battle against shrub
and tree invasion through the nineteenth century. On some fronts they
ultimately lost the war. At the turn of the century one chronicler of
Calapooia Valley history, looking back onto the landscape of the past,
remarked that previously the small hills and buttes rising from the floor
of the valley had been "free from timber and covered with beautiful
grass. . . . The Indians had kept the brush burned down, burning over
the hills each year. The white man neglected to do this, and now in
many places the grass has given way to moss and timber." In the 1930s
a Calapooia resident remarked, "There was not so much brush in the
country then as now, because the Indians came through in little bands
and set fire to the range, thus keeping it down. The open country, free
from brush and undergrowth made hunting and cattle herding a much
easier task than it is now."[24]

In addition to the encroachment of shrubs and trees, other problems
beset farmers as well. In 1872 Frances Fuller Victor commented that
"one of the pests of Oregon farming is a large, coarse fern [bracken,
Pteridium aquilinum] . . . which is common to the forests, and which
encroaches on the improved lands contiguous to them. . . . It is very
difficult to eradicate, the roots penetrating to a great depth, and being
very tough and strong." As early as 1852 Thomas Kendall had noted
that bracken covered some areas of the valley so densely "as to prevent
a heavy coat of grass, rendering [these lands] far inferior, for stock, to
the rich grass of the plains."[25]

Calapooia residents resorted to various techniques of dealing with
bracken. Fannie Adams Cooper's family found the best way to eradicate
it. On the spot selected for their garden on the upper Calapooia,
bracken grew "two and three feet high and brush everywhere." Cooper's husband rolled an immense pile of logs onto the garden and set
them afire, burning the soil "deep and black far in the ground." The
result was that "never a weed grew there," though Cooper had to admit
that bracken "once in a while" did return. Since some Calapooia residents could not beat them, they joined them, finding ingenious ways to

use bracken. On a trip up the Calapooia Valley in 1861, George A. Waggoner and a companion had dinner and spent the night with a local settler. After the main course, Waggoner and his friend expressed surprise when their host presented them with a "fern pie." This dessert so impressed Waggoner's traveling companion that he immediately wrote to inform his wife to "experiment with [bracken] as food, in different forms."[26]

When they attempted to engage in agriculture, settlers found they also had to contend with the invasion of a number of other native and exotic plants, such as "blue pod" (a native vetch, *Vicia* sp.), thistles (*Cirisium* spp.), and dog fennel (*Foeniculum vulgare*, an exotic), all of which readily colonize disturbed sites, particularly tilled soil. Calapooia settler John Wigle recalled that geese and ducks grazed on young wheat, stunting it, so that "the blue pod and thistles would come on and hinder the growth of the wheat." Several early valley residents noted the inability of mill screens to separate blue pod from the wheat, and thus much of it ended up in flour and "women complained of it bitterly." Sarah Cornett's diary reveals problems with thistles and dog fennel. For instance, on 4 July 1885, her husband John "finished mowing in the Orchard and then some in the field," while the hired hand, Hunter, "killed thistles." Cornett also mentioned that another hired hand "pulled dog fennell the rest of the day" on 21 August 1885. Later that month, he spent two more days on the pesky weed, finishing up on the twenty-ninth by "pulling and mowing" it.[27]

Market agriculture in the Calapooia and the southern Willamette Valley in the late nineteenth century caused other changes in the ecosystem. In addition to the draining of the plains, which reduced fowl and aquatic animal populations, enclosing open lands and the invasion of shrubs resulted in the decrease on the prairies of certain other animal species, such as the white-tailed deer. One Calapooia pioneer descendant declared, "Deer seldom came out on the valley floor much after the settlement was well started, but earlier settlers say that they formerly roamed in herds all over the valley." Another noted, "White tailed deer are more an animal of the open valley than the smaller black-tailed deer. . . . Now I presume they are all gone, though it may be possible that there are still a very few of them in the woods and among the small wooded islands there."[28]

Beginning in the 1850s, Calapooia settlers set out to fulfill Kendall's dream that the "central portions of the prairies" would "one day be the great agricultural spots." In some ways they achieved this pastoral dream. The Donation Land Claim Act placed virtually all of the Willamette Valley's cultivable land into private hands by the mid 1850s.[29] Through drainage, settlers converted much of this land into farmland. Between 1850 and 1890, depending on location in the Calapooia, Linn County, or the Willamette Valley at large, improved acres of farmland equaled between 50 and 80 percent of total claimed land (table 5).

Agricultural development in the Willamette, however, did not necessarily spiral continuously upward. Large segments of claimed land remained unimproved through the end of the century. In part, responsibility for this situation lay with the original generosity of the Donation Land Claim Act. One geographer found that in the four middle and southern counties of the Willamette Valley—Marion, Benton, Linn, and Lane—the ratio and absolute amount of improved land declined after 1880. Also, although the amount of wheat harvested in the Calapooia, Linn County, and the Willamette between 1850 and 1890 increased, the total amount of acres of wheat declined in Linn County and the Willamette between 1880 and 1890 (table 3). Reasons for abandonment of cultivable lands include exhaustion of soil, a shift in the center of wheat industry in the Pacific Northwest to the Inland Empire after 1880, and the shift in husbandry and agriculture to dairying and orchards in the later nineteenth century.[30]

But the central agricultural district in the southern Willamette Valley, Linn County in particular, remained the plains rather than the foothills through the end of the century. The plains were no more fertile than the land cultivated along the foothills, but there were more cultivable acres and more cultivable acres per claim. And on the plains, farmers improved more land than they did in the hills.[31] In the narrower Calapooia Valley, forest and foothills became obstacles to cultivation on a large scale. Farms along the foothills had more acres of woodland and fewer acres in cultivated fields than did their counterparts on the prairies (table 6).

In a sense, farmers relatively though not absolutely fulfilled Kendall's 1852 expectation. The open prairies west of the Calapooia foothills definitely became the center of agriculture in the region. But development proceeded in a halting fashion. Important changes in residents' attitudes and perceptions of land accompanied the claiming of the prairies. Claiming and cultivating the prairie had severe repercussions for the environment as well. Some of these changes that Calapooia and

TABLE 6

CALAPOOIA FARMLAND, 1880

	Prairies	Foothills
Number of farms	82	127
Average size in acres	308.1	272.5
Acres in tilled and fallow fields	157.5 (51.1%)[a]	55.6 (20.4%)
Acres in meadows, pastures, and orchards	97.2 (31.5%)	50.8 (18.6%)
Acres in woodland and other unimproved land	53.4 (17.3%)	166.1 (61%)

SOURCE: Agricultural Manuscript Census, Linn County, 1880.

[a]Percentage of total acreage, rounded to the nearest one-tenth. Because of rounding, percentages for prairie lands add up to 99.9.

other Willamette residents unwittingly initiated also came back to bedevil them. The invasion of blue pod, thistles, bracken, dog fennel, and brush was a natural reaction to changes in the environment that humans had initiated. Despite these and other impediments to cultivation and success—such as loss of soil fertility and even abandonment—agriculture on the plains continued to dominate the economy of Linn County and the Calapooia Valley.

At the same time, locals also saw the utility of the landscape in terms of industrial potential and thus established manufactories around which grew up towns. As with the extension of husbandry and agriculture in the Calapooia, we can see changes in human attitudes toward the environment by analyzing early industry and town development.

TOWN BUILDING AND INDUSTRIAL DIVERSIFICATION

In 1853 James Blakely, with the help of local resident and surveyor Luther White, laid out the town of Brownsville on his claim along the banks of the Calapooia where the stream flows out onto the plains of the Willamette Valley. Blakely named the village in honor of his uncle and nearby settler, Hugh Brown, who had established a small store in the vicinity as early as 1849–50.[32] Modified and refined expressions of residents' attitudes about landscape and the environment are detectable in the founding and growth of this and other early Calapooia towns.

In 1859 the partnership of Brown, Blakely, James McHargue, and Robert A. Johns established Brownsville's first manufactory, a flour mill. The mill needed a water race. But because a minor heir of Eliza Spalding held the title to the best property for the race, the mill partners had to request special permission from the territorial government to purchase a right-of-way. Forty-three locals signed the petition. In their supplication, they pointed out that "the erection of extensive flouring mills and other machinery in the vicinity . . . [is] needed to promote the public convenience, and develop the resources of an extensive agricultural region." The petitioners sweetened the prospect when they implied that such improvements would tend to "enhance the value of said lands." In this instance, the first establishment of manufacture in Brownsville, local citizens suggested that the needs of their community—especially public convenience—would be best met by using the landscape for industrial purposes. At the same time, such use would result in further development of the local economy. Once constructed, the millrace itself would impart value back to the landscape. To a degree, this prospect did indeed come to pass, and the millrace eventually powered the industrial center of Brownsville.[33]

This first manufacturing establishment on the Calapooia was promoted by a group of Brownsville residents who continued to influence development of the town over the next few decades. In 1860, a year after the establishment of the flour mill, the population of Brownsville had already reached ninety-nine. On 24 November of that year, residents R. H. Crawford, Timothy Riggs, William T. Templeton, E. M. Griffin, and Joseph Hamilton put their heads and money together with the intention of creating a new industry for Brownsville: a woolen mill. The woolen mill had great economic potential. County-fair promotion and especially national demand during the cotton shortages engendered by the Civil War stimulated the growth of the woolen industry in the Willamette during the 1860s. In 1865, Linn County yielded 132,148 pounds of wool, making it the leading producer among Willamette Valley counties. Brownsville entrepreneurs, in hopes of an increasing national demand, incorporated the Linn County Woolen Mills, contracting with the McHargue flour mill for fourteen horsepower of water from its race. By the spring of 1860 they had constructed buildings on the north bank of the Calapooia, but they did not receive looms, carding machines, and spinners (shipped from New Jersey) until 5 June 1863. Although the Linn County Woolen Mills burned down on 29 March

1865, the local directorship of Hugh Brown, William Kirk, Arnold Bassett, Hugh Dinwiddie, and E. E. Wheeler opened the newly organized Eagle Woolen Mills one year later. In August 1866 the mill employed fifty people, produced five hundred yards of cloth a day, and paid wages of about $50,000 a year. Because of litigation and economic difficulties, the Eagle Woolen Mills closed at the end of 1868.[34]

The woolen mill reopened in 1873, and the town continued to grow. By 1880 its population had reached 450. In the middle of the decade the gristmill, valued at $15,000, produced 150 barrels of flour a day. A sash and door factory (figure 4), valued at $8,000, turned out 500,000 board feet of lumber annually. The woolen mill had a value of $75,000, worked 9,500 pounds of wool monthly, employed twenty-six, and had an additional tailor shop with twelve workers. Other commercial interests included a picture gallery, two furniture stores, a notions dealer, and several professional offices for physicians and attorneys. Brownsville's growth, while slow, continued through the end of the century. In 1890 its population reached 580, and in 1900, 698.[35]

Established as the first town on the Calapooia, Brownsville remained the largest and most important in the valley proper through the nineteenth century, but it had competition. In 1850 the Reverend Wilson Blain founded on his claim the town of Union Point, named for the United Presbyterian Church he had already established there. Blain originally hoped to develop Union Point into a cultural center based on the territorially commissioned academy he headed. During the 1850s the town included some small commercial establishments—a blacksmith, a gunsmith, and a store—but Union Point never succeeded, partly because no major source of waterpower flowed through it. The academy closed in 1857, and citizens had part of the town plat legally vacated in 1858.[36]

The history of another Calapooia town, Crawfordsville, differed from Union Point. Just upstream from Richard Finley's gristmill, where Brush Creek flows into the Calapooia, Philemon Vawter Crawford laid out the town of Crawfordsville on properties he acquired in about 1869. Crawford built a sawmill and carding mill, both powered by water drawn from Brush Creek, but Crawfordsville remained not much more than a hamlet. In 1880 its population reached fifty-eight, and according to the immigration agent's report in 1887, the town had "two harness and saddle shops, two blacksmith shops, one ax manufactory, one planing mill, two dry goods stores, one boot and shoe shop, one drug store, one tannery and one hotel."[37]

Figure 4.   John M. Moyer's sash and door factory, 1878. Moyer purchased this sash and door factory in Brownsville in 1863. Note the millrace leading into the factory along the left side of the picture. Source: *Illustrated Historical Atlas Map of Marion and Linn Counties, Oregon.*

Located well into the forested foothills of the Cascade Mountains, Crawfordsville depended principally on the lumber industry, which fed primarily a local market. Small water-powered sash-frame mills such as Richard Finley's, P. V. Crawford's, and Timothy Rigg's existed on the upper Calapooia and Brush Creek as early as the 1850s. By the 1870s larger mills had made their appearance. David Allingham's forty horse-power steam mill, the largest, had a capital investment of $6,300. It conducted business six months of the year and employed six men over sixteen years of age. McDowell and Company's thirty-five horsepower, water-driven mill had a capital investment of $3,000 and operated year-round with a work force of eight and total lumber production value of $13,200.[38]

Allen, Robinson and Company, a large lumber firm located on the Willamette River in Albany, logged on the upper Calapooia above Craw-fordsville for a more extensive market. Allen, Robinson owned a con-trolling interest in the Calapooia Boom Company. In 1876 the state legislature granted this company exclusive rights to "improve" about

Calaposia River,
Albany, Ore.

Figure 5.   Mills on the lower Calapooia River, 1895. The Calapooia River was
both a means of transporting logs to Albany and a source to power the lumber
mills. Courtesy of Print Collection, A9415, Special Collections, Knight Library,
University of Oregon, Eugene (negative number CN 924).

forty miles of the Calapooia River from Crawfordsville to the Willamette in order to float logs to the Allen, Robinson mill. Once this work
was completed, loggers felled timber into the Calapooia and Brush
Creek above Crawfordsville for several months of the year, then waited
for the winter rains to float the logs the forty-plus miles to the mills in
Albany. Figure 5 shows some of the mills on the lower Calapooia in
Albany.[39]

Log drives on the Calapooia, which began in 1878, commonly occurred in fall and winter. One newspaper account reported that the
Allen, Robinson loggers felled up to five million feet of timber into the
upper Calapooia River and Brush Creek in anticipation of autumn
rains. On 12 December an Albany newspaper reported, "On Thursday
of last week they were running so fast and thick at Crawfordsville that
men could cross the river on them, and we are informed that on last
Monday the entire drive had passed there." From her farm on the
Calapooia some twenty-five miles below the timber belt, Sarah Cornett

noted in her diary in January 1885, "Jo and George went over to Mr. Farwells then up to the dam to see the logs come over the rest of us staid at home." Two days later she casually remarked, "The logs went by to day."[40]

Although a number of firms—essentially small mills save for Allen, Robinson—exploited the forest of the upper Calapooia, the amount of timber taken remained limited during this period. Because of the inaccessibility of the steep and rugged valley of the upper Calapooia, loggers took only trees along the banks of the river. Because of unreliability of the Calapooia itself as a highway for logs to Albany, a fifteen-year cessation of log drives on the river began in about 1890.[41] Not until well into the twentieth century did increasing regional and national demand and technological improvement allow for the extensive logging of Calapooia forests.

The cutting of forests along the banks of the Calapooia, while limited, and the "improvement" of the stream for drives between 1876 and 1890 did have environmental consequences. Logging increased erosion and runoff. In improving the river, Allen, Robinson eliminated sloughs and minor courses, removed trees and debris, tore out drifts, and confined floating, stationary logs to the stream's banks (known in the trade as booming) in order not to obstruct the central channel. This work, coupled with the loss of riparian forest from local logging, altered the nature of the Calapooia. On the one hand, floods still occurred and perhaps increased in ferocity, but on the other hand, humans forced the river into a narrower channel, actively and continually separating it from its flood plain. On its flood plain, in its sloughs, and among its forested banks, the river had prehistorically deposited large amounts of sediment. In addition, the original riparian forests traditionally reduced erosion. In their absence, and with the river unable to unload much of its organic material, the Calapooia naturally increased in turbidity as well as nutrients, increasing algae and decreasing stream clarity, and thereby decreasing fish populations. Before stream improvement, the higher water table added to marshlands, home to a multitude of aquatic animals and fowl. Now, during log drives on both the Calapooia and Brush Creek, logs blocked the migration of some fish and scoured the riverbed, reducing fish habitat and destroying aquatic plant communities. The floating logs also shed bark, which sank to the bottom and destroyed fish spawning grounds. Decomposing bark removed needed oxygen from the water, and log rafts blocked sunlight from plants on the riverbed.[42]

As a thriving community, Crawfordsville depended for prosperity on the early logging industry, but locals also exploited other forest products, such as cascara bark or chittim, which was used in laxatives. In the 1880s and 1890s, cascara bark collecting became a prosperous cottage industry, and residents removed tons from the forest, in the process killing large numbers of cascara trees. One east Linn County inhabitant, Joseph Stein, shipped sixty-eight tons of chittim in June 1890. Fannie Adams Cooper remembered that her husband collected bark and "packed it out of the woods on his back." She would "scrape off the moss and spread it to dry," and her husband would then "put it in a big deep box and chop it with a spade and sack it." In town, the Coopers exchanged the bark for groceries, shoes, and other necessities. Cooper recalled that it "took a lot of bark at 2 cents a pound to buy things."[43]

In addition to the exploitation of forest products, Crawfordsville residents also had other commercial interests. The same individuals who gave impetus to the town, Richard Finley and P. V. Crawford, worked together in 1858–59 to establish a new and larger gristmill and town out on the plains of the Willamette. Finley's original mill on the upper Calapooia had primarily served the local economy of the Calapooia and the southern Willamette Valley. A typical order in 1856, revealing the limited nature of his operations, was the milling of four bushels of wheat for three dollars. As more settlers moved into other areas of the southern Willamette, other millers constructed flour mills. In 1860 the census taker counted four flour mills in Linn County. One of the larger of these, the Magnolia Flour Mill, was constructed in Albany on the Calapooia where it flows into the Willamette River (figure 6). Finley's mill, well up the Calapooia and now distant from the population and thriving trade centers, began losing business.[44]

To recapture his lost market, as well as take advantage of the growing population in the Willamette Valley, Finley formed a partnership with Crawford and Alexander Brandon to begin a new mill, the Boston Mills, several miles downriver on the plains of the Willamette. Finley acquired land from Americus Savage and water rights from Robert Elder, enabling him to construct a dam across the Calapooia for milling purposes. He cut and hewed the timbers for the mill near Crawfordsville and hauled them to the new town site, some twelve miles away. Eventually a carding mill came to the area. Although the mill burned down a couple of years after its completion, its owners rebuilt it. Near the mills, Richard Finley laid out the town of Boston, which included a central

Figure 6.   Magnolia Flour Mill, 1878. The Magnolia Flour Mill, built near the confluence of the Calapooia and Willamette rivers at Albany, drew much of the business away from Richard C. Finley's small flour mill on the upper Calapooia. Note the steamboat on the Calapooia at the right edge of the picture. Because of the small size of the Calapooia, steamboats never ascended above its mouth. Source: *Illustrated Historical Atlas Map of Marion and Linn Counties, Oregon.*

town square surrounded by several blocks divided into building lots. Although the community remained small, it did have a store, blacksmith, and the carding and flouring mills, and it also became an important stage stop.[45]

The town of Boston had a very short life, however, and its history reflects the general pattern of events in latter nineteenth-century Calapooia and Willamette Valleys. In short, although Boston's beginnings were closely tied to happenings in the Calapooia foothills, its demise was determined by events occurring on the plains of the Willamette. On 8 December 1870, less than a decade after Finley laid out Boston, Ben Holladay's Oregon and California Railroad, coming from the north, reached Albany, the seat of Linn County. In June 1871 it extended onto the central portions of the county's prairie west of the Calapooia Valley and just one and one-half miles west of Boston. Now off the main transportation route, Boston withered away while its population moved west to meet the railroad. Because of the railroad—in the middle of open farmlands—the town of Shedd sprang up, as did a neighboring village, Halsey, five miles south.[46]

Four years after its founding, Shedd had two general stores, a blacksmith, shoemaker, hotel, two warehouses, and one church. Halsey had a population of 250 and a long list of commercial establishments including four general merchandisers, two blacksmiths, a telegrapher, a sash and door factory, a hotel, and five warehouses. Although neither town even existed in 1870, 306 people lived in Halsey and 55 in Shedd in 1880, ten years later, Shedd had a population of 355.[47] Located in the center of Linn County's vast agricultural district on the plains of the Willamette, both towns became shipping centers for the county's wheat and other produce.

The Oregon and California Railroad never reached Brownsville, but local promoters there finally acquired a connection to the Oregon Railway Company's narrow-gauge line on 28 December 1880. During the preceding nine years, between the time the Oregon and California came to the valley and Brownsville received a railroad connection, commercial interests in Brownsville had difficulty accepting the phenomenal growth of their two new competitors, Halsey and Shedd. Brownsville residents argued that there was no natural reason for Shedd's and Halsey's existence: "What has made the town of Halsey? Has she any real, natural advantages? . . . Is the land around there any better, or more productive? We say not a bit." In promotional articles and editorials week after week, the *Brownsville Advertiser* demanded that the railroad come to its hamlet. The *Advertiser* constantly threw disgruntled barbs at growing communities like Halsey whose very existence seemed artificial. And just as constantly they promoted the natural resources and situation of Brownsville:

> The large section of country covered with heavy timber above us, would resound with the lumber-man's axe . . . ; town property would be increased; more people would come in with capital; more houses would be built; more goods would be sold; . . . this town would grow up into a great manufacturing center, situated as we are with almost unlimited water power, and an endless supply of timber of the finest quality, within easy reach, and good farming land on every side, who can say what the future of Brownsville would be, with Rail Road and river connection in Albany?[48]

In this example of the idea of community building, the theme of utility is fully pronounced. At the same time, the relationship between utility and landscape changed through the long process of estrangement of the Calapooians from the natural landscape. No longer did they see landscape itself as the sole provider of resources; instead, these resources could be made profitable only through the acquisition of more and better technology, in this case the railroad. In other words, the citizens of Brownsville realized that they could not place the future of their community solely in the landscape, either its primitive or pastoral prospects. Rather, having witnessed the rapid development of Halsey and Shedd, they came to believe that it was really mechanization that would allow them to progress. Asking themselves, "Why all this difference?" between Halsey and Shedd and their own town, they summed up the answer in their response, "The railroad is the reason!"[49] Though the Calapooians did not forget the primitive and pastoral beauty of the land, their narrowing and intensifying focus on mechanization, profit, and better access to outside markets—which was also seriously affecting the environment—would ultimately have severe consequences for their psychological relationship to the land.

With the establishment and growth of towns on the banks of the Calapooia, not only industry but also personal occupations grew and diversified. The first census of the Calapooia Valley in 1850 listed 219 people. Out of the 39 people who gave an occupation, 32 described themselves as farmers. In 1860, 915 people lived in the valley; 114 worked as farmers or farm laborers, while day laborers accounted for 37 and stockraisers and herders 14. Most significant was the appearance of 19 other occupations accounting for some 50 people, including 2 sawyers, 5 blacksmiths, 3 cobblers, and 4 schoolteachers, as well as merchants, grocery clerks, and physicians. The 1870 and 1880 censuses reported more new occupations: engineers, photographers, coopers, wagon makers, justices of the peace, telegraphers, gardeners, and woolen-mill workers.[50]

Population growth related directly to the diversification of occupation, nascent industries, the establishment of towns, the improvement of transportation, and the extension of agriculture. (Table 7 shows the increase in population in the Calapooia area and comparison figures for Linn County and the Willamette Valley.) The economic historian James Tattersall has pointed out that population grew in Oregon during the 1850s because of both the California gold strikes and the Donation Land Law. Population growth slowed down during the 1860s, as immigrants chose more often to go to California than to Oregon, but it

TABLE 7

POPULATION GROWTH, 1850–90

	Calapooia		Linn County		Willamette Valley	
1850	219		994		11,631	
1860	915	(318%)[a]	6,772	(581%)	34,851	(200%)
1870	1,104	(21%)	8,717	(29%)	49,659	(42%)
1880	2,338	(112%)	12,676	(45%)	73,994	(49%)
1890[b]	3,000	(28%)	16,265	(28%)	108,802	(47%)

SOURCES: Manuscript Census Returns for Population, Linn County, 1850, 1860, 1870, 1880; U.S. Department of Commerce, Bureau of the Census, *Statistics of the Population of the United States . . . Ninth Census* (1872), 57; *Statistics of the Population of the United States . . . Tenth Census* (1883) 1:304; *Report on Population of the United States . . . Eleventh Census, 1890* vol. 50, pt. 8 (1896), 286.

[a]Percent increase from previous figures, rounded to the nearest percent.

[b]The 1890 Manuscript Population Census Returns is missing for the Calapooia: therefore, population is estimated based on local precinct returns.

continued to grow because of more gold strikes in the Pacific Northwest. Population growth picked up in the 1870s because of the extension of transportation and the entry of northwestern agricultural and forest products into world markets. Population continued to grow, but again at a slower pace, through the end of the century.[51]

While following the general population trends for Oregon and the Willamette Valley, Linn County and the Calapooia differed in rates and reasons for growth. For instance, in the 1850s the growth rate of the Linn County and Calapooia population was greater than that of the Willamette as a whole. Since Linn County and the Calapooia are near the southern end of the valley, where initial settlement occurred later, more land was open for settlement and a greater proportion of immigrants could be absorbed during the years of the Donation Land Law (1850–55). Population growth slowed greatly in the 1860s as land supplies diminished and as the county still remained somewhat cut off from markets during this period—again in part because of the Donation Land Law, as discussed above. Furthermore, the general population of Oregon expanded, thanks partly to the lumber industry; the expansion was greatest in the northern valley at the confluence of the Willamette and Columbia rivers. But Linn County, located in the southern valley and lacking adequate means of lumber transport, could not take advantage of the wider regional timber trade during these years. By 1880 the population of Linn County and the Calapooia again burgeoned with the coming of the railroad, and it kept climbing through the end of the century.

Calapooia residents founded early towns, with the exception of Union Point (significantly, it failed within seven years), on the principle of utility derived from the landscape. The examples of Brownsville's flour mill and the town's demand for a railroad connection demonstrate how human changes in the natural landscape could increase the utilitarian potential of the landscape. The example of Crawfordsville shows how the extraction of timber and the use of the Calapooia as a log highway could limit the ability of the environment to rejuvenate what settlers had first recognized as most valuable—in this case, fertile soils. The rise and fall of Boston discloses a pattern first of the plains becoming more important than the foothills, and then the location of the railroad becoming more important than anything else. The growth of Shedd and Halsey demonstrates the importance of the proliferation of technology during the nineteenth century.

The founding of communities; the establishment of manufacturing and industry; the rise of logging; the increase in agricultural production; the building of roads, steamboats, and railways; the imposition of the cadastral survey and land claiming laws that forced adherence to it; and the growth of the population—all of these reveal how in the later nineteenth century the Calapooia settlement and the environment increasingly became integrated into a world that stretched far beyond the walls of the valley. Accompanying the economic integration of the Calapooia into the region, nation, and world was a change in the residents' attitudes to and psychological relationship with the environment. The settlers had once considered the landscape to be in some ways separate from humans and in many ways something on which humans depended; over time, though, the landscape increasingly became just the object of utilitarian desires and economic demand. Throughout this process, however, the environment was also an actor, and it responded in ways that proved costly to its inhabitants.

CHAPTER VII

Life and Reflection
on a Transformed Landscape

Within the space of about fifty years, from the 1840s to the 1890s, the environment of the Willamette Valley underwent incredible and rapid change. By 1890 the Kalapuya had completely disappeared, and with them went an age-old landscape, ecological balance, natural abundance, and a cosmology that viewed the land and its animals in spiritual relationship to people. Although white-tailed deer and migrating and resident fowl still remained in or frequented the valley, their numbers had been greatly reduced. By the 1890s some native animals, among them the grizzly, cougar, and wolf, were locally either extinct or near extinction. Exotic species such as cattle, swine, and horses had replaced them. Nonnative and native grasses, shrubs, and trees had invaded the prairies, from which various native grasses and large expanses of camas had disappeared. Euro-Americans had also introduced to the valley a number of cultivated plants—wheat, oats, and garden vegetables. The once scantily timbered foothills supported denser forests, while streamside woodlands had become sparser. Some soils in the valley had been exhausted. Erosion had increased on certain streams, and at the same time flood plains had been diminished and many marshes eliminated. Fish habitat and spawning grounds were impaired or altogether destroyed. And the valley was now divided into parcels of privately owned property.

This enormous disruption and change occurred because one group of people, Euro-Americans, replaced another, Native Americans. But the Kalapuya had altered the environment as well. They did so most strikingly with the annual use of fire, preventing continuous forests from covering the Willamette Valley. For basic needs of food and shelter, the natives, working within the limits of natural possibilities, created in the valley an environment that included, among other things, an abundance of camas meadows, oak groves, forest-prairie edges, tarweed, and white-tailed deer. But merely listing the separate components of the environment does an injustice to the complex ecological relationships among animals, plants, climate, and people that existed in the Willamette during prehistoric times. The environment that the Kalapuya and nature wove together in the Willamette remained in ecological balance for at least several hundred years. The people, and the environmental change they induced, followed a continuous seasonal cycle year after year after year. Of course, this cycle may not have continued indefinitely had not Europeans and Euro-Americans arrived on the scene. Larger, slower changes have occurred in the Willamette, with the climate varying between dry/warm and moist/cool periods. These changes have influenced and will continue to influence vegetation and animal life as well as human occupancy.

Euro-American settlers replaced the Kalapuya in the Willamette Valley within a brief period of time. Because the culture of the Kalapuya and the Willamette were closely intertwined, the tumultuous disruption of native culture also represented a convulsive change in the ecological balance of the valley. As the Kalapuya vanished, so, too, did the environment they and nature had created. Nature, however, remained a constant, and Euro-Americans working within its possibilities and responding to growing and distant markets created a new, relatively unstable environment in the valley. Euro-Americans entered the Willamette with a set of cultural assumptions much different from the one their predecessors had held. The new inhabitants conceived of their whole history of westward migration as one of continual progress. They had a sense of time as linear, not cyclical. They hoped to transform the valley into an environment based on the vision of their history and future: towns, farms, wheat fields, pastures, fences, private property, factories. Essentially, they wanted to create a pastoral landscape. With the pastoral in mind, Euro-Americans believed that they depended less directly on the primitive environment than had their predecessors. This belief may have led them to take the environment for granted; it certainly encouraged them to take less care of it.

The evidence I have collected here certainly supports some of the conclusions of other environmental historians interested in explaining the differences between native and Euro-American cultures and economies and the environments they create.[1] But I am primarily interested in asking and answering other questions about the relationship between settlers and the western environment: How did settlers respond to the primitive environment of the West? How did the western environment influence settlement culture? What role did Native Americans play in the cultural-environmental relationships of Euro-Americans settlers? What changes in peoples' minds accompanied changes in the environment? And how did Euro-Americans feel about the changes in the landscape as it altered over the course of settlement?

Mid nineteenth-century western settlers responded to the environment of the Willamette in a number of positive ways. They appreciated its primitive beauty, they valued some of its "wilderness" qualities, they worked within its possibilities, and they even incorporated some of its natural attributes into their vision of a future pastoral community. The initial settlement of the Calapooia Valley shows that Euro-American pioneers, on levels from material culture to aesthetic responses to emotional connection, intimately interacted with and felt positively about their surroundings.

Environmental historians accept without question that when Euro-Americans moved West and imposed their culture on a new landscape, they necessarily altered the environment in significant ways, with both short-term and long-term consequences. But historians still debate whether or not the western environment—more precisely, the frontier—influenced the mind and therefore the institutions of the American people. The history of the settlement of the Willamette demonstrates that Euro-Americans did indeed alter the environment. This history also shows that the environment did subtly influence the culture and attitudes that settlers brought with them from the Ohio Valley. For instance, housing styles remained the same, but settlers realized these styles with new materials. Settlers found the Willamette Valley initially easier to clear as the forests were already diminished because of Kalapuya burning. Similarly, farmers found the sod of the Willamette easier to plow than the sod of the Midwest, but they had to give up the cultivation of corn. Settlers continued to raise livestock in their new home for the same reasons they had in the Ohio Valley, but the nature of the Willamette, with its grasslands, camas meadows, and mild climate, allowed livestock to forage year-round. In addition, early settlers recognized and appreciated their new home's milder climate, lack of summer humidity, dearth of thunder storms, and healthier atmosphere. Finally, Euro-Americans had to balance themselves with the idiosyncrasies of the landscape, especially the nature of its foothills and prairies, thus making the Willamette settlement process a unique experience in the West. Although subtle, these environmental differences between the frontiers of the Willamette and cis-Appalachia underlie cultural differences between the Midwest and the Far West, particularly western Oregon.

An examination of the Euro-American settlement process in the Willamette Valley demonstrates that Native Americans played a role in shaping the settler-environment relationship, influencing settlement culture, and conditioning the vision Euro-Americans held of their own future in the valley. For example, the Kalapuya were largely responsible for the location of wood and summer water sources in the valley, and thus for early Euro-American settlement patterns and the settlers' intimate connection with the environment. The Kalapuya were also partly responsible for the abundance of deer and fowl that settlers depended on and appreciated. And the Kalapuya created the prairies that settlers looked at in pastoral terms. Undoubtedly, mid nineteenth-century Americans would have held much the same pastoral vision of their future regardless of where they settled, but the Kalapuya-created grasslands of the Willamette captivated settlers' imaginations.

As a case study of the West, the example of the Calapooia and Willamette valleys demonstrates that settlers had an intimate and often positive relationship with the primitive landscape; that they altered the environment; and that the environment, which the natives had been instrumental in shaping, modified the culture Euro-Americans brought with them from other western frontiers and also influenced their vision of the valley's possibilities. The last and perhaps most important question this study has centered on, and which the remainder of this chapter assesses, concerns Euro-Americans' changing feelings and attitudes about the primitive environment and the pastoral landscape of the Willamette. To shed light on this fundamental question of nineteenth-century settlement in the Far West, this study has employed the metaphor of movement between the foothills and the plains of the Willamette Valley.

FROM FOOTHILLS TO VALLEY FLOOR:
FLUX IN THE LATE NINETEENTH CENTURY

During the early years of frontier settlement, Euro-Americans avoided the open prairies of the southern Willamette Valley, instead taking refuge among the foothills of the periphery and secondary valleys such as the Calapooia. Settlers consciously sought out the forest-prairie ecotone along the foothills, for this environment afforded the various resources they needed during this primitive phase of living in the Willamette: wood, water, and well-drained soil, as well as the prairie grasslands. During this initial phase of settlement, and because of a plethora of factors (including access to resources, poor transportation, aesthetic appreciation, lack of a developed market economy, land-claim laws, and psychological need), settlers of the foothills developed a direct and intimate relationship with the environment. But they also brought with them to the Willamette Valley a vision of a civilization they wished to create there, and they constantly looked away from the foothills to the plains as the refuge for this ideal, which was a brand of pastoral or garden imagery.

By the late nineteenth century, the population center of the Calapooia and southern Willamette valleys had indeed moved out onto the plains. By 1887 four-fifths of Linn County's population, which reached more than sixteen thousand in 1890, lived on the open prairies on farms, in Albany (the county seat) along the Willamette River, or in villages that the railroad had created, such as Shedd and Halsey. In this same year the plains region contained eleven-twelfths of all taxable property in Linn County. Of inestimable value to the early settlers, foothills had at one time been taxed at a higher rate than the prairies. But during the shift of the center of economy and population, the value of prairie land actually rose above foothill land (table 8). The impending arrival of the railroad in 1870–71 had the greatest influence on the change in value of prairie land. Between 1864 and 1870 the taxable value of prairie land rose 110.6 percent higher than what it had been in 1864. Simultaneously, the market value of prairie land skyrocketed over lands along the foothills. In 1875 prairie land ranged from $20 to $40 per acre while foothill land was only $3 to $15. The proximity of the railroad had a direct bearing on these figures. Land within five to six miles of a shipping point sold for at least $30 per acre.[2]

By the late nineteenth century, residents of the southern Willamette

TABLE 8

TAXABLE VALUE OF CALAPOOIA LANDS, 1858–78

	Foothills		Prairies	
	Sample Size (in Acres)	Value/Acre	Sample Size (in Acres)	Value/Acre
1858	17,330	$3.45	5,346	$2.84
1861	14,138	$3.36	13,844	$3.24
1864	10,788	$2.87	9,045	$3.57
1870	10,734	$3.94	11,771	$7.52
1878	13,441	$5.06	14,662	$9.67

SOURCES: Linn County Tax Registers, Oregon State Archives, Salem.

Valley considered the most valuable land to be the open prairies. There, too, concentrated the bulk of the southern valley's population. Calapooians achieved this transformation through a number of means: the Donation Land Claim Act, modern transportation (the steamboat and the railroad), prairie drainage, a developed market economy, and manufactories. In achieving the future, the Calapooians also cultivated a new relationship with the landscape. In the case of the Finley gristmill, utilitarian values of the landscape became preeminent in the fledgling community, and traditional mores concerning land claiming fell by the wayside. The Donation Land Claim Act forced new and old settlers alike to abide by arbitrary and invisible survey lines, no longer allowing them to place claims on the landscape according to the natural setting. The same survey also shunned property boundaries recognized by the land's natural features.

    With the growth of the livestock trade in the 1850s, the open prairies' utilitarian values became most pronounced, and a struggle ensued over who would control these grasslands. One of the results of this battle was a decided effort to fence the land. Eventually, improved transportation, the growth of a commercial market, and the drainage of wet prairies all combined to allow human occupation and exploitation of these very same lands. In the midst of these prairies, towns sprang up practically overnight. Finally, with the establishment of manufactories and the growth of technology came the full development of the land's utility. The diversion of the Calapooia's waters allowed the establishment of grist, lumber, and woolen mills. And the railroad became the most promising way to allow the landscape's utility to be fully realized. Within a few years, the earliest Calapooians and their descendants had created a pastoral landscape, simultaneously cultivating a new relationship with the landscape as well.

THE GARDEN REALIZED

A comparison of two panoramic views of the Willamette Valley one dating from 1847 (figure 1) and the other from 1888 (figure 7), reveals the great transformations that the landscape had undergone. The 1888 sketch shows the forests of 1847 cut down, with only patches confined to the geometrical divisions conforming to fence and DLCA survey lines. No longer are natural divisions between forest and prairie discernible. Furthermore, the three deer in the foreground of figure 1, representing the valley's primitive nature, have yielded in 1888 to three Euro-American inhabitants of the valley, representing civilization. The 1888 picture also shows a variety of fences and fields disunifying the scene, with a village barely visible in the hazy distance.

As early as 1855, Blain had seen the beginnings of this transformation, as he noted in a letter after returning from a spring trip to the lower part of the Willamette: "I was on the whole much pleased with the evidence of extensive improvement which every where met the eye. New houses, barns, and farms clothed many portions of the road, with which I had been familiar, with the novelty of a new country."[3] Blain, as we have seen, appreciated the natural beauty of the valley as well as its primitive, even wilderness aspects. Indeed, he revealed equivocal feelings about the effects of continued Euro-American settlement on the primitive nature of the valley.

Late nineteenth-century Euro-Americans' relationship to, and perception of, the transformed, pastoral Willamette landscape were as complex and multifaceted as Blain's and others' initial responses to the primitive landscape. What is most intriguing about this later generation's reactions to the transformed landscape, however, was their concentration on the beauty it still possessed. To late nineteenth-century Willamette and Calapooia valley inhabitants, human artifice, such as villages, farmsteads, and mills, coupled with the valley's remaining primitive qualities, created a scene of domestic enchantment that they considered beautiful in its own right. Thus commented the *Willamette*

CHEHALEM VALLEY.-THE GREAT FRUIT GROWING SECTION OF OREGON.

Figure 7.   The transformed landscape of the Willamette Valley, 1888. Compare this sketch of the Chehalem area of the Willamette Valley (near Newberg) with Paul Kane's rendition of the valley in 1847 (fig. 1). Unlike Kane's painting, which depicts an uncultivated landscape inhabited only by wildlife, this 1888 illustration emphasizes the Euro-American presence—humans, fences, rectangular fields, a village in the distance, and abrupt divisions between prairies and forest patches. Courtesy of the Oregon Historical Society, Portland (negative number ORHI 35543).

Farmer in 1873: "Neither can there be a more charming spot of earth than this blessed valley which offers us a home, with its delightful climate, rich and certain harvests and with its undeveloped resources." One year later the same newspaper commented, "Is this a dream? Beautiful fields of golden grain, green orchards, meadows, the Willamette River, like a silver belt, glistening in the sunlight."[4] In both these instances, the observer paired the valley's natural beauty with utility and human artifice.

More vividly, in 1882 an observer of the Willamette Valley scene, E. Ingersoll, wrote at length about the confluence of nature and human artifice on the valley's landscape.[5] Ingersoll began by describing average Willamette Valley farms that "follow one another from the river back into the wooded foot-hills." He then turned his attention to the houses, "which are almost invariably of frame, and of good size, with far more attention paid to comfort and attractive surroundings than it is customary in the Eastern States." He also noted the "little villages scattered here and there," as well as schoolhouses and churches. The vision he describes conveys to his reader an idea of a domesticated landscape.

Significantly, nature had a role here, too, for it provided a charming setting within which Willamette Valley inhabitants built their community. Ingersoll mentioned, for instance, the "many scattered oaks," "yellow pines," and "stately firs," which "gave an opportunity not lost sight of to place one's house where the effect would be that of an ancient homestead, around whose sacred altars trees planted in grandfather's youth had had time to become of great size and dignity." This "pleasant description," Ingersoll explained, "is seen everywhere; and it *is* deceptive, . . . giving an impression of a country occupied for centuries and full of traditions."

For Ingersoll, human occupation of the land transformed nature, turning elements of the landscape into embellishments of a domestic garden. From this immediate scene, which he himself termed one of "domestic felicity," Ingersoll then described the greater surrounding landscape: "The whole wide basin lies open to the eye, robed in green, but green of what infinite variety of tint and shading, between the emerald squares of the new wheat and the opaque mass of the far-away hill forests sharply serrate against the sky, or melting into farther and farther indistinctness of hill and haze. The foreground, too, is always pleasantly sketchy."[6] Reminiscent of Blain's descriptions of the Willamette and Calapooia valleys just thirty years earlier, Ingersoll's verbal rendition of a visual experience, however, is punctuated by the hand of man, though in a positive way, as seen in the "emerald squares of the new wheat." Ingersoll continued, "if you think my picture lacks color, look at that . . . brown patch of freshly ploughed ground; at this brilliant red barn and white farmhouse half hidden in its blossoming orchard!" For Ingersoll, only with the addition of human artifice— houses, barns, plowed fields, and orchards—could the true beauty of the landscape be appreciated.

The overwhelming beauty found in the now domesticated, pastoral Willamette Valley was commented on by observers of the Calapooia area and Linn County as a whole. A correspondent for the *Willamette Farmer* who traveled from Lebanon to Shedd in May 1877 declared of the view near the foot of Saddle Butte, "The scenery was magnificent.

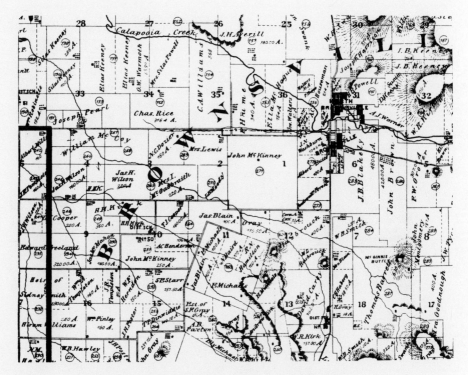

Map 8.   Land claims at the mouth of the Calapooia Valley, 1878.

SOURCE: *Illustrated Historical Atlas Map of Marion and Linn Counties, Oregon.*

We could count twenty-one teams putting in grain, in going one mile. Linn County is literally one grand wheat field." Another correspondent wrote later the same season about the view as he and his companion headed southeast from Halsey to the foothills, "passing nearly all the way over prairies as rich as need be, showing everywhere comfortable homes."[7]

Much of the area through which they traveled, the once formerly open, uninhabited plains of the Willamette Valley west of Brownsville at the mouth of the Calapooia Valley, is shown in map 8. Note that on this map, executed one year after the newspaper correspondent traversed the area, the landscape is divided into numerous farms. Figure 8 allows us to glimpse the plains of the Willamette adjacent to the Calapooia River as they appeared in 1878. This lithograph shows the formerly avoided prairies now transformed into a realm of domestic bliss. It reveals neatly kept farms, with fences dividing and therefore

Figure 8.   D.P. Porter's farm and residence, 1878. Located near the town of Shedd, Porter's residence is an example of the pastoral achievement of southern Willamette Valley inhabitants in the late nineteenth century. Source: *Illustrated Historical Atlas Map of Marion and Linn Counties, Oregon.*

putting into captivity prairies that have now been changed into productive fields and pastures. Barns, other outbuildings, and young orchards embellish the scene, while men busily attend grain fields, and farm animals laze about the barnyard. The lithograph even captures a croquet match in progress. All these adornments and activities however, serve only as embroidery for the most important feature of the scene, the domestic abode, standing in a central, stately location.

In this lithograph and the period descriptions, the natural beauty of the primitive valley has given way to the utilitarian beauty of the transformed landscape. The meaning of this landscape had also changed. We see this most graphically in the comments of an 1884 correspondent to an Albany newspaper. This writer first described the panorama of the valley as viewed from "a slight eminence on the [east] edge of the Willamette valley," where the town of "Brownsville stands in her glory." This correspondent appears to have stood in almost exactly the same place where Wilson Blain had stood thirty-three years earlier when he "gazed with rapture" across a valley that combined, in the most "remarkable manner, variety, beauty, and sublimity, in the natural world."[8]

But the vision of the 1884 observer, while superficially similar to Blain's, is in fact quite different. He begins by regarding the "background made up of the Cascade range and with a front view of the beautiful Willamette valley and its native scenery." He continues, "But a little beyond this scenery is the Coast range, which has been termed the dyke of the great Pacific." What made this scenery most "beautiful, indeed romantic" to this viewer, however, was not simply its natural and sublime beauty—as it had been for Blain—but the fact that he heard a special message "echoing" over the valley, reverberating from the heights of the Coast Range. That message was "business."

Notes on the beauty of the transformed Calapooia scenery were not limited to panoramic vistas alone, for observant eyes dissected this landscape, isolating its important utilitarian features, such as the Calapooia River itself. Regarded as the "leading element" in North Brownsville's prosperity as of 1878, observers saw the Calapooia as "splendid and never-failing [in] water power . . . which drives all . . . mills and factories." Eleven years later another viewer of the Brownsville scene remarked that the dam built across the Calapooia turned "almost the entire river into a race." One year later, another enumerated the manufactories the river powered in Brownsville: "a woolen mill, flour mill, saw mill, sash and door factory, furniture factory, etc." He ended his commentary by noting that there was yet "plenty of power to spare." Commentators on the Calapooia positively assessed this realization of the river's utility; indeed, in 1876 one resident of Crawfordsville suggested that the river was so important that it deserved "a better name than it bears."[9]

Even individual towns and their situations were considered idyllic scenes. In 1878 a viewer described South Brownsville as "picturesquely-situated and flourishing . . . at the entrance to the valley of the Calapooia River, and more beautiful surroundings than it possesses would be hard to conceive." The twin towns of South and North Brownsville together had "picturesque dwellings, neatly-arranged grounds, in the cool shade of innumerable trees, present[ing] a picture of comfort which no other town can excel and few equal." Even Brownsville's small industrial area around the woolen mills had a domestic lure, according to one late nineteenth-century observer: "Surrounding, and in near proximity to the mill, are the dwellings of the operatives, and the observer will be pleased with the general air of neatness and comfort pervading this section of the city, most of the houses being built and surrounded by orchards and gardens prolific in their yield."[10]

The late nineteenth-century Calapooia, as well as the whole of the Willamette Valley, may not in reality have been the tranquil pastoral landscape that its inhabitants so gloriously proclaimed. In fact, these descriptions ignore some of the reality of environmental degradation under which these people suffered. But it is important to note that this is how they wished to view the world they and nature had created. Here, comfortable houses and productive farms dotted the prairies, industrious villages reposed among shade trees, and bustling rivers powered factories. All this they viewed as a jewel set in the beautiful green basin of the Willamette.

Late nineteenth-century Willamette and Calapooia residents believed they lived in an actual garden. Immigration agent C. G. Burkhart, who lived in Linn County his entire life, argued in 1887, "It is stated that if the Willamette Valley is the garden spot of the state, Linn County is the garden spot of the valley. The comparison is now extended and the statement confidently made that, if Linn County is the garden spot of the valley," the prairie extending west of the Calapooia "is the garden spot of the county." In other words, these open prairies that the Calapooia community once hoped would become a garden had, by the end of the nineteenth century, far exceeded all expectations and had become literally the garden spot of the garden spot of the garden spot of the entire state.[11]

Burkhart and his successor, B. F. Alley, marketed the garden image of the Willamette plains adjacent to the Calapooia during the end of the 1880s. Burkhart noted, "In all this plain the land is all taken and converted into fine farms." In another reference he remarked that the "belt from the Willamette River to the foothills . . . is an open, level prairie country, the most productive in the valley. . . . Wheat, oats, barley and all kinds of vegetable and fruits are grown here with the greatest success." Elsewhere he pointed out,

> In all parts of the country, along the river and creek bottoms and all through the foot hills, fruits of most kinds are grown in the greatest abundance and the quality is unsurpassed by that of any other state. Apples of all varieties, pears in size and quality call out the unstinted praise of all who see them, plums as large as hen eggs, rich and juicy, cherries that in both quality and

quantity challenge comparison with similar fruits grown anywhere else, prunes that delight the eye and taste of all.[12]

Alley described the fertile plains of the Willamette, "stretching away to the west and south" from the Calapooia, as "carpeted with numberless fields of grain, dotted with farm houses and settlements, showing a prosperous and successful people." He also wrote of "the beauty and fertility" of the prairies surrounding the town of Halsey and of "the unmistakable healthfulness of its climate." According to Alley, "All the essentials that go to make up a desirable country abound here."[13]

These descriptions of the Calapooia's prairies in particular, and the Willamette Valley in general, rely on the image of the garden. Settlers dreamed of such a garden at an early date and then realized it through a variety of interdependent natural and human factors: fertility of soil, drainage of the valley's plains, a variety of natural resources, a salubrious climate, the growth of markets and their accessibility through improved transportation, a growing population, development of early manufacturing and the utilization of rapid streams, and the expansion of agriculture. Here, indeed, a garden thrived.

The beauty and utility of the landscape, however, were as two-dimensional as the descriptions and sketches of the Calapooia's gardenlike appearance. Scratch the surface of these lithographs and we find that the grazing cattle and rooting swine, coupled with the cessation of burning by the Kalapuya, helped destroy the grasslands of the plains on which settlers once gazed with pleasure. Fencing diminished the Calapooia as a wildlife habitat. The draining of prairies destroyed the valley's natural sloughs, home to waterfowl and animals. Furthermore, the early lumber industry not only felled the native trees but converted the Calapooia into a highway for logs, with harmful effects on the stream and its ability to replenish the floodplain. And nature reacted. The environment continued to act independently of its human inhabitants, as it had during early pioneer years. But its reaction in these later years was magnified because the changes humans attempted to make were more environmentally significant. Although settlers could alter prairies and woodlands, they could not stop natural succession. Soon, invasions of brush and weeds, native and exotic, and the depletion of soil fertility made life difficult for the civilization that unwittingly initiated the change.

From at least the 1890s and well into the twentieth century, longtime settlers recognized changes in the land, many of which they lamented. John Minto noted just after the turn of the century, "These damp-land and water fowls and animals, which once found here their breeding places, have gone forever, unless farmers in the near future construct artificial fish ponds, and reservoirs for irrigation when needed." A Calapooia Valley old-timer remarked to a historian at about the same time, "You can not imagine the beauty of this country when we first came here." Another Calapooian remarked in the late 1930s of the vanished white-tailed deer, "Now I presume they are all gone, though it may be possible that there are still a very few of them in the woods and among the small wooded islands."[14] Lamentation over the lost wildlife and primitive landscape of the Calapooia and Willamette valleys certainly composed part of residents' responses to the transformed environment.

One can also find at the end of the nineteenth century a human-landscape relationship truncated by a myriad of intermediaries now separating the two. Living in this garden, valley inhabitants lacked a certain depth in their relationship to the landscape, for the process undertaken to achieve this garden actually amputated the third dimension of intimacy, a closeness to the primitive landscape that the early settlers enjoyed. Lacking this third dimension, residents' relationship to the land collapsed into two-dimensionality. They still went about their activities, but they felt a significant loss that they were unable exactly to describe. This change, and the necessity of leaving the foothills for the prairie where future development would take place, resulted in the loss of a certain quality of life. By the end of the nineteenth century, valley inhabitants were looking back to the foothills, and their still relatively primitive nature, for this vanished quality of life, and aspects of the foothills were celebrated in literature and deemed desirable. If the garden qualities of the Willamette could be so widely glorified, the foothills, too, had their own benefits, which were missing from the plains.

FOOTHILLS IN RETROSPECT

When George Atkinson traveled through the western portion of the mid Willamette Valley in 1848, he kept a diary of his journey. On 15 July he noted in his journal that he had met along the way a Mr. B. (possibly Glen O. Burnett), who evidently mentioned that "a man can live [in the Willamette] with half the labor done in the States." Three years later

Wilson Blain reported that he had "heard an Illinois farmer sum up the character of Oregon in a very few expressive words. 'It is a great country . . . for a lazy man; for in no other could such a man live with so little care or labour.' " Blain went on, however, to note how "great" the country was "for an industrious man."[15]

Some thirty years later, an important change in the message that Atkinson and Blain related can be detected. In 1887 the Linn County Immigration Agent wrote, "This County is not a paradise. It requires labor and industry, indefatigable to win a fortune here. It requires earnest effort to make a living here. If a person cannot sacrifice this much of self, he should not make this his home." This message to prospective immigrants was probably designed, in part, to weed out what the Immigration Agent called "sluggards." But it also reveals a clue to a changed relationship with environment of the Willamette and Calapooia valleys.[16]

From late nineteenth-century valley literature, we hear complaints from inhabitants about the life they led. Some of these complaints came from farmers whose agricultural practices had changed, or at least intensified, since the early years. Drawn into a market economy, they extended cultivation onto the Willamette prairies, which they had to drain of excessive winter and spring waters. In time the fertility of these same lands declined, forcing the complete abandonment of some areas.

In response to this environmental change, one valley farmer wrote to the *Willamette Farmer* in 1872, "When the soil was new and rich, it did not seem to take much thought how to farm; but, as the fertile prairies have been used for many years in constant cropping, men began to see the necessity of more thorough farming." Two techniques required for this "more thorough" type of cultivation, and on which this farmer commented, were draining and subsoiling, both arduous tasks. He then commented that although Oregon farmers should write to the *Willamette Farmer* for advice, they were unlikely to do so: "The truth is farmers, after the toils of the day, feel more like resting than writing [to your paper for successful advice]."[17]

In response to growing markets, the Willamette Valley farmers demanded increased yields, which required extensive cultivation techniques and resulted in complex and perplexing ecological responses, and in turn caused the wearisome toil they experienced. As we have seen, the cessation of Kalapuya burning, for instance, encouraged shrubs to invade prairies now used for cultivated crops. When commenting on the "brush invasion," one valley farmer prefaced his remarks by noting, "It is natural for man to shun hard labor." But in combating ecological succession, this same farmer submitted, "It requires not only a strong head but strong muscles." The invasion of other plants, such as bracken, added to these problems and were themselves "very difficult to eradicate."[18]

Burkhart, the Linn County immigration agent and a lifetime resident of the area, noted, however, that there existed refuge from such wearisome toil. This refuge could be found in the landscape itself:

> Situated in and rising out of this [Willamette] plain are quite a number of buttes or single circular hills from three to five hundred feet high, covered more or less with timber or brush though some are destitute of both.
>
> Bubbling from the sides of these hills are to be found springs of pure, living water, as well as rich nutritious grass. . . . Dotted over these hills are many romantic, shady groves, where, in spring and summer time people from all surrounding country hold their picnic, grange, and other outdoor gatherings to recuperate from the exhaustion brought on by the toils and burdens of every day life.[19]

The description of this geographical refuge suits well the land the first settlers, such as Thomas Ward (map 6), took up in the late 1840s and early 1850s before extensive settlement on the prairie proper. Figure 9 shows one such butte as it appeared in 1878.

Retreated to out of necessity during early days, and then considered of secondary importance as later arrivals realized the potential of the valley's floor, the small buttes and foothills of the valley now became "romantic" refuges where locals "from all surrounding country" could "recuperate" from everyday toils. Some locals have left references about such retreats. For instance, during the mid 1880s Sarah Cornett noted in her diary the daily weather conditions as well as the innumerable chores she, her husband, and other members of the family performed every day. Sunday, though, was usually a day of rest. On Sunday, 10 May 1885, she wrote of a family outing to Soda Springs in the foothills: "quite warm has some appearance of rain John and I and Mother and Mary all went to Soda to day we had a very nice time." Living in the shadow of the isolated Saddle Butte, Cornett simply mentioned on another Sunday, "John and I went to the butte this evening." In 1866, Jasper Cranfill remarked, "Ploughed one half the day. Remainder I passed off in going to the largest Buttes on a hunting tour & pleasure trip."[20]

But Burkhart's comment on "the exhaustion brought on by the toils

Figure 9.   Small butte in northern Linn County, 1878. Conical buttes, such as the one pictured here, and surrounding foothills offered southern Willamette Valley inhabitants a romantic refuge from the drudgery of everyday life. Note the dense forest on the north (left) side of the butte and the sparser woodland on the drier south side. Source: *Illustrated Historical Atlas Map of Marion and Linn Counties, Oregon.*

and burdens of every day life" had a broader meaning than just the laborious work experienced in rural living as farmers attempted to produce more efficiently for wider markets. When looking to the foothills, Burkhart, like other Calapooia and Willamette Valley citizens, was actually looking away from the complexities of life in the late nineteenth century. Another valley inhabitant summed up the problem—after glorifying the amenities of life that might be enjoyed in the foothills—with his remark, "If some of us must wear our lives out in the drudgery of town work, we hope the people of the hill country will appreciate their privileges and use them right."[21]

Commentators celebrated at length the privileges of living among the foothills: "The water is better and the air is purer in the hills"; "It must be healthier in the hills, and where there is health there is happiness"; "A single day among these hills will make any man who has eyes for beauty and lungs for fresh air." The practical qualities the earliest set-

tlers noted about the foothills, especially good drainage but also access
to water, timber, and good pasturage, were all once again discussed at
the end of the nineteenth century.[22]

Observers realized that practical considerations were not the only
qualities of the foothills to be enjoyed. What became the most significant feature in this celebration of the foothills was the "natural" quality
of life available there and its psychological implications for residents.
Thus on a trip to the foothills, one valley inhabitant remarked about a
particularly memorable moment "not beyond the reach of settlement
where the foothills wear inviting aspects and the sounds of civilization
seem an actual invasion of Nature's domain."[23]

Linn County and Calapooia residents desired the release that nature
afforded them during the late nineteenth century. Some residents, not
always able to go to the foothills, substituted a wilder area of their
farms. Jasper Cranfill, for instance, did not always have time to retreat
to the hills, but he still needed to get away from everyday toil. Thus, he
"went down into the timber for diversion" on more than one occasion
in the late 1860s.[24]

Another telling incident is recorded in Sarah Cornett's diary. As
noted in chapter 4, Cornett's forebears on the Calapooia in the late
1840s and early 1850s, Agnes Courtney and Elizabeth Blain, domesticated their wilderness claims by planting flowers. In the 1880s Cornett
also had a flower garden in which she took great pride. She lamented in
her diary on 19 January 1883, for instance, that it was "very cold last
night" and "froze all of our flowers." Another time she was apparently
delighted when Allie Elder stopped in "and brought me some dahlah
bulbs." While Cornett enjoyed her garden very much, her domestic
flowers did not always provide her with the satisfaction she desired.
One day, when "Ada and Nellie were here . . . we went down to the
timber to get some wild current blossoms." Agnes Courtney and Elizabeth Blain used flowers to domesticate their wilderness claims during
early settlement; Sarah Cornett used a bit of the "wild" to embellish her
domesticated surroundings in the 1880s.[25]

Western Oregon resident Frances Fuller Victor noted the significance
of wooded corners of inhabitants' claims and labeled them "truly 'Arca-
dian' groves." On one occasion in the 1870s, Victor lamented at length
the abuse of one of these patches of timber. On visiting the home of one
valley farmer, she declared it "a sort of profanation that [he] . . . has
allowed one of these grand forest cathedrals to be used as a shelter for

his stock, and so to become defiled." In essence, Victor criticized what had transpired in the Willamette over the past few years when she chided her own view as having neither "utilitarian, nor even humanitarian" values. To Victor, utility and "humanity" had wrought havoc on the naturalness of the valley. In making a deep bow to these forces, Victor also averred that there was still something mystical in remnant stands of "these giants of centuries old" to which impermanent humans (specifically their cattle which "are born and die in half a dozen years") had no right "to bring grief."[26]

While wooded corners of late nineteenth-century farms provided havens for valley inhabitants, as they had for Cranfill, Cornett, and Victor, the foothills, with vaster areas of what appeared to be natural or wild, became the focus of attention. Descriptions of little valleys like the Calapooia and nearby foothills tended to concentrate on the more natural surroundings than could be found on the plains of the Willamette: "The prospect is better and the scenery more varied. The groves of oak timber are a delight to the eye." The following lengthy description of Brownsville's setting also shows a concern to point out the natural beauty of the Calapooia and not the signs of human habitation. Brownsville, we are told, is situated

> at the entrance to the charming little valley of the Calapooia, where the first low hills rise from the level plains of the Willamette Valley, and stretch in rolling landscape, hill upon hill, away toward the snow clad Cascades. The village has a population of something like six hundred, and is nestled along the margin of the Calapooia Creek, about one-half on the grass covered hills that reach down almost to the sparkling waters of the stream, and the other on the south bank, whence the level bottom land extends out for miles toward the ever green hills. [It] is the most romantically situated of any village in the country, and is remarkable for its pleasant surrounding.[27]

Breathing fresh air, drinking pure water, and looking onto the foothills' scenery lent a certain "naturalness" to life that had been lost on the valley floor. The late nineteenth-century way of life in the foothills, particularly in the small valley of the Calapooia, allowed residents to participate in what might appear to be a completely different realm of psychology:

> This rolling, hilly region is interspersed with little skirts of prairie bottoms here and there along the creeks and rivers that wend their way to the Willamette River from the snows of the Cascades. These little valleys along these streams are a thing of beauty, a joy forever to those who are so lucky as to

find a home in them. So varied and romantic in their form and appearance as
to excite the admiration of all who are of poetical inclinations.[28]

Thus, the variety of elements the foothills mysteriously possessed made
it possible to lead in them a life of romance. In fact, those "so lucky as to
find a home in them" might even live a life there that replicated poetry.
These surroundings would induce, according to another observer, a
certain quality of thought in its residents so that one day "some of the
best brains and truest hearts of future generations will come from 'The
Hills.' "[29] Essentially what these people noted about the foothills was
that their primitive qualities still existed and were vital for psychological
health.

Psychologist Harold F. Searles has noted that the "advancement of
our technology has made for a psychological distancing of man
from . . . innumerable . . . elements of his non-human environment."
This distancing has been caused by a loss of "contact with nature,"
resulting in a "profound sense of meaninglessness."[30] The history of
Euro-American settlers and their relationship to the environment along
the banks of the Calapooia in the nineteenth century is a history of
humans becoming estranged from the land. The earliest settlers sought
out the foothills along valleys like the Calapooia as the best place to
settle. There they developed a close relationship with the land. In time,
the various values of this land went down as settlers and their descendants exploited the expanse of the Willamette plains. But by the end of
the nineteenth century, people looked back to the little valleys and
foothills for something they apparently no longer experienced on the
floor of the Willamette Valley. If the plains of the Willamette west of the
Calapooia had become a two-dimensional garden spot, then the smaller
valleys like the Calapooia, with their numerous foothills and small
patches of prairie, held within their geographical form the psychological
third dimension missing from the complex life on the expansive plains
of the Willamette.

History had come nearly full circle. Retreating to the foothills to
make a living during the early years, settlers looked wistfully on the
open prairies. On those plains they believed a pastoral community
would be created. In reality, when looking onto the plains from the
vantage of the foothills, they looked into their future. Unable to know
what the realization of this future would mean—most important, a
changed relationship with the landscape—they set about working to-

ward it. When sitting on their farms of the prairies at the end of the nineteenth century, however, valley inhabitants noticed a void in their lives, a void that could be traced to their changed relationship with the land. Thus, when they looked to the foothills for the answer, they were, metaphorically, looking into their own past.

Notes

INTRODUCTION

1. In referring to the Midwest and Upper South, I use *cis-Appalachia* rather than the more common *trans-Appalachia* to emphasize my regional perspective. *Cis-Appalachia* means, literally, "this side of the Appalachian Mountains," whereas *trans-Appalachia* means "across or beyond the Appalachians." From the viewpoint of Oregon settlers and those of us in the West, *cis-Appalachia* is more appropriate.

2. Huth, *Nature and the American*; Ekirch, *Man and Nature in America*; Nash, *Wilderness and the American Mind*. See also Stilgoe, *Common Landscape of America*, 7–12; and Miller, *Errand into the Wilderness*, chap. 1.

3. Nash, *Wilderness and the American Mind*, 24.

4. Smith, *Virgin Land* (see particularly book 3, "The Garden of the World"); Marx, *Machine in the Garden*; Novak, *Nature and Culture*. See also Kolodny's two studies, *The Lay of the Land* and *The Land Before Her*, which look first at early American men's and then early American women's attitudes, particularly fantasies, about the North American landscape and environment. Kolodny's earlier work, which concerns men and the environment, falls into the first interpretive strand of American intellectual relationship with the environment that I have outlined. Kolodny basically argues that the masculine interpretation was rapacious and saw the North American environment as a virgin to be controlled and dominated. In her second work, Kolodny argues that women were not bent on "massive exploitation and alteration" of the environment but rather were more interested in creating gardens in the West (xiii).

5. Mitchell, *Witnesses to a Vanishing America*, xiii.

6. For example, White, *Land Use* and Cronon, *Changes in the Land*.

1. VALLEY OF THE LONG GRASSES

1. Moir and Mika, "Prairie Vegetation," 7–13, describes native prairie grasses of the Willamette Valley; for origins of the word *kalapuya*, see Leila Hallan, "History of Calapooias," 8. Early documents reveal a wide variety of spellings for "Calapooia"—"Call-law-poh-yea-as," "Callapuya," "Kelus-suyas," and "Vale Puyas," to name only a few. The accepted spelling for the tribe is now "Kalapuya." The "Calapooia" spelling was first applied to the small valley under discussion in 1850. Two other features in western Oregon, a mountain range and a creek, have been dubbed "Calapooya." McArthur, *Oregon Geographic Names*, 102; Carey and Hainline, *Brownsville*, 12.

2. Bramwell, in Haskin, Oral History.

3. Baldwin, *Geology of Oregon*, 1–3, 47–50, 53, 60; McKee, *Cascadia*, 157–58, 164–67, 175; Franklin and Dyrness, *Natural Vegetation*, 16; Smith, *Physical and Economic Geography*, 144, 147; Dicken and Dicken, *Two Centuries of Oregon Geography* 2:46.

4. McKee, *Cascadia*, 164, 167; Dicken and Dicken, *Two Centuries of Oregon Geography* 2:46; W. Smith, *Physical and Economic Geography*, 144, 147. Oregon City is today located above this basalt cliff, which forms the Willamette Falls.

5. Baldwin, *Geology of Oregon*, 52–53; Franklin and Dyrness, *Natural Vegetation*, 16.

6. Baldwin, *Geology of Oregon*, 52; Allen, Burns, and Sargeant, *Cataclysms on the Columbia*.

7. Detling, *Flora of the Pacific Northwest*, 34–36.

8. Ibid.; Thilenius, "*Quercus garryana* Forests," 1124–33; Minor et al., *Cultural Resources Overview*, 32–34.

9. Minor et al., *Cultural Resources Overview*, 32–34; Beckham, *Indians of Western Oregon*, 23.

10. Aikens, *Archaeological Studies*, 26; Detling, *Flora of the Pacific Northwest*, 35; Minor et al., *Cultural Resources Overview*, 34; Franklin and Dyrness, *Natural Vegetation*, 42, 110; U.S. Congress, House, *Columbia River* 5:1775, 1992, 2003 (see also appendix J, part 1, plate 2).

11. The Willamette Valley is about 110 miles long. The southern terminus is approximately 420 feet above sea level and only 320 feet higher than the point where the river flows over the basalt cliff in the northern valley. This lack of relief over such a great distance gives the valley a relatively flat character, especially in the southern portion, where relief is sometimes as little as one foot to the mile. The entire drainage area for the Willamette River is 11,250 square miles. Of this, the Calapooia drains about 362 square miles, or about 3.3 percent of the total. The banks of the Willamette River are estimated to have been about 1.5 to 3 yards higher than the surrounding land at the time of settlement. Such low riverbanks, along with low relief and a large drainage area, made the course of the Willamette and its tributaries quite changeable over the last few millennia. Especially during the period from 500 B.C. to the mid nine-

teenth century, these same factors caused the floor of the Willamette Valley, particularly the southern portion, to be much moister than at present. See Sedell and Froggatt, "Importance of Streamside Forests," 1829–30. When Charles Wilkes traversed the Willamette Valley in the 1840s, he commented on Willamette River floods: "The sudden rises of the river are somewhat remarkable and difficult to be accounted for. . . . The perpendicular height of the flood is, at times, as much as thirty feet, which was marked very distinctly on the trees growing in its banks." Wilkes, *Narrative* 4:358. See also U.S. Congress, House, *Columbia River* 5:5, 1711, 2249; W. Smith, *Physical and Economic Geography*, 144, 147; Dicken and Dicken, *Two Centuries of Oregon Geography*, 46; Baldwin, *Geology of Oregon*, 47–50; McKee, *Cascadia*, 175.

12. Franklin and Dyrness, *Natural Vegetation*, 110, 116, 124–25; Towle, "Woodlands in the Willamette Valley," 48. For more information on the "original" vegetation of the Willamette Valley, see also Habeck, "Original Vegetation," Johannessen et al., "Vegetation of the Willamette Valley" and Towle, "Willamette Valley Woodlands," 66–67.

13. Although western hemlock is the climax species over much of the western portion of the Pacific Northwest, most botanists believe that the Willamette Valley's climate is too warm and dry for this tree to compete successfully with other species; see Franklin and Dyrness, *Natural Vegetation*, 126–29; Thilenius, "*Quercus garryana* Forests," 1126–32. Through the study of growth rings on tree stumps, we know that Indians were already using fire regularly in the mid 1600s; Aikens, *Archaeological Studies*, 28.

14. Minor et al., *Cultural Resources Overview*, 43, 47; Beckham, *Indians of Western Oregon*, 43; Ratcliff, "What Happened to the Kalapuya?" 28; Frachtenberg, "Ethnological Researches," 89; Kroeber, *Cultural and Natural Areas*, 215–16.

15. Kroeber, *Cultural and Natural Areas*, 30. Boyd, "Strategies of Indian Burning," 67, discusses some of the similarities and differences between the Kalapuya culture and the Northwest Coastal and Columbia River Plateau cultural divisions.

16. Ratcliff, "What Happened to the Kalapuya?" 27, has limited population estimates to around three thousand. Boyd, "Strategies of Indian Burning," 69, argues persuasively that the population was much larger and that the generally accepted figure of three thousand is an underestimate based on faulty firsthand reports. See Zucker, Hummel, and Høgfoss, *Oregon Indians*, 8–10, 33, for population densities. For more on the Coast Salish of Puget Sound, see White, *Land Use*, 14–34.

17. The quotation is from Wilkes, *Narrative* 4:344–45. Ratcliff, "What Happened to the Kalapuya?" 29; Jacobs, *Kalapuya Texts*, 24–25; Minor et al., *Cultural Resources Overview*, 56, 59.

18. Zucker, Hummel, and Høgfoss, *Oregon Indians*, 29–31; Minor et al., *Cultural Resources Overview*, 38. Camas was the staple of the Kalapuya diet, but it is not given much discussion in Boyd's otherwise superb article "Strategies of Indian Burning."

19. Douglas, *Oregon Journals* 2:130, 132; Brackenridge, *Brackenridge Journal*, 58; Applegate, *Recollections of My Boyhood*, 69.

20. On Willamette prairie-forest composition, see Moir and Mika, "Prairie Vegetation," 12–13; Towle, "Woodlands in the Willamette Valley," 35–36.

21. Douglas, *Oregon Journals*, 130; Lewis Judson as quoted in Boyd, "Strategies of Indian Burning," 77. On Native American burning strategies, edges, and deer, see Lewis, *Patterns of Indian Burning*, 17; Towle, "Settlement and Subsistence," 19; Leopold, "Deer"; and Boyd, "Strategies of Indian Burning."

22. Wilkes, *Narrative* 5:222. For information on the use and effects of fire on grasses and trees, see Minor et al., *Cultural Resources Overview*, 56, 58; Cooper, "Ecology of Fire," 150–51; Humphrey, *Range Ecology*, 151–52; Towle, "Settlement and Subsistence," 18–19; Ratcliff, "What Happened to the Kalapuya?" 29. Recent historical scholarship has emphasized Native Americans' conscious role in shaping the natural environment rather than simply inhabiting a "virgin wilderness." This shaping of America's environment was in large part done through the use of fire. For a general, theoretical discussion of this point, see Cronon and White, "Indians in the Land," 18–25. For specific histories, see Cronon's *Changes in the Land*, which includes a discussion of New England tribes during the colonial period, and White's *Land Use*, which discusses the role of the Salish in the Puget Sound area of the Pacific Northwest. For the history of fire and its uses, see also Pyne, *Fire in America*. On acorn use, see Ratcliff, "What Happened to the Kalapuya?" 29; Minor et al., *Cultural Resources Overview*, 56, 58. On Native Americans in California, see Lewis, *Patterns of Indian Burning*, 19; see also Boyd, "Strategies of Indian Burning," 74–81.

23. Clarke, *Pioneer Days of Oregon History* 1:91. On the *battue*, see also Collins, "The Cultural Position of the Kalapuya," 29; and Boyd, "Strategies of Indian Burning," 74–75.

24. As quoted in Boyd, "Strategies of Indian Burning," 78.

25. Ratcliff, "What Happened to the Kalapuya?" 29; Minor et al., *Cultural Resources Overview*, 57–58; McCoy, *Biography of John McCoy*, 35. For further discussion of Pacific Northwest tribes' use of plant foods, see French, "Ethnobotany of the Pacific Northwest Indians," 378–82.

26. Zucker, Hummel, and Høgfoss, *Oregon Indians*, 35–36; Minor et al., *Cultural Resources Overview*, 38; Ratcliff, "What Happened to the Kalapuya?" 27.

27. Zucker, Hummel, and Høgfoss, *Oregon Indians*, 35–36; Minor et al., *Cultural Resources Overview*, 38, 58; Ratcliff, "What Happened to the Kalapuya?" 27.

28. Zucker, Hummel, and Høgfoss, *Oregon Indians*, 21, 24, 29–31; Minor et al., *Cultural Resources Overview*, 38, 58; Ratcliff, "What Happened to the Kalapuya?" 29.

29. Momaday, "Native American Attitudes," 84. This beautiful creation story is recorded in Ramsey, *Coyote Was Going There*, 106–10.

30. John B. Hudson, descendant of the Santiam Kalapuya tribe, quoted in Beckham, *Indians of Western Oregon*, 85; Mackey, *Kalapuyans*, 80–81.

31. Clark, *Indian Legends*, 100.

32. For a general discussion of this point, see Cronon and White, "Indians in the Land." For more specific cases, see Cronon, *Changes in the Land*; White, *Land Use*, 26–34.

33. Clara C. Morgan Thompson, in Haskin, Oral History. There has been much debate over the exact nature of the "fever and ague" that struck the Native Americans of the Northwest in 1830–33, but the best scholarship indicates that it was malaria. See especially Boyd, " 'Fever and Ague' "; Cook, "Epidemic of 1830–1833." See also Mackey, *Kalapuyans*, 21; Ratcliff, "What Happened to the Kalapuya?" 27; Minto, "Number and Condition." Figures for the declining Kalapuya population come from Boyd, " 'Fever and Ague,' " 136. I have drawn largely on Boyd's article for the malaria analysis; see also Wilkes's reports in *Narrative* 4:362, 370, and 5:140, 218, 350 (the last gives an 1841 eyewitness account).

34. Lee and Frost, *Ten Years in Oregon*, 39. Numbers for the Kalapuya population are from Ratcliff, "What Happened to the Kalapuya?" 31.

35. Ratcliff's, "What Happened to the Kalapuya?" offers intriguing possibilities in this vein. Ratcliff, however, attempts to use direct European contact too forcefully to explain the demise of the Kalapuya. His evidence does not support his thesis, and I draw a narrower conclusion from his evidence.

36. Jacobs, *Kalapuya Texts*, 69; Ramsey, *Coyote Was Going There*, 104.

37. Marx, *Machine in the Garden*. See also Barbara Novak, *Nature and Culture*; Bermingham, *Landscape and Ideology*.

38. Wilkes, *Narrative* 5:221–22.

39. Matthieu, "Reminiscences," 88; Warre and Vavasour, "Documents," 52.

40. Palmer, *Journal of Travels*, 99.

41. Douglas, *Oregon Journals* 2:128, 158; Henry, *New Light* 2:815.

42. Warre and Vavasour, "Documents," 52; Wilkes, *Narrative* 4:353 and 5:218; Atkinson, "Diary," 348, 350; U.S. Congress, Senate, "Memorial of William A. Slacum," 15.

43. Hines, *Voyage Round the World*, 321.

44. Henry, *Journal* 2:811; Howison, "Report," 43; Hines, *Voyage Round the World*, 326; Wilkes, *Narrative* 4:344.

2. LIFE AND CULTURE ON AN OLD LANDSCAPE

1. Stanard, "Old Stuff and New," 20 July 1924.

2. Rose B. Anderson, Albany, Oreg., to author, 20 June and 12 July 1987; U.S. Department of Commerce, Bureau of the Census, Seventh Census, Manuscript Population Census Returns, Linn County, 1850. (Hereafter, manuscript census returns will be cited by topic, area, and date.)

3. For an excellent general history of the early cis-Appalachian West, see Malcolm J. Rohrbough, *Trans-Appalachian Frontier*. For further consideration of town and urban life in the early settling years of that region, see Wade, *Urban*

Frontier; and Hine, *Community on the American Frontier*. For further discussion of early politics in the region, see Cayton, *Frontier Republic*.

4. Biographical information for the statistical information that follows derives primarily from the following sources: Genealogical Forum of Portland, *Genealogical Materials*; Haskin, Oral History; the genealogical and biographical files of the Oregon Historical Society, Portland; *Illustrated Historical Atlas Map of Marion and Linn Counties, Oregon*; Miller, *Millers of Richardson Gap*; Miles and Milligan, *Linn County, Oregon, Pioneer Settlers*; the private files of Richard R. Milligan, Albany, Oreg.; and Manuscript Population Census Returns, Linn County, 1850, 1860, 1870, and 1880. For more on the origins of early Oregon Country and Willamette Valley settlers, see Douglas, "Origins," tables 3 and 4; and Bowen, *Willamette Valley*.

5. Bowen, *Willamette Valley*, 48, notes that while those people listed in the Oregon 1850 census who had origins in Missouri and Illinois dominated the population, "Kentuckians were found in more frontier homes and were related to more persons born outside their home state than any of the other . . . states or Canada. . . . [Kentucky] with its more extensive family ties and larger related population possessed a greater potential for cultural ascendancy" in the Willamette Valley. The origins of the cis-Appalachian region's population have been well documented by other scholars. See in particular Merk, *History of the Westward Movement*, 163–72; Faragher, *Sugar Creek*, 45, 51, 56; Parker, *Iowa Pioneer Foundations* 1:76; O'Brien et al., *Grassland, Forest, and Historical Settlement*, 58–59; Power, *Planting Corn Belt Culture*, 1–3, 26–34. For dispersal of upper-South pioneers north of the Ohio River, see Hart, "Middle West," 260; Sauer, "Homestead and Community," 4; Moynihan, "Abigail Scott Duniway of Oregon," 69.

6. Willis, *William Shields Family*; Abraham. J. Wigle, Reminiscences. On the general movement of settlers across cis-Appalachia, see Power, *Planting Corn Belt Culture*, 34; Faragher, "Midwestern Families in Motion," 30–31.

The Robnett family provides a fascinating example of cross-country migration, as described in Turnbow, *Robnett Family Record*. Samuel, the patriarch of the Robnett family in America, was born in England in 1669 and emigrated with his parents to Pennsylvania in 1682, where he died in 1745. His son, Nathan, was born in Pennsylvania in 1717 and continued his family's migration by moving to Maryland where he died in about 1787. John Robnett, the next in line, was born in Maryland in 1755. He married twice, first to Catharine Carr in Virginia, where they had three children by 1783. By 1788, after Catharine's death, he had emigrated to Covington County, Kentucky, where he married Rebecca Frazier. John and Rebecca had nine children between 1790 and 1810, all of whom were born in Bourbon County, Kentucky. Joseph Robnett, from John's first marriage to Catharine, was born about 1783 in Monongalia County, Virginia. He had moved with his father to Kentucky by 1788. In 1806 in Bourbon County, Kentucky, he married Nancy Barker. They remained in Kentucky and had seven children by 1824. In that year they headed to Boone County, Missouri, where they had one more child in 1830. Joseph died in Boone

County in 1835. All eight of Joseph and Nancy's children eventually completed the family's journey to the Willamette Valley. William Robnett was born in Kentucky in 1812, headed to Missouri in 1824, and came to the Calapooia in 1847; he died there in 1886. Lucinda Robnett, who was a twin of William, emigrated to Oregon in 1847 with her husband, Thomas Hall, and later settled on the Calapooia. Pleasant, Joseph, Samuel, and James Robnett all emigrated to Oregon in 1847 with their brother William and sister Lucinda. Stephen Robnett, born 1807 in Bourbon County, Kentucky, moved to Boone County, Missouri, in 1824, to Benton County, Arkansas, in 1833, and to Oregon in 1851. John Robnett was born in 1809 in Kentucky, went to Missouri in 1832, and headed to the Calapooia Valley in 1851.

7. Moore, *Frontier Mind*, 13; Bogue, *From Prairie to Corn Belt*, 5. On trees and soil fertility, see also Hart, "Middle West," 259; on woodlands culture, see also Buley, *Old Northwest* 1:168.

8. Faragher, *Sugar Creek*, 27, 26. On Native Americans in the general pioneering scheme of the Ohio Valley, see also Moore, *Frontier Mind*, 61–67; Merk, *History of the Westward Movement*, 153–62, 168–72; Buley, *Old Northwest* 1:18–20. On the native perspective, see particularly Edmunds, *Tecumseh*.

9. On early surveying, see Thrower, *Original Survey and Land Subdivision*, 1–5; Hughes, *Surveyors and Statesmen*, 4–5; Power, *Planting Corn Belt Culture*, 102; Tatter, *Preferential Treatment*, 12–13.

10. Gates, "Tenants of the Log Cabin," 14, 16, 17. This chapter is very good for understanding Kentucky settlers problems with land claiming, but see also Moore, *Frontier Mind*, 71–75; O'Brien et al., *Grassland, Forest, and Historical Settlement*, 67. Antislavery sentiment was another important reason for southerners to move north of the Ohio; see Faragher, *Sugar Creek*, 48; Moynihan, "Abigail Scott Duniway," 37, 47, 60.

11. On initiation of the rectangular survey in the Ohio Valley, see Hart, "Middle West," 264; Johnson, *Orderly Landscape*, 7, 16; Johnson, *Order upon the Land*; Johnson, "Rational and Ecological Aspects," 338; Stilgoe *Common Landscape of America*, 100–105; Buley, *Old Northwest* 1:115–23; Carstensen, *Public Lands*, xv; Ernst, *With Compass and Chain*, maps on pages 200, 236, 251.

12. For theories on avoidance of the midwestern prairie, see especially Sauer, *Land and Life*; Malin, *History and Ecology*; McManis, *Initial Evaluation*; Kolodny, *Land Before Her*; Yi-Fu Tuan, *Topophilia*; Buley, *Old Northwest* 1:229; Hart, "Middle West."

The point concerning the relationship between soil fertility and trees has generated debate. As early as 1964, McManis wrote that the "claim that settlers considered the prairies infertile and hence unfit for cultivation because of their treelessness is not supported by the literature of the period" (*Initial Evaluation*, 50). McManis found that only in later reminiscences did older settlers indicate that this belief was widely held. As recently as 1986, however, Faragher (*Sugar Creek*, 62–63) found evidence that some settlers in Illinois felt a lack of prairie vegetation indeed indicated a lack of soil fertility. Moore notes that some early travelers through cis-Appalachia, such as F. A. Michaux, who visited Kentucky in 1802, commented on trees and their relationship to soil fertility (*Frontier Mind*, 12). It appears, then, that early settlers in the Midwest did hold some superstitions about trees and soil fertility.

13. Abraham J. Wigle, Reminiscences; Parker, *Iowa Pioneer Foundations* 1:100; McManis, *Initial Evaluation*, 44–49, 86–88; O'Brien et al., *Grassland, Forest, and Historical Settlement*, 45–49.

14. On hunting and livestock raising culture of Ohio Valley settlers from the upper South, see Hart, "Middle West," 265; McManis, *Initial Evaluation*, 26; Sauer, "Homestead and Community," 4; Parker, *Iowa Pioneer Foundations* 1:287–89; Buley, *Old Northwest* 1:158–59. On the cultural interpretation of western settlers as backwoodsmen fleeing society, see H. Smith, "Daniel Boone," in *Virgin Land*, 51–58; and as materialists, see Hofstadter, *Age of Reform*.

15. Faragher, *Sugar Creek*, 65–66.

16. Parker, *Iowa Pioneer Foundations* 1:288; see also Hart, "Middle West," 266; McManis, *Initial Evaluation*, 26–27.

17. Kendall, "Letter," 190.

18. Parker, *Iowa Pioneer Foundations* 1:245, 250–52; Buley, *Old Northwest* 1:169, 170–74; McManis, *Initial Evaluation*, 52–53; Faragher, *Sugar Creek*, 63; Sauer, "Homestead and Community," 4.

19. Bowen, in *Willamette Valley*, 17–20, gives a brief but excellent discussion of reasons midwesterners went to Oregon; Hussey, *Champoeg*, 124–27, gives a cursory discussion of patriotism and emigration to Oregon; Johansen, "Working Hypothesis," emphasizes the pulls of migration to Oregon rather than the pushes; Baker, "Oregon Pioneer Tradition," discusses pioneers' retrospective views of some of their reasons for migrating. For more general discussions of the overland experience, see particularly Unruh, *Plains Across*; Faragher, *Women and Men*.

20. Abraham J. Wigle, Reminiscences; Timothy A. Riggs to Goodall, 76.

21. Kendall, "Letter," 188–89; Abraham J. Wigle, Reminiscences; Lucy M. King to Swank; William McHargue to McHargue; Bennett-Browning, "Pioneer Keeney Family."

Scholars have recognized the primacy of disease and health as leading causes for the migration to Oregon. Year after year, malaria, measles, tuberculosis, smallpox, meningitis, influenza, scarlet fever, ophthalmia, cholera, typhoid fever, and erysipelas plagued settlers of the region. See particularly Pickard and Buley, *Midwest Pioneer*; Buley, *Old Northwest* 1:240–314; Bowen, *Willamette Valley*, 18–19; Faragher, *Sugar Creek*, 89–91; McManis, *Initial Evaluation*, 41–44.

3. MATERIAL CULTURE

1. In the Oregon Treaty of 15 June 1846, Great Britain ceded to the United States its claims to the Oregon Country below the forty-ninth parallel. The

Pacific Northwest then became a part of the United States. For an overview of
the Oregon Country diplomacy during this period, see Johansen and Gates,
Empire of the Columbia; for a treatment in depth, see Merk, *Oregon Question*.

2. Gibson, *Farming the Frontier*, 130; Hussey, *Champoeg*, 43–61. Statistics for population growth are for Euro-Americans and Europeans only; Native
Americans are not included. See Gibson, *Farming the Frontier*, 134–36; Hussey, *Champoeg*, 126, 129; Johansen and Gates, *Empire of the Columbia*, 178.
There is little agreement on the number of immigrants to Oregon during the
years 1840–45. See Young, "Oregon Trail," 370; Hussey, *Champoeg*, 130;
Gibson, *Farming the Frontier*, 134–36.

The early Willamette Valley settlement was without law and order other
than the persuasion and cajoling from Fort Vancouver or the Methodist Mission. In 1841 settlers began working to establish a system for the maintenance
of peace and the protection of property, eventuating in the formation of the
provisional government two years later. Although Oregon became part of the
United States in 1846 and then an official U.S. Territory in 1848, it was not until
early 1849 that the new territorial government relieved the provisional government. Hussey, *Champoeg*, 137–72, has an excellent account of the provisional
government's formation.

3. Works Progress Administration Writers' Program (hereafter WPA), *History of Linn County*, 2–3; U.S. Department of Commerce, Bureau of the Census, *Seventh Census*, 988–1013.

4. The following section deals in depth with settlement patterns of the
Calapooia. General texts for settlement in the Willamette Valley include Bowen,
Willamette Valley; Head, "Oregon Donation Land Claims."

5. These and following surveyors' descriptions of the Calapooia are taken
from the surveyor's notes for townships 13 and 14 south, ranges 1, 2, and 3
west and 14 south, range 1 east of the Willamette meridian, written during the
winter of 1852–53, U.S. Department of the Interior, Bureau of Land Management, Cadastral Surveyors' Notes and Maps (hereafter cited as Surveyors'
Notes).

6. Stilgoe, *Common Landscape of America*, 341; on this theme, see also
the classic study by Marx, *Machine in the Garden*.

7. The following section and chapter 4 sketch life and culture on the
Calapooia frontier between 1846 and 1860. In cases where sources are limited
and where essential changes have not occurred, I have drawn on evidence from
later in the nineteenth century and from greater Linn County and the Willamette
Valley to support my argument.

8. Benjamin Freeland to Brother (hereafter cited as Freeland, Letter); WPA,
History of Linn County, 6–7; Associated Reformed Presbyterian Church,
Calapooia, Linn County, Minute Book, 1849, quoted in Stanard, "Old Stuff
and New," 20 July 1924.

9. Surveyors' Notes.

10. John L. Wigle, Reminiscences; John Grath Bramwell, in Haskin, Oral
History.

11. J. Fred McCoy, *Biography of John McCoy*, 10; John Cornett, in Haskin, oral history.

12. WPA, *History of Linn County*, 7; Wilson Blain, Union Point, Linn County, Oregon Territory, to David Kerr, Pittsburgh, Penn., 5 Mar. 1851, Blain Collection.

13. Kendall, "Letter," 190, 195; Archie Frum, in Haskin, Oral History.

14. Balancing natural resources during settlement has been a theme of anthropological scholarship; see Jochim, *Strategies for Survival*.

15. Kendall, "Letter," 195.

16. From 1 December 1850 to the winter of 1852–53, settlement continued in the Calapooia until the survey was imposed there. During these years land claims had to adhere to straight north-south, east-west boundary lines that would conform to accepted survey lines once the survey reached the Calapooia. Claims taken before 1 December 1850 did not have to conform to survey lines.

17. Head, "Oregon Donation Land Claims," 53.

18. Oregon Provisional and Territorial Government Papers, item 121817; Oregon Territorial Government, *Oregon Archives*, 35; Oregon Provisional and Territorial Government, *Laws*, 72.

19. Oregon Provisional and Territorial Government Land Claim Records, A-2, 8:72; 4:267, 261, 318; 7:9, 214. The latter examples are taken from claims of Agnes and John Courtney, James McHargue, and Richard Finley.

20. Timothy A. Riggs to Goodall, 76; John L. Wigle, Reminiscences; McCoy, *Biography of John McCoy*, 11; "Browns Play Important Part in Oregon State's History." For cis-Appalachian architectural styles, see especially O'Brien et al., *Grassland, Forest, and Historical Settlement*, 232, 251–57; O'Brien also has a useful bibliography for further consideration; but see also Buley, *Old Northwest* 1:142–45.

21. Kendall, "Letter," 189.

22. Reynolds, "Evolution," 32. Reynolds found that in his study area some people remarked on the ease of plowing, but others commented that the Oregon soil was tougher than the soil was in Illinois. My research suggests that cultivation proved more difficult only in areas of the valley that were overgrown with shrubs and fern. Universally, however, the open prairies of the Willamette and Calapooia were easily plowed; see Towle, "Woodlands in the Willamette Valley," 34. My evidence presented in this paragraph comes from Hines, *Voyage Round the World*, 342; Atkinson, "Diary," 349; Howison, "Report," 51; Earl, Reminiscences; John L. Wigle, Reminiscences; McCoy, *A Biography of John McCoy*, 12.

23. Ingersoll, "In the Wahlamet Valley," 768; Manuscript Agricultural Census Returns, Linn County, 1850; U.S. Department of Commerce, Bureau of the Census, *Seventh Census*, 1007.

24. Thomas Bird Sprenger, in Haskin, Oral History; Blain, Oregon City, Oregon Territory, to Kerr, Autumn 1850; Albert Waggoner, in Haskin, Oral History; Minto, "From Youth to Age," 153; Kendall, "Letter," 191–92. The Oregon Historical Society's collection of Blain's letters is in typescript, edited by

J. Orin Oliphant. In a footnote to Blain's mention of Bashan, Oliphant writes that Bashan was "a fruitful land on the east side of Jordan, famous for its oaks, its fine cattle, and its rich pastures"; Ezekiel 39:18, Isaiah 33:9.

25. Oregon Provisional and Territorial Government Papers, item 9161 (emphasis is in the original document); Kendall, "Letter," 191–92.

26. Manuscript Agricultural Census Returns, Linn County, 1850; *Linn County, Oregon: Early 1850 Records*, 31–45. Chapters 5 and 6 look more closely at the livestock economy of the early Calapooia, as well as the role of livestock in fomenting community division and leading to estrangement from the landscape.

27. Albert G. Waggoner, in Haskin, Oral History.

28. Priaulx, "Lumber Industry"; McCoy, *Biography of John McCoy*, 11; Lewis Tycer, Redman Pearl, and Silas V. Barr, in Haskin, Oral History.

29. *Albany Herald*, 28 Apr. 1876, 3, as cited in WPA, Federal Writers' Project Collection, series 1, box 41, Linn County, Fauna file; Jasper Cranfill, Diary, 26 Nov. 1866, in Isom Cranfill, Diaries and Papers (hereafter cited as Cranfill, Diary); Andrew Kirk, in Haskin, Oral History. For more particulars on wildfowl in the Willamette, see Minto, "From Youth to Age," 152; U.S. Department of the Interior, Bureau of Sport Fisheries and Wildlife, *Willamette National Wildlife Refuge*.

30. James Worth Morgan, Andrew Kirk, Thomas Bird Sprenger, and Redman Pearl, in Haskin, Oral History; John L. Wigle, Reminiscences; WPA, *History of Linn County*, 11.

31. Earl, Reminiscences. Charles Wilkes noted when he traveled through the northern Willamette Valley in the early 1840s that cougars, or "Oregon tigers," were "voracious animals . . . numerous and bold"; Wilkes, *Narrative* 4:348.

32. McCoy, *Biography of John McCoy*, 14; Albert Waggoner, in Haskin, Oral History. Black bears are also indigenous to the Willamette Valley, but their presence was noted less often during the settling years because they proved more docile than the larger, more notorious grizzlies. The grizzly was extirpated in Oregon in the 1930s according to U.S. Department of Agriculture, Bureau of Biological Survey, *Mammals and Life Zones of Oregon*, 326. For more tales of grizzlies in the early Willamette Valley, see especially Douglas, *Oregon Journals*.

33. Howison, "Report," 49; Wilkes, *Narrative* 5:222; Hussey, *Champoeg*, 145–49; and S. Young, *Wolf in North American History*, 92. "Small wolves" may very well have been coyotes; Oregon Provisional and Territorial Government Papers, items 3420, 3645, 3781, 12186; Oregon Territorial Government, *Statutes of a General Nature*, 275; Linn County Court Journal 7:481, Clerk's Vault, Courthouse, Albany, Oreg., rep. in *Albany States Rights Democrat*, 23 Aug. 1872, 1; both court journal and article are in WPA, Federal Writers' Project Collection, series 1, Linn County, Fauna file.

34. Mrs. James P. Miller to Banks, 426.

35. "History of the Hugh L. Brown Family"; Timothy A. Riggs to Goodall, 75, 76.

36. Bennett-Browning, "Pioneer Keeney Family"; Timothy A. Riggs to

Goodall; Blain, Union Point, Oregon Territory, to Kerr, 30 Oct. 1855 and ca. 31 Aug. 1855.

During both the Cayuse War, which broke out after the Whitman Massacre at the Waiilatpu Mission in November 1847, and the Rogue River wars in the 1850s, Calapooia settlers responded by taking up arms. At the time of the Cayuse War, James Blakely helped form a company of volunteers near his home in the Calapooia, while all of Linn County came together and formed the Mounted Riflemen. During the Rogue River wars, Jonathan Keeney, Oliver P. Coshow, and other Calapooia residents served. WPA, *History of Linn County*, 13–14; Standish, "Indian Wars Affect Linn County." For particulars on these conflicts, see Johansen and Gates, *Empire of the Columbia*, 221–25, 252–53; Beckham, *Requiem for a People*; Robbins, "Indian Question in Western Oregon."

37. On the history of treaties between the United States and the Kalapuya, see Mackey, *Kalapuyans*, 136–43.

38. Wilkes, *Narrative* 4:362; Warre and Vavasour, "Documents," 2; and Blain, Union Point, Oregon Territory, to Kerr, 14 Feb. 1853.

39. Lewis Tycer, in Haskin, Oral History; Cranfill, Diary, 18 Jan. and 21 Jan. 1866; U.S. Congress, House, *Columbia River* 10:1710, 1956, 2018; Michael Plaster, Business Accounts; WPA, *History of Linn County*, 40.

The flood on the Calapooia River in 1861 was extensive and costly. Floodwater inundated 35,080 acres of agricultural land, 120 acres of urban and suburban land, and 600 acres of stream courses. The economic losses amounted to $5,648,000 in agriculture, $770,000 in roads and bridges, $450,000 in commercial and industrial properties, $165,000 in urban and suburban areas, and $125,000 in streets, sewers, and other utilities. Estimates indicate that at peak flow of the Willamette River, the 1861 flood had 500,000 cubic feet of water per second, the 1881 flood 428,000, and the 1890 flood 450,000, compared to the seasonal summer low before 1954 of 2,500 cubic feet per second. Gleeson, *Return of a River*, 5; U.S. Congress, House, *Columbia River* 10:1710, 1899, 1903, 1956, 1903, 2020–21.

40. WPA, *History of Linn County*, 6–7. A similar route, following the base of foothills on the west side of the Willamette, became the west-side Territorial Road; Alexander Kirk and Morgan Kees, "Report of the Road Commissioners, Linn County," 28 May 1848, copy in Roads file, Amelia Spalding Brown History Room.

41. Thomas Bird Sprenger and Catharine Louise McHargue Hume, in Haskin, Oral History; Freeman, "Territorial Road," 58; *Brownsville Advertiser*, 28 Feb. 1878, 3; Cornett, Diary, 7 Jan. 1883, 29 Jan. 1883, 14 Apr. 1883.

42. Cranfill, Diary, 16 Jan. 1865, 15 January 1866; Blain, Union Point, Oregon Territory, to Kerr, 14 Feb. 1853.

43. Hines, *Voyage Round the World*, 335–36. For a study of the influence of weather, particularly rain, on the culture of the Pacific Northwest, see Brown, "Rainfall and History."

44. Burkhart, *Settler's Guide*, 37; Blain, Union Point, Oregon Territory, to John Gray, Preble County, Ohio, July 1851; Cranfill, Diary, 1 Sept. 1866.

45. Kendall, "Letter," 189; Howison, "Report," 50.

46. Kendall, "Letter," 188–89; see also Hines, *Voyage Round the World*, 336; Pickard and Buley, *Midwest Pioneer*, 11–12.

47. On malaria and its disappearance, see Boyd, " 'Fever and Ague' "; Larsell, *Doctor in Oregon*, chap. 17.

48. Kendall, "Letter," 189; Blain, Union Point, Oregon Territory, to Kerr, 1 Apr. 1851; Blain, Oregon City, Oregon Territory, to Kerr, Autumn 1850(?) and late 1850(?); Fielding Lewis to "Friends in the States" (hereafter cited as Lewis, Letter).

49. Blain, Union Point, Oregon Territory, to Gray, July 1851 (emphasis in excerpt is Blain's); Herman Gragg, Brownsville, to Sister, Monroe, Oreg., 5 Mar. 1885, Gragg Family Papers; Burkhart, *Settler's Guide*, 35; Blain, Union Point, Oregon Territory, to Kerr, 15 Dec. 1854; W. B. Mealey, to Parents, in McCoy, *Biography of John McCoy*, 36–38; Boyd, " 'Fever and Ague,' " 144–45.

4. AESTHETICS

1. McLoughlin, *Letters* 4:15–17.

2. This cultural interpretation is best exemplified in R. Nash, *Wilderness and the American Mind*; Ekirch, *Man and Nature in America*; Huth, *Nature and the American*; and Miller, *Errand into the Wilderness*, chap. 1.

3. Duncan, *Covenanters by the Willamette*, 5.

4. Blain, Union Point, Oregon Territory, to Kerr, 5 Mar. 1851; Blain, Oregon City, Oregon Territory, to Kerr, late 1850 (?); Carey and Hainline, *Brownsville*, 32.

5. Blain, Union Point, Oregon Territory, to Kerr, 5 Mar. 1851.

6. The following section is based on Blain, Union Point, Oregon Territory, to John B. Dales, 1 Apr. 1851.

7. Blain, Union Point, Oregon Territory, to Kerr, 5 Mar. 1851; Blain, Union Point, Oregon Territory, to Dales, 1 Apr. 1851.

8. Kendall, "Letter," 195–96: Freeland, Letter; Waggoner, *Stories of Old Oregon*, 20; Goodall, "Upper Calapooia," 70.

9. Elizabeth Reinhart Weber, in Haskin, Oral History (Weber attended Amelia during the latter's invalidism); John L. Wigle, Reminiscences.

10. See in particular Jackle, Brunn, and Roseman, *Human Spatial Behavior*; and Lynch, *Image of the City*.

11. Catharine Louise McHargue Hume, in Haskin, Oral History; Waggoner, *Stories of Old Oregon*, 20.

12. Tuan, *Topophilia*, 28; see also Kolodny, *Land Before Her*, 6.

13. The following is based on materials in the Lewis Tycer and Eliza Finley Brandon interviews in Haskin, Oral History.

14. See R. Nash, *Wilderness and the American Mind*; Miller, *Errand into the Wilderness*.

15. The following stories are from the Andrew Kirk and Catharine Louise McHargue Hume interviews in Haskin, Oral History.

16. This section is based on Blain, Union Point, Oregon Territory, to Kerr, 15 Sept. 1854.

17. On forests and valleys offering protection, see Tuan, *Topophilia*, 28; Bogue, *From Prairie to Corn Belt*, 5; Kolodny, *Lay of the Land*; Kolodny, *Land Before Her*, 6.

18. Kendall, "Letter," 195; Freeland, Letter; Blain, Union Point, Oregon Territory, to Dales, 1 Apr. 1851; Atkinson, "Diary," 348.

19. Smith, *Virgin Land*, 124.

20. Freeland, Letter; Blain, Oregon City, Oregon Territory, to Kerr, late 1850 (?); Kendall, "Letter," 193–94.

21. Blain, Union Point, Oregon Territory, to Kerr, 5 Mar. 1851; Blain to Kerr, Autumn 1850 (?); Blain to Dales, 1 Apr. 1851; Kendall, "Letter," 195.

22. Manuscript Population Census Returns, Linn County, 1850. The 1860 census reveals that 156 of 164 households in the Calapooia area contained one- or two-parent families; the other eight households were composed of single men. Also, although the number of males was 508, there was a substantial number, 407, of females. Adult males outnumbered adult females in the Calapooia and Linn County throughout the settlement period, but the single men were almost always attached—usually as laborers—to a household within which resided an adult female, usually a mother of the family, or a father and his children. Furthermore, of the 174 Donation Land claimants of the Calapooia— those who had the most direct influence over the landscape—121 either were married or widowers at the time they claimed land (five widows also received land in the Calapooia). Twenty-nine of the remaining men married within a few years, sometimes within a few months, of settling their claims. For the other nineteen claimants, all men, we have insufficient records. Sources: Manuscript Population Census Returns, Linn County, 1860; Genealogical Forum of Portland, *Genealogical Materials*; Miles and Milligan, *Linn County, Oregon, Pioneer Settlers*; Richard R. Milligan's personal files, Albany.

On men's and women's spheres in agricultural communities on American frontiers and the influence of women and the domestic ideal on westering men, see Jeffrey, *Frontier Women*; Faragher, *Women and Men*; Ryan, *Cradle of the Middle Class*. Unfortunately, studies of men's and women's spheres and the penetration of domestic ideals on the early Pacific Northwest frontier are limited. Carlson, "Rural Family," deals with the family in the later nineteenth century and indicates that domestic ideology was prevalent in the Willamette Valley certainly by the 1870s. Carlson also shows that single male farm laborers were almost always treated as members of, and integrated into, the families for whom they worked. Often these laborers were sons of neighboring farmers. On the early Pacific Northwest, see also Moynihan, *Rebel for Rights*.

On churches, religion, and revival meetings, see Pleasant Butte Baptist Church sketch in Church file, Amelia Spalding Brown History Room; Stanard, "Rev. H. H. Spalding"; Stanard, "Old Stuff and New," 4 Nov. 1923 and 20

July 1924; Drury, *Pioneer of Old Oregon*, 353–54; Duncan, *Covenanters by the Willamette*; Mrs. William Bland Anderson and James Worth Morgan, in Haskin, Oral History.

23. Freeland, Letter; Mrs. Elias Marsters, in Haskin, Oral History; Stanard, "Old Stuff and New," 20 July 1924; Mrs. James P. Miller, to Banks, 425.

24. Blain, Oregon City, Oregon Territory, to Kerr, late 1850 (?); Blain, Union Point, Oregon Territory, to Kerr, 5 Mar. 1851; Kendall, "Letter," 196.

25. Kendall, "Letter," 190, 195; Waggoner, *Stories of Old Oregon*, 20; Freeland, Letter; Blain, Union Point, Oregon Territory, to Kerr, 5 Mar. 1851.

26. Kendall, "Letter," 190; Freeland, Letter; Surveyors' Notes; Provisional and Territorial Government Papers, item 9161.

27. Blain, Union Point, Oregon Territory, to John Gray, July 1851, and Blain, Union Point, Oregon Territory, to Kerr, 5 Mar. 1851, are examples.

28. Henry Nash Smith and Leo Marx, leading commentators on the destructive influence of industry and commerce on the nineteenth-century garden image, have suggested that these debilitating forces came from outside the garden. In fact, Smith and Marx do not recognize the possible negative consequences of the garden's metaphors of growth and increase that I argue for. What is most important to note in the case of the Calapooia and southern Willamette valleys is not the problem of "steam working through river boats and locomotives" in the destruction of the garden, as Smith suggests (124), but rather a loss of intimacy with the landscape. In the Calapooia, at least, these very forces allowed a version of the garden image to be realized by the end of the nineteenth century (see chapters 5 and 6). But once this garden was achieved, the inhabitants of the Calapooia and Willamette valleys became aware that they had lost a quality of life that they once enjoyed through the intimate connection to the natural landscape. See Smith, *Virgin Land*; Marx, *Machine in the Garden*.

5. EARLY ECONOMIC, ATTITUDINAL, AND ENVIRONMENTAL CHANGE ON THE CALAPOOIA

1. Cronon, *Changes in the Land*; White, *Land Use*; White, "The Altered Landscape"; Robbins, *Hard Times in Paradise*; Faragher, *Sugar Creek*; de Buys, *Enchantment and Exploitation*.

2. Associated Reformed Presbyterian Church Minutes, Josiah Osborn, Clerk of the Church, 18 June 1849, Calapooia, Linn County, Oregon, quoted in Stanard, "Old Stuff and New," 20 July 1924; Oregon Provisional and Territorial Land Claim Records, A-2, 3:41, 4:318 (emphasis is mine).

3. Oregon Territorial Government, *Laws*, 72 (sec. 1); Tatter, *Preferential Treatment*, 39–41. Most oral tradition does not recall the name of the original land claimant but only that he was indeed a member of the Courtney family. One strand of oral tradition states that his name was McAllister. Official documents for the time, however, show John R. Courtney as selecting this property, and in fact no McAllister or a person with a derivation of that name is to be found in the records. Also, family genealogist Rose Anderson of Albany does

not know of a McAllister in the Courtney family. Records show that about six years after the events discussed took place, a Lewis McAllister purchased land from Agnes Courtney, but he did not come to Oregon until September 1852. What is most important is not the exact names, but rather the events and their repercussions. Throughout this narrative, I will use "John R. Courtney," as found in official records, rather than McAllister, as found in oral interviews. Sources: Hugh Dunlap, Eliza Finley Brandon, and Andrew Kirk, interviews by Leslie Haskin, and Haskin's own research in the late 1930s for the Works Progress Administration, in Haskin, Oral History. Haskin interviewed Eliza Finley Brandon twice. George Finley interview by Everett Earl Stanard in Haskin, Oral History; Rose B. Anderson, Albany, Oreg., to author, 29 June 1987; Genealogical Forum of Portland, *Genealogical Materials* 2:129.

4. Tatter, *Preferential Treatment*, 39–41.

5. Bennett-Browning, "Pioneer Keeney Family."

6. Bowen, *Willamette Valley*, 70–72; see also Tobie, "Joseph Meek," 250–51; Pratt, "Twenty-two Letters of David Logan," 259–60; Faragher, *Sugar Creek*, 55, discusses settlers' support of others who improved lands, though left them temporarily.

7. Turnbow and Turnbow, *Charles Rice*, 154–55; Ramstead, "Pioneer of Oregon"; Bennett-Browning, "Pioneer Keeney Family," 23; W. C. Cooley and Leander Kirk, in Haskin, Oral History; Manuscript Population Census Returns, Linn County, 1850.

8. Ramstead, "Pioneer of Oregon," 4; W. C. Cooley, in Haskin, Oral History; Oregon Donation Land Claim maps for townships 13 and 14 south, ranges 3 and 4 west, Land Office, Bureau of Land Management, Portland.

9. W. C. Cooley, Leander Kirk, and Andrew Kirk, in Haskin, Oral History; Ramstead, "Pioneer of Oregon," 3.

10. Leander Kirk and Andrew Kirk, in Haskin, Oral History; Turnbow and Turnbow, *Charles Rice*, 155; Hugh Dunlap and Andrew Kirk, in Haskin, Oral History; George Finley, in Stanard, Oral History.

11. I use *ostensible* here because, as discussed below, the Blakelys, Browns, and Kirks had much to gain from the establishment of a gristmill on the Calapooia, and it seems likely that they had planned some commercial endeavor before settling on the Calapooia.

12. Newspaper clipping, 1909, in James Blakely Collection; Eliza Finley Brandon, Hugh Dunlap, and John McKercher, in Haskin, Oral History. Finley's claim description is identical to Courtney's, Oregon Territorial and Provisional Government Land Claim Records, A-2, 4:261.

Early Calapooia literature is filled with references to the long journey to Oregon City just to have flour ground; see, for instance Goodall, "Upper Calapooia," 70–77; *Sunday Portland Oregon Journal*, 16 Feb. 1919, newspaper clipping in the James Blakely Collection. Local historians dubbed Richard Finley's flour mill the first gristmill south of Oregon City. This is inaccurate. The first gristmill in the valley, according to Corning in *Willamette Landings*, 82–83, was at Champoeg, several miles southwest of Oregon City. As early as

June 1841, Charles Wilkes noted a visit to the Methodist Mission gristmill southeast of what later became Salem; Wilkes, *Narrative* 4:353; see also Work, "John Work's Journey," 241. Moreover, it is not clear why settlers were forced to travel all the way to Oregon City to have their wheat ground, since these other mills existed. By 1850, there were fourteen gristmills in the Willamette Valley, but Finley's mill was the most southerly in Oregon; Bowen, *Willamette Valley*, 63; U.S. Department of Commerce, Bureau of the Census, *Seventh Census*, Manuscript Census of Products of Industry, Oregon.

13. Hugh Dunlap, Andrew Kirk, Eliza Finley Brandon, and John McKercher, in Haskin, Oral History, and Haskin's own research attached to the Kirk interview; and George Finley, in Stanard, Oral History.

14. George Finley, in Stanard, Oral History.

15. Eliza Finley Brandon, first interview, in Haskin, Oral History.

16. Tattersall, "Economic Development," 39; Gibson, *Farming the Frontier*, 139–47; Blok, "Evolution," 48–49, 50; Halbakken, "History of Wheat-Growing," 35.

17. Kendall, "Letter," 193; Manuscript Agricultural Census Returns, Linn County, 1850.

18. Catharine Louise McHargue Hume, in Haskin, Oral History; "History of the Hugh L. Brown Family."

19. *Sunday Portland Oregon Journal*, 16 Feb. 1913, newspaper clipping in James Blakely Collection; Andrew Kirk, in Haskin, Oral History.

20. Eliza Finley Brandon, in Haskin, Oral History; Bowen, *Willamette Valley*, 66–67, 68–69, 77; Gibson, *Farming the Frontier*, 140; Blok, "Evolution," 48–49; Bennett-Browning, "Pioneer Keeney Family," 23.

21. WPA, *History of Linn County*, 6–7; Linn County, Record of the Proceedings 1:57; Alexander Kirk and Morgan Kees to the Clerk of Linn County, 28 May 1848.

Kirk's ferry was actually seasonal, for in the summer the flow of the Calapooia diminishes enough that it can be crossed unaided. Kirk and Morgan's letter already refers to the road they surveyed as the Territorial Road and notes that they had been appointed by the Legislature of the Oregon Territory. Although the boundary dispute between Great Britain and the U.S. had been solved in 1846, the Oregon Country did not officially become a territory until August 1848, and it would not be until the spring of 1849 that the Oregon Territorial Legislature would convene. Kirk and Morgan's appointment probably came from the provisional government in anticipation of territorial status debated in the U.S. Congress in the spring and summer of 1848.

22. Tattersall, "Economic Development," 40; Blain is quoted in WPA, *History of Linn County*, 49; Blok, "Evolution," 52.

23. No study has detailed early differences between the agricultural and economic development of the northern Willamette and the southern. Most works to date concentrate on the northern Willamette's development and thus suggest that the effects of the gold rush on agricultural development and the economy were the same throughout the valley. In fact, this was not the case. For

studies that pertain primarily to the northern Willamette, and thus rely on this thesis, see Gibson, *Farming the Frontier*; Blok, "Evolution"; Tattersall "Economic Development"; Olsen, "Beginnings of Agriculture."

24. Oliphant, *Cattle Ranges of Oregon*, 42–43; U.S. Department of Commerce, Bureau of the Census, *Seventh Census*, 1006–7; Freeland, Letter.

25. Manuscript Agricultural and Population Census Returns, Linn County, 1850.

26. Freeland, Letter; Fielding Lewis, Letter; Blain, Union Point, Linn County, Oregon Territory, to John Gray, July 1851.

27. Kerr, "Calapooya," 167–68; Hainline, "Past Times," 1 Dec. 1977.

28. Moir and Mika, "Prairie Vegetation," 17, 18, 19; Lewis, *Patterns of Indian Burning*, 19; Cooper, "Ecology of Fire," 151; Galbreath and Anderson, "Grazing History of the Northwest," 8; Victor, *All Over Oregon and Washington*, 184; Kendall, "Letter," 191, 193; Ratcliff, "What Happened to the Kalapuya?" 31.

29. Linn County Petitioners, ca. 1856, and Lane County Petitioners, 1856, Oregon Provisional and Territorial Government Papers, items 9161, 9171 1/2. Emphasis is in the original petition.

30. Minto, "From Youth to Age," 153; Oregon Provisional and Territorial Government Papers, items 7680, 9600–9604.

31. John Cornett, in Haskin, Oral History. The "Battle of Bunker Hill" has been given various interpretations. It has been speculated that the fight was over whose horse was faster. But the best source, John Cornett, grandson of Americus Savage, said the quarrel was over hogs. This seems to be the most reasonable explanation not only because Cornett's mother was Savage's daughter but also because Elder and Savage signed opposing petitions dealing with swine. Cornett erred, however, in stating that Elder was the one who kept hogs. This is probably a mix-up since Haskin's interview with Cornett took place at the end of the 1930s, some eighty years after the event described took place.

32. Oregon Provisional and Territorial Government, *Laws*, 203.

33. U.S. Congress, Senate, *Reports of Explorations* 6:82; James Ayers, in Haskin, Oral History; W. T. Templeton, [Calapooia Valley, Oreg.], to Robert Templeton, 13 Mar. 1879, Templeton Family Papers.

34. For a discussion of the shift of the cattle industry from the western to the eastern portion of the Pacific Northwest, see Oliphant's works: "Cattle Herds and Ranches"; "Eastward Movement"; and *Cattle Ranges of Oregon*.

35. On oats and barley, see *Oregon's First Century of Farming*, 10, 11; Hill et al., "Barley Production in Oregon"; Hill, "Oats Production in Western Oregon."

6. CHANGES IN LANDSCAPE, CHANGES IN MEANING

1. McCoy, *Biography of John McCoy*, 15.

2. Corning, *Willamette Landings*, 117, 119, 123; Reynolds, "Evolution," 40.

3. Holtgrieve, "Historical Transportation Routes," 36; Linn County, Record of the Proceedings 1:25.

4. Reynolds, "Evolution," 40; *States Rights Democrat* (Albany), 12 June 1869, 1. In the year 1869, Linn County produced 342,323 bushels of spring wheat and 136,971 bushels of winter wheat. Although some counties in the Willamette produced more winter wheat than spring, spring wheat was overall more important than winter through the nineteenth century. The total in 1869 for the Willamette as a whole was 1,658,476 bushels of spring wheat to only 428,350 bushels of winter wheat. U.S. Department of Commerce, Bureau of the Census, *Statistics of the Wealth and Industry of the United States . . . Ninth Census* (Washington, D.C.: Government Printing Office, 1872) 3:231; A.S. Mercer, *Material Resources of Linn County*, 16.

5. Corning, *Willamette Landings*, 116; Fite, *Farmers' Frontier*, 153; Johansen and Gates, *Empire of the Columbia*, 373.

6. Elizabeth Ritchey Donation Land Claim Certificate, Donation Land Claim Records on microfilm at the National Archives Branch, Seattle, microfilm 815, certificate 508.

7. U.S. Congress, *Statutes at Large* 9:498, chap. 76, sec. 6.

8. Thomas Wilcox Donation Land Claim Certificate, Donation Land Claim Records, microfilm 815, certificate 1948.

9. Oregon Provisional and Territorial Government, Land Claim Records 4:318, 7:214; Agnes Courtney Donation Land Claim Certificate, Donation Land Claim Records, microfilm 815, certificate 753.

10. Henry H. Spalding Donation Land Claim Certificate, Donation Land Claim Records, microfilm 815, certificate 2418.

11. James Andrews, Polk County, Oregon Territory, to Preston, 24 May 1853, Preston Collection, file A–C; S.D. Snowden, Champoeg, Oregon Territory, to Preston, 22 Mar. 1853, Preston Collection, file S; Joseph L. Evans, Lynn [*sic*] County, O[regon] T[erritory], to Preston, 6 Apr. 1853, Preston Collection, file D–G.

12. Cooper, "My Life as a Homesteader," 77.

13. Fox, *Jared Fox's Memmorandom*, 121.

14. Dick, *Lure of the Land*, 131.

15. Johansen and Gates, *Empire of the Columbia*, 232; *Willamette Farmer* (Salem), 24 Jan. 1874, 4.

16. Ingersoll, "In the Wahlamet Valley," 766.

17. Victor, *All Over Oregon and Washington*, 184–85.

18. Albert Waggoner, in Haskin, Oral History; *Willamette Farmer* (Salem), 4 May 1877, 6.

19. William T. Templeton, [Brownsville], to Robert Templeton, 13 Mar. 1879, Templeton Family Papers; Cornett, Diary, 27–31 Mar. and 2 Apr. 1883. See also Williams, "Drainage of Farm Lands," 3–31.

20. Albert Waggoner and Redman Pearl, in Haskin, Oral History; Minto, "From Youth to Age," 131–32; U.S. Department of the Interior, Bureau of Sport Fisheries and Wildlife, *Willamette National Wildlife Refuge*, 5.

21. Wilkes, *Narrative* 4:358.

22. *Willamette Farmer* (Salem), 13 Aug. 1875, 5, and 10 Sept. 1875, 10.

23. Cornett, Diary, 6 Feb. 1884, 21 Sept. 1883; Carlson, "Rural Family," 152.

24. Goodall, "Upper Calapooia," 70; A. T. Morris, in Haskin, Oral History.

25. Victor, *All Over Oregon and Washington*, 187; Kendall, "Letter," 190.

26. Cooper, "My Life as a Homesteader," 75–76; Waggoner, *Stories of Old Oregon*, as quoted in Carey and Hainline, *Sweet Home*, 12–13. Waggoner wrote that in later years people often chided him for this story about bracken pie, but he swore that it was true. Of course, bracken played an important role in the diet of Native Americans in the Pacific Northwest.

27. John L. Wigle, Reminiscences; McCoy, *Biography of John McCoy*, 14; Cornett, Diary, 4 July and 21, 28, 29 Aug. 1885.

28. Thomas Bird Sprenger and Redman Pearl, in Haskin, Oral History.

29. Kendall, "Letter," 194; Head, "Oregon Donation Acts," 87.

30. Towle, "Woodland in the Willamette," 78, 79; U.S. Department of Agriculture, Bureau of Chemistry and Soils, *Soil Survey of Linn County*; Halbakken, "A History of Wheat-Growing."

31. Towle, "Woodlands in the Willamette," 77. In terms of soil fertility, 1880 is the only year for which we have per-acre production statistics for wheat. Unfortunately this census, enumerating the results of the 1879 harvest, caught the valley wheat crop suffering from "rust." However, since rust struck Linn County evenly, we can still compare production per acre for a variety of local lands. From the 3,071 acres sown to wheat in 1879 on farms along the foothills, 32,731 bushels were harvested, or 10.7 bushels per acre. From the 5,948 acres of wheat on the valley floor, 70,570 bushels were harvested, or 11.9 bushels per acre—that is, slightly more than one bushel per acre over the foothill farms; Manuscript Agricultural Census Returns, Linn County, 1880.

The Calapooia and Willamette Valley soils are made up of numerous deposits of river alluvia, which vary in their individual characteristics. A look at a soil map for the area shows a multiplicity of soil types, most of which are in narrow bands and small spots here and there. A historic comparison of each soil's fertility would be extremely difficult, if not impossible, since most farms have included a variety of soil types. The *Soil Survey of Linn County* (U.S. Department of Agriculture, Soil Conservation Service) shows that on a generalized soil map, prairie lands are no more fertile than foothill lands. The "white lands" on the prairie are the poorest drained and the least fertile and would be most susceptible to early exhaustion and abandonment. The best land for agricultural purposes is a narrow strip along the Calapooia from midway between the towns of Brownsville and Crawfordsville to midway between Shedd and Halsey.

32. WPA, *History of Linn County*, 14; Carey and Hainline, *Brownsville*, 2.

33. Oregon Provisional and Territorial Government Papers, item 11635. Theoretically, the establishment of this mill north of the Calapooia founded North Brownsville, eventually incorporated in 1876. In 1895 North Brownsville and Brownsville united. Brownsville also includes the townsite of Amelia,

platted in 1858 by Henry Harmon Spalding and named for one of his daughters; see Carey and Hainline, *Brownsville*, 30–31.

34. Manuscript Population Census Returns, Linn County, 1860. For this section, I am indebted to Lomax, *Pioneer Woolen Mills in Oregon*, esp. 82–85. Other useful information I drew from Stanard, "Seventy-fifth Anniversary of Brownsville Mills"; Hainline, "Past Times," 14 Nov. 1985; and Lomax, *Later Woolen Mills*.

35. U.S. Department of Commerce, Bureau of the Census, *Statistics of the Population of the United States . . . Tenth Census* (Washington, D.C.: Government Printing Office, 1883) 1:304; Mercer, *Material Resources of Linn County*, 48–51; WPA, *History of Linn County*, 20; U.S. Department of Commerce, Bureau of the Census, *Report on the Population of the United States . . . Eleventh Census: 1890* (Washington, D.C.: Government Printing Office, 1895), 286.

36. Standish and Carey, *Brownsville*, 32.

37. WPA, *History of Linn County*, 38–40; Burkhart, *Settler's Guide*, 40, 71; U.S. Department of Commerce, Bureau of the Census, *Statistics of the Population of the United States . . . Tenth Census* (Washington, D.C.: Government Printing Office, 1883), 304.

38. Manuscript Industrial Census Returns, Linn County, 1870; Priaulx, "Lumber Industry."

39. *Oregon Cultivator* (Albany), 26 Oct. 1876, 8; *Albany City Directory, 1878*, 39; Kerr, "Calapooya," 169; Farnell, "Calapooia River Navigability Study."

40. See Farnell, "Calapooia River Navigability Study"; Cornett, Diary, 18 and 20 Jan. 1885.

41. Farnell, "Calapooia River Navigability Study," 12–13.

42. See Sedell and Froggatt, "Importance of Streamside Forests," 1828–34; U.S. Department of Agriculture, Forest Service, Pacific Northwest Forest and Range Experiment Station, "Water Transportation and Storage of Logs."

43. Priaulx, " 'Chittim Bark' "; Cooper, "My Life as a Homesteader," 75–76.

44. Richard C. Finley, Mill Accounts; Manuscript Agricultural Census Returns, Linn County, 1860.

45. Turnbow and Turnbow, *Charles Rice*, 156–57; Hainline, "Past Times," 1 Dec. 1977; Carey and Hainline, *Shedd*; WPA, *History of Linn County*, 49–50. It is believed that two settlers from New England, Americus Savage from Maine and Richard Farwell from New Hampshire, influenced the naming of the town of Boston; Carey and Hainline, *Shedd*, 14. The former Boston Mills, now called Thompson's Mills, is still in operation at this writing.

46. See Carey and Hainline, *Shedd* and *Halsey*.

47. Mercer, *Material Resources of Linn County*, 46, 51–52; U.S. Department of Commerce, Bureau of Census, *Statistics of the Population of the United States . . . Tenth Census* 1:344; id., *Report on Population of the United States . . . Eleventh Census: 1890*, 286.

48. *Brownsville Advertiser*, 28 Feb. and 4 Mar. 1878. For more particulars

on the narrow gauge, see Leslie M. Scott, "History of the Narrow Gauge Railroad."

49. *Brownsville Advertiser*, 14 Mar. 1878.

50. Manuscript Population Census Returns, Linn County, 1850, 1860, 1870, and 1880. This analysis does not include occupations such as housewife and student. In 1850 only four other occupations were listed: laborer, minister, carpenter, and merchant.

51. Tattersall, "Economic Development," 43–45, 86–92.

7. LIFE AND REFLECTION ON A TRANSFORMED LANDSCAPE

1. See, for example, White, *Land Use*; Cronon, *Changes in the Land*.

2. Burkhart, *Settler's Guide*, 21; Mercer, *Material Resources of Linn County*, 20; see also Blok, "Evolution," 65.

3. Blain, Union Point, Oregon Territory, to Kerr, spring 1855.

4. *Willamette Farmer* (Salem), 14 June 1873, n.p., and 14 Aug. 1874, supplement, n.p.

5. Ingersoll, "In the Wahlamet Valley," 766–67.

6. Ibid.

7. *Willamette Farmer* (Salem), 4 May 1877, 6; 27 July 1877, 4.

8. *States Rights Democrat* (Albany), 18 Jan. 1884, n.p.; Blain, Union Point, Oregon Territory, to Dales, 1 Apr. 1851.

9. *Illustrated Historical Atlas Map*, 26 1/2; *Brownsville Times*, 18 July 1890, n.p., copy in Linn County Historical Museum, Brownsville, Box: Newspapers, Brownsville; *Oregon Cultivator* (Albany), 13 Apr. 1876, 7.

10. *Illustrated Historical Atlas Map*, 26 1/2; Alley, *Linn County*, 61, 63.

11. Burkhart, *Settler's Guide*, 21–22.

12. Ibid., 21–22, 23, 27.

13. Alley, *Linn County*, 61, 66.

14. Minto, "From Youth to Age," 131–32; Goodall, "The Upper Calapooia," 70; Redman Pearl, in Haskin, Oral History; see also Mitchell, *Witnesses to a Vanishing America*. Baker, "Oregon Pioneer Tradition," argues that Oregon pioneers in the late nineteenth century looked back on the progress they had made in the Pacific Northwest with approval. At the same time, however, they questioned the quality of civilization they had created and looked back on their past with nostalgia.

15. Atkinson, "Diary," 349; Blain, Union Point, Oregon Territory, to Dales, 1 Apr. 1851.

16. Burkhart, *Settler's Guide*, 8. Burkhart repeatedly makes this assessment in his guide: "The sluggard will find it hard to make a living here, and should not come. The shiftless will wage an unequal warfare in the battle of life here as he does elsewhere. There is no room for him here. It is the man who seeks a permanent home for himself and his family, who has energy, spirit, and disposition to build up the country in building up himself, that should seek a home here" (19). Later, Burkhart notes, "The kind of people needed here are those

who can take off their coats and, by hard labor and industry, make the wild forests to blossom as the rose" (20).

17. *Willamette Farmer* (Salem), 24 Feb. 1872, 1.

18. *Willamette Farmer* (Salem), 3 Aug. 1875, 5; Victor, *All Over Oregon and Washington*, 187.

19. Burkhart, *Settler's Guide*, 23. The same passage appears in *States Rights Democrat* (Albany), 18 Jan. 1884, 1.

20. Cornett, Diary, 10 May 1885, and 11 Dec. 1883; Cranfill, Diary, 13 Apr. 1866.

21. *Willamette Farmer* (Salem), 27 July 1872, 4.

22. Ibid. Examples include: *Willamette Farmer* (Salem), 27 July 1872, 4; 22 Nov. 1873, 1; 13 Aug. 1875, 1; 31 Dec. 1875, 1; *Albany Register*, 8 June 1877, 2; Burkhart, *Settler's Guide*.

23. *Willamette Farmer* (Salem), 13 Aug. 1875, 1.

24. Cranfill, Diary, 13 Aug. and 16 July 1865.

25. Cornett, Diary, 19 Jan. and 8 Mar. 1883, and 17 Mar. 1885.

26. Victor, *All Over Oregon and Washington*, 187.

27. *Willamette Farmer* (Salem), 27 July 1872, 4; S. Mercer, *Material Resources of Linn County*, 47.

28. Burkhart, *Settler's Guide*, 16–17. The last sentence in this quotation from Burkhart is grammatically incorrect in the original.

29. *Willamette Farmer* (Salem), 27 July 1872, 4.

30. Searles, "Role of the Nonhuman Environment," 32, 33; see also Searles, *Nonhuman Environment*.

BIBLIOGRAPHY

ABBREVIATIONS

OHQ   *Oregon Historical Quarterly*
OHS   *Oregon Historical Society, Portland*
PNQ   *Pacific Northwest Quarterly*

PRIMARY SOURCES

UNPUBLISHED

Amelia Spalding Brown History Room. Vertical and genealogy files. Browns-
    ville Community Library, Brownsville.
Blain, Wilson. Letters, 1848–57, and Notes. Manuscript 1035, Blain Collec-
    tion. OHS.
Blakely, James. Collection. CA B583, Special Collections. Knight Library, Uni-
    versity of Oregon, Eugene.
Blakely, Margaret (Baird). Interview by M. Sophia Robertson (c. 1940). Amelia
    Spalding Brown History Room.
Blakely, M. M., Pendleton, Oreg., to Mrs. Dougherty, Brownsville, 26 Feb.
    1925. Box: Misc. Documents. Linn County Historical Museum, Browns-
    ville.
Cornett, Sarah Jane (Savage). Diary. In the possession of E. H. Margason,
    Shedd, Oreg.
Cranfill, Isom. Diaries and Papers, 1847, 1860, 1863–77. AX 127, Special
    Collections. Knight Library, University of Oregon, Eugene. (Contains Jasper
    Cranfill's diaries.)
Earl, Robert. Reminiscences. Manuscript 793. OHS.

Finley, Richard C. Documents and Correspondence, 1854–90, and Papers, 1852–68. Manuscript 725. OHS.

Freeland, Benjamin, Calapooia, Linn County, Oregon Territory, to Brother, 3 Feb. 1854. Photostatic copy, Manuscript 811. OHS.

Gragg Family Papers. AX 139 1, Special Collections. Knight Library, University of Oregon, Eugene.

Haskin, Leslie. Oral History Interview Collection. Federal Writers' Project, Works Progress Administration. Photostatic copies in Amelia Spalding Brown History Room.

King, Lucy M., Louisville, Clay County, Ill., to James W. Swank, Brownsville, Oreg., 9 Aug. 1852. Photostatic copy in Swank Genealogy file. Amelia Spalding Brown History Room.

Kirk, Alexander, and Morgan Kees, Oregon City, Oregon Territory to Clerk of Linn County, Oregon Territory, 28 May 1848. Photostatic copy in Oregon: Early Roads and Railroads file. Amelia Spalding Brown History Room.

Lewis, Fielding, Linn County, Oregon, to "Friends in the States," 18 May 1853. Typescript copy in Lewis Genealogy file. Amelia Spalding Brown History Room.

Oregon Historical Society. Genealogy and biographical files. Portland.

Plaster, Michael. Business Accounts, Weather Log, and Family Records, 1858–1901. In possession of Geneva Barry, Indian Valley, Idaho.

Preston, John B. Preston Collection. Letters from Donation Land Claimants, 1853, to John B. Preston, Surveyor General. Manuscript 914. OHS.

Stanard, Everett Earl. Oral History Interviews. Amelia Spalding Brown History Room.

Templeton Family Papers, 1862–1953. Manuscripts 1332 and 1332B. OHS.

Wigle, Abraham J. Reminiscences [1898]. Manuscript 587. OHS.

Wigle, John L. Reminiscences of Crossing the Plains and Early Settlement in Oregon. Amelia Spalding Brown History Room.

Works Progress Administration. Federal Writers' Project Collection. Oregon State Library, Salem.

PUBLISHED WORKS

Albany City Directory, 1878. Albany: Mansfield & Monteith, 1878.

Alley, B. F. *Linn County, Oregon, Description and Resources, Its Cities and Towns*. Albany: Royce & Ribler, [1889].

Applegate, Jesse. *Recollections of My Boyhood*. Roseburg, Oreg.: Press of Review Publishing Company, 1914.

Atkinson, George H. "Diary of Rev. George Atkinson, D.D., 1847–1858." Edited by E. Ruth Rockwood. *OHQ* 40, no. 4 (Dec. 1939): 343–61.

Brackenridge, W. D. *The Brackenridge Journal for the Oregon Country*. Edited by O. B. Sperlin. Seattle: University of Washington Press, 1931.

Burkhart, C. G. *Settler's Guide to Homes in the Willamette Valley, Oregon, For the Use and Information of Immigrants*. Albany: By the author, Immigration Agent for Linn County, [1887].

Cooper, Fannie Adams. "My Life as a Homesteader." Edited by Leonard A. Whitlow and Catharine Cooper Whitlow. *OHQ* 82, nos. 1–2 (Spring–Summer 1981): 65–84, 152–68.

Douglas, David. *The Oregon Journals of David Douglas of His Travels and Adventures among the Traders and Indians in the Columbia, Willamette and Snake River Regions During the Years 1825, 1826, and 1827.* Edited by David Lavender. 3 vols. Ashland: Oregon Book Society, 1972.

Fox, Jared. *Jared Fox's Memmorandom Kept from Dellton, Sauk County, Wisconsin, toward California and Oregon, 1852–1854.* Edited by Stephen Calvert. Benton, Wis.: Cottonwood Hill, 1990.

Henry, Alexander. *New Light on the Early History of the Greater Northwest: The Manuscript Journals of Alexander Henry and of David Thompson, 1799–1814.* Edited by Elliott Coues. 3 vols. New York: Francis P. Harper, 1897.

Hines, Gustavus. *Voyage Round the World.* Buffalo, N.Y.: George H. Derby, 1850.

Howison, Neil M. "Report of Lieutenant Neil M. Howison on Oregon, 1846: A Reprint." *OHQ* 14, no. 1 (Mar. 1913): 1–60.

Illustrated Historical Atlas Map of Marion and Linn Counties, Oregon, 1878. San Francisco: Edgar Williams and Co., 1878.

Ingersoll, E. "In the Wahlamet Valley of Oregon." *Harper's New Monthly Magazine,* Oct. 1882, 764–71.

Jacobs, Melville. *Kalapuya Texts.* University of Washington Publications in Anthropology 11. Seattle: University of Washington Press, 1945.

Kendall, Thomas S. "Letter on Oregon Agriculture, 1852." Edited by J. Orin Oliphant. *Agricultural History* 9, no. 4 (Oct. 1935): 187–97.

Lee, Daniel, and J. H. Frost. *Ten Years in Oregon.* New York: By the authors, 1844. Rpt. *Sunday Oregonian* (Portland), 11 Oct. 1903–10 Jan. 1904.

Linn County, Oregon: Early 1850 Records. Portland: Boyce-Wheeler, 1983.

McHargue, William, Chariton County, Mo., to James McHargue, Calapooia, Oregon Territory, 22 Jan. 1853. Published in Everett Earle Stanard. "Old Stuff and New." *Sunday Democrat* (Albany), 15 July 1923, 5.

McLoughlin, John. *The Letters of John McLoughlin, From Fort Vancouver to the Governor and Committee, Second Series, 1839–44.* Edited by E. E. Rich with an introduction by W. Kaye Lamb. The Publications of the Hudson's Bay Record Society 4. London: The Champlain Society for the Hudson's Bay Record Society, 1943.

Matthieu, F. X. "Reminiscences of F. X. Matthieu." Edited by H. S. Lyman. *OHQ* 1, no. 1 (Mar. 1900): 73–104.

Mealey, W. B., Linn County, Muddy Creek Settlement, to Parents, 1 Sept. 1852. Published in J. Fred McCoy. *A Biography of John McCoy with a Brief History of Linn County, Oregon.* Albany: R. R. Milligan, [1983].

Mercer, A. S. *Material Resources of Linn County, Oregon, Embracing Detailed Descriptions and Business Directory.* Albany: Brown and Stewart, 1875.

Miles, John, and Richard Milligan. *Linn County, Oregon Pioneer Settlers: Oregon Territory Donation Land Claim Families to 1855.* 8 vols. Lebanon, Oreg.: John Miles, 1983.

Miller, Mrs. James P., Albany, Oreg., to Rev. Joseph Banks, Jan. 1852. *Evangelical Repository* 10 (Jan. 1852): 425–27.

Nash, Wallis. *Oregon: There and Back in 1877.* Foreword by J. Kenneth Munford. London: Macmillan, 1878.

Palmer, Joel. *Journal of Travels over the Rocky Mountains, to the Mouth of the Columbia River; Made During the Years 1845 and 1847.* Cincinnati: J. A. & U. P. James, 1847. Rpt. March of America Facsimilie Series no. 83. Ann Arbor, Mich.: University Microfilms, 1966.

Pratt, Harry E. "Twenty-two Letters of David Logan, Pioneer Oregon Lawyer." *OHQ* 44, no. 3 (Sept. 1943): 253–85.

Ramsey, Jarold, ed. *Coyote Was Going There: Indian Literature of the Oregon Country.* Seattle: University of Washington Press, 1977.

Riggs, Timothy A., Albany, Oreg., to George O. Goodall, 21 Sept. 1901. *OHQ* 4, no. 1 (Mar. 1903): 74–77.

Victor, Frances Fuller. *All Over Oregon and Washington: Observation of the Country, Its Scenery, Soil, Climate, Resources, and Improvements.* San Francisco: John H. Corning, 1872.

Warre, Henry J., and Mervyn Vavasour. "Documents Relative to Warre and Vavasour's Military Reconnoissance in Oregon, 1845–46." Edited by Joseph Schafer. *OHQ* 10, no. 1 (Mar. 1909): 1–99.

Wilkes, Charles. *Narrative of the United States Exploring Expedition During the Years 1838, 1839, 1840, 1841, 1842.* 13 vols. Philadelphia: Lea & Blanchard, 1845.

Work, John. "John Work's Journey from Fort Vancouver to Umpqua River and Return in 1834." Edited by Leslie M. Scott. *OHQ* 24, no. 3 (Sept. 1923): 238–68.

PUBLIC DOCUMENTS

Linn County, Oregon. Clerk. Record of the Proceedings of the County Court. Vol. 1: 1849–61. Court Journal. Vol. 7. Transcribed by Charles Crane. Oregon Historical Records Survey Project. Portland, July 1940. Oregon State Library. Works Progress Administration, Federal Writers Project. Series 1, box 41.

————. Tax Assessor. Tax Registers for 1858–59, 1861, 1864, 1870, 1878. Oregon State Archives, Salem.

Oregon Provisional and Territorial Government. Land Claim Records. Oregon State Archives. Salem.

————. Papers, 1843–59. Microfilm. Special Collections, Knight Library, University of Oregon, Eugene.

Oregon Territorial Government. *Laws of a General and Local Nature Passed by the Legislative Committee and Legislative Assembly, 1843–1849.* Salem: Asahel Bush, 1853.

————. *The Oregon Archives, Including the Journals, Governors' Messages and Public Papers of Oregon,* by LaFayette Grover, Commissioner. Salem: Asahel Bush, 1853.

——. *Statutes of a General Nature: Legislative Assembly*. Salem: Asahel Bush, 1851.

U.S. Congress. *The Statutes at Large and Treaties of the United States of America from December 1, 1845, to March 3, 1851*. Edited by George Minot. Boston: Charles C. Little and James Brown, 1851.

——. House. *Columbia River and Tributaries, Northwestern United States*. 81st Cong., 2d sess. House Doc. 531. Vol. 5. Washington, D.C.: Government Printing Office, 1951.

——. Senate. "Memorial of William A. Slacum, Praying Compensation for His Services in Obtaining Information in Relation to the Settlements on the Oregon River, December 18, 1837." 25th Cong., 2d sess. Sen. Exec. Doc. 24.

——. Senate. *Reports of Explorations and Surveys, to Ascertain the Most Practicable and Economical Route for a Railroad from the Mississippi River to the Pacific Ocean, 1854–1855*. 36th Cong., 1st sess. Sen. Exec. Doc. 56.

U.S. Department of Agriculture. Bureau of Biological Survey. *The Mammals and Life Zones of Oregon*, by Vernon Bailey. North American Fauna Series no. 55. Washington, D.C.: U.S. Deparment of Agriculture, 1936.

——. Bureau of Chemistry and Soils in cooperation with the Oregon Agricultural Experiment Station. *Soil Survey of Linn County, Oregon*, by A.E. Kocher, E.J. Carpenter, W.G. Harper, E.F. Torgerson, and R.E. Stephenson. Washington, D.C.: U.S. Department of Agriculture, 1923.

——. Forest Service, Pacific Northwest Forest and Range Experiment Station. "Water Transportation and Storage of Logs," by James R. Sedell and Wayne S. Duval. In *Influence of Forest and Rangeland Management on Anadromous Fish Habitats in Western North America*. Edited by William R. Meehan. Forest Service General Technical Report, PNW-8. Portland: U.S. Department of Agriculture, 1985.

——. "Willamette Floodplain Research Natural Area, Grassland and Oregon Ash Forest on Wet Bottom Land in Oregon's Willamette Valley." In *Federal Research Natural Areas in Oregon and Washinton: A Guidebook for Scientists and Educators, Willamette Floodplain Research Natural Area*. Portland: U.S. Deparment of Agriculture, 1972.

——. Soil Conservation Service in cooperation with U.S. Department of Interior, Bureau of Land Management, and Oregon Agricultural Experiment Station. *Soil Survey of Linn County Area, Oregon*, by Russell W. Landridge. [Corvallis, Oreg.]: U.S. Department of Agriculture, [1987].

U.S. Department of Commerce. Bureau of the Census. *The Seventh Census of the United States: 1850*. Washington, D.C.: Robert Armstrong, Public Printer, 1853.

——. Seventh Census, 1850. Manuscript Census, Linn County.

——. *The Eighth Census of the United States: 1860*. Washington, D.C.: Government Printing Office, 1864. (Separate volumes have varying titles, publication dates.)

——. Eighth Census, 1860. Manuscript Census, Linn County.

——. *The Ninth Census of the United States: 1870*. Washington, D.C.: Government Printing Office, 1872. (Separate volumes have varying titles, publication dates.)

———. Ninth Census, 1870. Manuscript Census, Linn County.

———. *The Tenth Census of the United States: 1880.* Washington, D.C.: Government Printing Office, 1883. (Separate volumes have varying titles, publication dates.)

———. Tenth Census, 1880. Manuscript Census, Linn County.

———. *The Eleventh Census of the United States: 1890.* Washington, D.C.: Government Printing Office, 1895. (Separate volumes have varying titles, publication dates.)

U.S. Department of the Interior. Bureau of Land Management. Cadastral Surveyors' Notes and Maps. Bureau of Land Management Offices, Portland.

———. Donation Land Claim Records. Bureau of Land Management Offices, Portland, Oreg., and National Archives, Seattle.

———. Bureau of Sport Fisheries and Wildlife. *Willamette National Wildlife Refuge: Muddy Creek Division, Ankeny Division, Baskett Slough Division; Development and Management Plan.* [1966].

NEWSPAPERS

Albany Democrat, 1888–1900
Albany Register, 1868–80
Brownsville Advertiser, 1878–79
Brownsville Banner. Miscellaneous editions at the Linn County Historical Museum, Brownsville.
Brownsville Times. Miscellaneous editions, pre-1900, at the Linn County Historical Museum, Brownsville.
Daily Herald (Albany), 1880–82
Oregon Cultivator (Albany), 1875–77
States Rights Democrat (Albany), 1865–1900
Willamette Farmer (Salem), 1869–87

SECONDARY SOURCES

Aikens, C. Melvin. *Archaeological Studies in the Willamette Valley, Oregon.* University of Oregon Anthropological Papers no. 8. Eugene: University of Oregon, 1975.

Allen, John Eliot, Marjorie Burns, and Sam C. Sargeant. *Cataclysms on the Columbia: A Layman's Guide to the Features Produced by the Catastrophic Bretz Floods in the Pacific Northwest.* Portland: Timber Press, 1986.

Baker, Abner Sylvester. "The Oregon Pioneer Tradition in the Nineteenth Century: A Study of Recollection and Self Definition." Ph.D. diss., University of Oregon, 1968.

Baldwin, Ewart M. *Geology of Oregon.* 3d ed. Dubuque, Iowa: Kendall/Hunt, 1981.

Beckham, Stephen Dow. *Requiem for a People: The Rogue Indians and the Frontiersmen.* Civilization of the American Indian Series 108. Norman: University of Oklahoma Press, 1971.

———. *The Indians of Western Oregon: This Land Was Theirs*. Coos Bay, Oreg.: Arago Books, 1977.

Bennett-Browning, Elsie. "The Pioneer Keeney Family: Members Came to This Area with Earliest Settlers." *Times* (Brownsville), 17 June 1976, 23.

Bermingham, Ann. *Landscape and Ideology: The English Rustic Tradition, 1740–1860*. Berkeley and Los Angeles: University of California Press, 1986.

Blok, Jack H. "The Evolution of Agricultural Resource Strategies in the Willamette Valley." Ph.D. diss., Oregon State University, 1973.

Bogue, Allan G. *From Prairie to Corn Belt: Farming on the Illinois and Iowa Prairies in the Nineteenth Century*. Chicago: University of Chicago Press, 1963.

Bowen, William A. "Mapping an American Frontier: Oregon in 1850." *Annals of the Association of American Geographers* 65, no. 1 (Mar. 1975): map supplement no. 18.

———. *The Willamette Valley: Migration and Settlement on the Oregon Frontier*. Seattle: University of Washington Press, 1978.

Boyd, Robert T. "Another Look at the 'Fever and Ague' of Western Oregon." *Ethnohistory* 22, no. 2 (Spring 1975): 135–54.

———. "Strategies of Indian Burning in the Willamette Valley." *Canadian Journal of Anthropology/Revue Canadienne d'Anthropologie* 5, no. 1 (Fall 1986): 65–86.

Brown, Richard Maxwell. "Rainfall and History: Perspectives on the Pacific Northwest." In *Experiences in a Promised Land*. Edited by Carlos A. Schwantes and G. Thomas Edwards, 11–27. Seattle: University of Washington Press, 1986.

"Browns Play Important Part in Oregon State's History." Unpublished manuscript. Copy in Brown Genealogy file, Amelia Spalding Brown History Room, Brownsville Community Library.

Buley, R. Carlyle. *The Old Northwest Pioneer Period, 1815–1840*. 2 vols. Bloomington: Indiana University Press, 1951.

Carey, Margaret Standish, and Patricia Hoy Hainline. *Brownsville: Linn County's Oldest Town*. Brownsville: Calapooia Publications, 1976.

———. *Halsey: Linn County's Centennial City*. Brownsville: Calapooia Publications, 1977.

———. *Shedd: Linn County's Early Dairy Center and Memories of Boston*. Brownsville: Calapooia Publications, 1978.

———. *Sweet Home in the Oregon Cascades*. Brownsville: Calapooia Publications, 1979.

Carlson, Christopher Dean. "The Rural Family in the Nineteenth Century: A Case Study in Oregon's Willamette Valley." Ph.D. diss., University of Oregon, 1980.

Carstensen, Vernon, ed. *The Public Lands: Studies in the History of the Public Domain*. Madison: University of Wisconsin Press, 1968.

Cayton, Andrew R. L. *The Frontier Republic: Ideology and Politics in the Ohio Country, 1780–1825*. Kent: Kent State University Press, 1986.

Clark, Ella E. *Indian Legends of the Pacific Northwest*. Berkeley and Los Angeles: University of California Press, 1953.

Clarke, S. A. *Pioneer Days of Oregon History*. Portland, Oreg.: J. K. Gill Company, 1905.

Collins, Lloyd R. "The Cultural Position of the Kalapuya in the Pacific Northwest." M.S. thesis, University of Oregon, 1951.

Cook, S. F. "The Epidemic of 1830–1833 in California and Oregon." In *University of California Publications in American Archaeology and Ethnology*, ed. E. W. Gifford, A. L. Kroeber, R. H. Lowie, T. D. McCown, D. G. Mandelbawm, and R. L. Olson, 43:303–25. Berkeley and Los Angeles: University of California Press, 1956.

Cooper, Charles F. "The Ecology of Fire." *Scientific American* 204, no. 4 (Apr. 1961): 150–60.

Corning, Howard McKinley. *Willamette Landings: Ghost Towns of the River*. 2d ed. Portland: Oregon Historical Society Press, 1973.

Cronon, William. *Changes in the Land: Indians, Colonists, and the Ecology of New England*. New York: Hill & Wang, Farrar, Straus & Giroux, 1983.

Cronon, William, and Richard White. "Indians in the Land." *American Heritage* 37, no. 5 (Aug.–Sept. 1986): 18–25.

de Buys, William. *Enchantment and Exploitation: The Life and Hard Times of a New Mexico Mountain Range*. Albuquerque: University of New Mexico, 1985.

Detling, Leroy E. *Historical Background of the Flora of the Pacific Northwest*. University of Oregon Museum of Natural History, Bulletin no. 13. Eugene: University of Oregon, 1968.

Dick, Everett. *The Lure of the Land: A Social History of the Public Lands from the Articles of Confederation to the New Deal*. Lincoln: University of Nebraska Press, 1970.

Dicken, Samuel N., and Emily F. Dicken. *Two Centuries of Oregon Geography*. Vol. 1, *The Making of Oregon: A Study in Historical Geography*. Vol. 2, *Oregon Divided: A Regional Geography*. Portland: Oregon Historical Society Press, 1982.

Douglas, Jesse S. "Origins of the Population of Oregon in 1850." *PNQ* 41, no. 2 (Apr. 1950): 95–108.

Drury, Clifford Merrill. *Pioneer of Old Oregon: Henry Harmon Spalding*. Caldwell, Idaho: Caxton Printers, 1936.

Duncan, Robert C. *Covenanters by the Willamette: United Presbyterian Pioneers in Albany and Linn County, Oregon, 1850–1900*. Kennewick, Wash.: By the author, 1972.

Edmunds, R. David. *Tecumseh and the Quest for Indian Leadership*. Edited by Oscar Handlin. Boston: Little, Brown, 1984.

Ekirch, Arthur A., Jr. *Man and Nature in America*. New York: Columbia University Press, 1963.

Ernst, Joseph W. *With Compass and Chain: Federal Land Surveys in the Old Northwest, 1785–1816*. New York: Arno Press, 1979.

Faragher, John Mack. "Midwestern Families in Motion: Women and Men on the Overland Trail to Oregon and California, 1843–1870." Ph.D. diss., Yale University, 1977.

————. *Sugar Creek: Life on the Illinois Prairie*. New Haven: Yale University Press, 1986.

————. *Women and Men on the Overland Trail*. New Haven: Yale University Press, 1979.

Farnell, James E. "Calapooia River Navigability Study." Unpublished report, 1980. Oregon Division of State Lands, Salem.

Fite, Gilbert C. *The Farmers' Frontier, 1865–1900*. New York: Holt, Rinehart & Winston, 1966.

Frachtenberg, Leo J. "Ethnological Researches among the Kalapuya Indians." *Smithsonian Miscellaneous Collections* 65, no. 6 (1916): 85–89.

Franklin, Jerry T., and C. T. Dyrness. *Natural Vegetation of Oregon and Washington*. Forest Service General Technical Report PNW-8. Portland, Oreg.: U.S. Department of Agriculture, 1973.

Freeman, Olga. "Territorial Road Extended into Lane County." *Lane County Historian* 24, no. 2 (Fall 1979): 58–62.

French, David H. "Ethnobotany of the Pacific Northwest Indians." *Economic Botany* 19, no. 1 (Jan.–Mar. 1965): 378–82.

Galbreath, Willam A., and E. William Anderson. "Grazing History of the Northwest." *Journal of Rangeland Management* 24, no. 1 (1971): 6–12.

Gates, Paul W. "Tenants of the Log Cabin." In his *Landlords and Tenants on the Prairie Frontier: Studies in American Land Policy*. Ithaca: Cornell University Press, 1973.

Genealogical Forum of Portland, Oregon. *Genealogical Materials in Oregon Donation Land Claims*. 5 vols. Portland: Genealogical Forum of Portland, 1957.

Gibson, James R. *Farming the Frontier: The Agricultural Opening of the Oregon Country, 1786–1846*. Seattle: University of Washington Press for the University of British Columbia Press, 1985.

Gleeson, George W. *The Return of a River: The Willamette River, Oregon*. Corvallis, Oreg.: Water Resources Research Institute, 1972.

Goodall, George O. "The Upper Calapooia." *OHQ* 4, no. 1 (Mar. 1903): 70–77.

Habeck, James R. "The Original Vegetation of the Mid-Willamette Valley, Oregon." *Northwest Science* 35, no. 2 (1961): 65–77.

Hainline, Patricia Hoy. "Past Times." *Times* (Brownsville), 1 Dec. 1977, 2; 10 Apr. 1980, 2; 24 Apr. 1980, 2; 10 Jan. 1985, 2; 7 Feb. 1985, 2; 14 Nov. 1985, 2.

Halbakken, David Sanstad. "A History of Wheat-Growing in Oregon During the Nineteenth Century." M.A. thesis, University of Oregon, 1948.

Hallan, Leila. "History of Calapooias Depicts the Unwitting Genocide of a People." *Oregon Herald* (Albany), for the week ending 24 Dec. 1979, n.p.

Hart, John Fraser. "The Middle West." *Annals of the Association of American Geographers* 62 (1972): 258–82.

Head, Harlow Zinser. "The Oregon Donation Acts: Background, Development, and Applications." M.A. thesis, University of Oregon, 1969.

————. "The Oregon Donation Land Claims and Their Patterns." Ph.D. diss., University of Oregon, 1971.

Hill, D. D. "Oats Production in Western Oregon." In Agricultural Experiment Station Bulletin no. 285. Corvallis: Oregon Agricultural Experiment Station and Oregon State Agricultural College, 1931.

Hill, D. D., D. E. Stephens, D. E. Richards, Roy E. Hutchinson, and J. F. Martin. "Barley Production in Oregon." In Agriculture Experiment Station Bulletin no. 355. Corvallis: Oregon Agricultural Experiment Station, 1938.

Hine, Robert V. *Community on the American Frontier: Separate but Not Alone*. Norman: University of Oklahoma Press, 1980.

"A History of the Hugh L. Brown Family." Unpublished manuscript. Copy in Amelia Spalding Brown History Room.

Hofstadter, Richard. *The Age of Reform: From Bryan to F.D.R*. New York: Knopf, 1955.

Holtgrieve, Donald Gordon. "Historical Transportation Routes and Town Populations in Oregon's Willamette Valley." Ph.D. diss., University of Oregon, 1973.

Hughes, Sarah S. *Surveyors and Statesmen: Land Measuring in Colonial Virginia*. Richmond: Virginia Surveyors Foundation and the Virginia Association of Surveyors, 1979.

Humphrey, Robert R. *Range Ecology*. New York: Ronald Press, 1962.

Hussey, John A. *Champoeg: Place of Transition, A Disputed History*. Portland: Oregon Historical Society in cooperation with the Oregon State Highway Commission and the National Park Service, U.S. Department of the Interior, 1967.

Huth, Hans. *Nature and the American: Three Centuries of Changing Attitudes*. Berkeley and Los Angeles: University of California Press, 1957.

Jackle, John A., Stanley Brunn, and Curtis C. Roseman. *Human Spatial Behavior: A Social Geography*. Prospect Heights, Ill.: Waveland Press, 1985.

Jeffrey, Julie Roy. *Frontier Women: The Trans-Mississippi West, 1840–1880*. American Century Series. New York: Farrar, Straus & Giroux, Hill & Wang, 1979.

Jochim, Michael A. *Strategies for Survival: Cultural Behavior in an Ecological Context*. New York: Academic Press, 1981.

Johannessen, Carl L., William A. Davenport, Artimus Millet, and Steven McWilliams. "The Vegetation of the Willamette Valley." *Annals of the Association of American Geographers* 61 (June 1971): 286–302.

Johansen, Dorothy O. "A Working Hypothesis for the Study of Migrations." *Pacific Historical Review* 36 (Feb. 1967): 1–12.

Johansen, Dorothy O., and Charles M. Gates. *Empire of the Columbia: A History of the Pacific Northwest*. 2d ed. New York: Harper & Row, 1967.

Johnson, Hildegard Binder. "Rational and Ecological Aspects of the Quarter Section: An Example from Minnesota." *Geographical Review* 47, no. 3 (July 1957): 330–48.

———. *Order upon the Land: The U.S. Rectangular Land Survey and the Upper Mississippi Country*. New York: Oxford University Press, 1976.

———. *The Orderly Landscape: Landscape Tastes and the United States Sur-*

vey. James Ford Bell Lectures no. 15. Minneapolis: Association of the James Ford Bell Library, University of Minnesota, 1977.

Kerr, Mildred. "The Calapooya." *OHQ* 44, no. 2 (June 1943): 163–71.

Kolodny, Annette. *The Land Before Her: Fantasy and Experience on the American Frontiers, 1830–1860*. Chapel Hill: University of North Carolina Press, 1984.

———. *The Lay of the Land: Metaphor as Experience and History in American Life and Letters*. Chapel Hill: University of North Carolina Press, 1975.

Kroeber, A. L. *Cultural and Natural Areas of Native North America*. Berkeley and Los Angeles: University of California Press, 1963.

Larsell, Olaf. *The Doctor in Oregon: A Medical History*. Portland: Binford and Mort for the Oregon Historical Society, 1947.

Leopold, A. Starker. "Deer in Relation to Plant Succession." In *Transactions of the Fifteenth North American Wildlife Conference, March 6–9, 1950*. Washington, D.C.: Wildlife Management Institute, 1950.

Lewis, Henry T. *Patterns of Indian Burning in California: Ecology and Ethnohistory*. Ramona, Calif.: Ballena Press, 1973.

Lomax, Alfred L. *Pioneer Woolen Mills in Oregon: History of Wool and the Woolen Textile Industry in Oregon, 1811–1875*. Portland: Binford and Mort, 1941.

———. *Later Woolen Mills in Oregon: A History of the Woolen Mills Which Followed the Pioneer Mills*. Portland: Binford and Mort, 1974.

Lynch, Kevin. *The Image of the City*. Cambridge: MIT Press, 1960.

McArthur, Lewis A. *Oregon Geographic Names*. 5th ed. Portland: Western Imprints, The Press of the Oregon Historical Society, 1982.

McCoy, J. Fred. *A Biography of John McCoy with a Brief History of Linn County, Oregon*. Albany: R. R. Milligan, [1983].

McKee, Bates. *Cascadia: The Geologic Evolution of the Pacific Northwest*. New York: McGraw-Hill, 1972.

Mackey, Harold. *The Kalapuyans: A Sourcebook on the Indians of the Willamette Valley*. Salem: By the author in cooperation with the Mission Mill Museum Association, 1974.

McManis, Douglas R. *The Initial Evaluation and Utilization of the Illinois Prairies, 1815–1840*. University of Chicago, Department of Geography Research Paper no. 94. Chicago: University of Chicago, 1964.

Malin, James C. *History and Ecology: Studies of the Grassland*. Edited by Robert P. Swierenga. Lincoln: University of Nebraska Press, 1984.

Marx, Leo. *The Machine in the Garden: Technology and the Pastoral Ideal in America*. London: Oxford University Press, 1964.

Merk, Frederick. *History of the Westward Movement*. New York: Knopf, 1978.

———. *The Oregon Question: Essays in Anglo-American Diplomacy and Politics*. Cambridge: Belknap Press, Harvard University Press, 1967.

Miller, Owen G. *Millers of Richardson Gap*. Rev. ed. Salem: By the author, 1979.

Miller, Perry. *Errand into the Wilderness.* Cambridge: Harvard University Press, 1956.

Minor, Rick, Stephen Dow Beckham, Phyllis E. Lancefield-Steeves, and Kathryn Anne Toepel. *Cultural Resource Overview of the BLM Salem District, Northwestern Oregon: Archaeology, Ethnology, History.* University of Oregon Anthropological Papers, ed. C. Melvin Aikens, no. 20. Eugene: University of Oregon, 1980.

Minto, John. "The Number and Condition of the Native Race in Oregon When First Seen by White Men." *OHQ* 1, no. 3 (Mar. 1900): 296–315.

———. "From Youth to Age as an American." *OHQ* 9, no. 2 (June 1908): 127–72.

Mitchell, Lee Clark. *Witnesses to a Vanishing America: The Nineteenth-Century Response.* Princeton: Princeton University Press, 1981.

Moir, William, and Peter Mika. "Prairie Vegetation of the Willamette Valley, Benton County, Oregon." Unpublished report, [1972]. On file at U.S. Department of Agriculture, Forestry Sciences Laboratory, Corvallis, Oreg.

Momaday, N. Scott. "Native American Attitudes to the Environment." In *Seeing with a Native Eye: Essays on Native American Religion*, edited by Walter Holden Capps. New York: Harper & Row, 1976.

Moore, Arthur K. *The Frontier Mind: A Cultural Analysis of the Kentucky Frontiersman.* Lexington: University of Kentucky Press, 1957.

Moynihan, Ruth Barnes. "Abigail Scott Duniway of Oregon: Woman and Suffragist of the American Frontier." Ph.D. diss., Yale University, 1979.

———. *Rebel for Rights: Abigail Scott Duniway.* New Haven: Yale University Press, 1983.

Nash, Roderick. *Wilderness and the American Mind.* 3d ed. New Haven: Yale University Press, 1982.

Novak, Barbara. *Nature and Culture: American Landscape and Painting, 1825–1875.* New York: Oxford University Press, 1980.

O'Brien, Michael J., Jacqueline A. Ferguson, Dennis E. Lewarch, Chad K. McDaniel, William M. Selby, Lynn M. Snyder, and Robert E. Warren. *Grassland, Forest, and Historical Settlement: An Analysis of Dynamics in Northwest Missouri.* Studies in North American Archaeology, edited by W. Raymond Wood. Lincoln: University of Nebraska Press, 1984.

Oliphant, J. Orin. "The Cattle Herds and Ranches of the Oregon Country, 1860–1890." *Agricultural History* 21, no. 4 (Oct. 1947): 217–38.

———. *On the Cattle Ranges of Oregon.* Seattle: University of Washington Press, 1968.

———. "The Eastward Movement of Cattle from the Oregon Country." *Agricultural History* 20, no. 1 (Jan. 1946): 19–43.

Olsen, Michael Leon. "The Beginnings of Agriculture in Western Oregon and Western Washington." Ph.D. diss., University of Washington, 1970.

Oregon's First Century of Farming: A Statistical Record of Achievements and Adjustments in Oregon Agriculture, 1859–1958. Corvallis: Federal Cooperative Extension Service, Oregon State College, [1956].

Parker, George F. *Iowa Pioneer Foundations*. 2 vols. Iowa City: State Historical Society of Iowa, 1940.

Pickard, Madge E., and R. Carlyle Buley. *The Midwest Pioneer: His Ills, Cures, and Doctors*. New York: Henry Schuman, 1946.

Power, Richard Lyle. *Planting Corn Belt Culture: The Impress of the Upland Southerner and Yankee in the Old Northwest*. Indiana Historical Society Publications 17. Indianapolis: Indiana Historical Society, 1953.

Priaulx, Arthur W. " 'Chittim Bark' Early Pocket Money Source." *Albany Democrat-Herald*, 25 Aug. 1948, sec. 3, p. 2.

———. "Lumber Industry Dates From Beginning of Linn History." *Albany Democrat-Herald*, 25 Aug. 1948, sec. 3, p. 2.

Pyne, Stephen J. *Fire in America: A Cultural History of Wildland and Rural Fire*. Princeton: Princeton University Press, 1982.

Ramstead, David A. "Pioneer of Oregon: Captain James Blakely." Unpublished manuscript, 1955. Copy in Amelia Spalding Brown History Room.

Ratcliff, James L. "What Happened to the Kalapuya? A Study of the Depletion of Their Economic Base." *Indian Historian* 6, no. 3 (Summer 1973): 27–33.

Reynolds, Wes Lee. "The Evolution of the Grass Seed Landscape: A Historical Geography of Agriculture in the Southern Willamette Valley." M.A. thesis, University of Oregon, 1977.

Robbins, William G. *Hard Times in Paradise: Coos Bay, Oregon, 1850–1986*. Seattle: University of Washington Press, 1988.

———. "The Indian Question in Western Oregon: The Making of a Colonial People." In *Experiences in a Promised Land*, edited by Carlos A. Schwantes and G. Thomas Edwards, 51–67. Seattle: University of Washington Press, 1986.

Rohrbough, Malcolm J. *The Trans-Appalachian Frontier: People, Societies, and Institutions, 1775–1850*. New York: Oxford University Press, 1978.

Ryan, Mary P. *Cradle of the Middle Class: The Family in Oneida County, New York, 1790–1865*. Interdisciplinary Perspectives on Modern History, edited by Robert Fogel and Stephan Thernstrom. Cambridge: Cambridge University Press, 1981.

Sauer, Carl Ortwin. "Homestead and Community on the Middle Border." *Landscape* 12, no. 1 (Autumn 1962): 3–7.

———. *Land and Life: A Selection from the Writings of Carl Ortwin Sauer*. Edited by John Leighly. Berkeley and Los Angeles: University of California Press, 1963.

Schwantes, Carlos A. *The Pacific Northwest: An Interpretive History*. Lincoln: University of Nebraska Press, 1989.

Scott, Leslie M. "History of the Narrow Gauge Railroad in the Willamette Valley." *OHQ* 20, no. 2 (June 1919): 141–58.

Searles, Harold F. *The Nonhuman Environment in Normal Development and in Schizophrenia*. Monograph Series of Schizophrenia no. 5. New York: International Universities Press, 1960.

———. "The Role of the Nonhuman Environment." *Landscape* 11, no. 2 (Winter 1961–62): 31–34.

Sedell, James R., and Judith L. Froggatt. "Importance of Streamside Forests to Large Rivers: The Isolation of the Willamette River, Oregon, U.S.A., from Its Floodplain by Snagging and Streamside Forest Removal." *Verhandlung International Vereinigen Limnologie* (Stuttgart) Dec. 1984, 1828–34.

Smith, Henry Nash. *Virgin Land: The American West as Symbol and Myth.* Cambridge: Harvard University Press, 1950.

Smith, Warren DuPre. *Physical and Economic Geography of Oregon.* Commonwealth Review of the University of Oregon, edited by F. G. Young, vol. 7, no. 4. Eugene: University of Oregon Press, 1925.

Stanard, Everett Earle. "Old Stuff and New." *Sunday Democrat-Herald* (Albany, Oreg.), 17 Dec. 1922, p. 5; 20 May 1923, sec. 2, p. 3; 4 Nov. 1923, sec. 2, p. 3; 20 July 1924, p. 5.

———. "Rev. H. H. Spalding." In *Official Program,* Linn County Pioneer Association, 44th Annual Reunion, June 1931. Brownsville, Oreg.: Privately printed, 1931.

———. "Seventy-fifth Anniversary of Brownsville Mills." *Brownsville Times,* 2, 9, 16 Aug. 1934.

Standish, John K. "Indian Wars Affect Linn County." *Champoeg Pioneer* (Aurora, Oreg.), July 1960, n.p.

Stilgoe, John R. *Common Landscape of America, 1580 to 1845.* New Haven: Yale University Press, 1982.

Tatter, Henry. *The Preferential Treatment of the Actual Settler in the Primary Disposition of the Vacant Lands in the United States to 1841.* New York: Arno Press, 1979.

Tattersall, James Neville. "The Economic Development of the Pacific Northwest to 1920." Ph.D. diss., Harvard University, 1960.

Thilenius, John F. "The *Quercus garryana* Forest of the Willamette Valley, Oregon." *Ecology* 46 (1968): 1124–33.

Thrower, Norman J. W. *Original Survey and Land Subdivision: A Comparative Study of the Form and Effect of Contrasting Cadastral Surveys.* Chicago: Association of American Geographers and Rand McNally, 1966.

Tobie, H. E. "Joseph Meek: A Conspicuous Personality." *OHQ* 40, no. 3 (Sept. 1939): 243–64.

Towle, Jerry Charles. "Woodlands in the Willamette Valley: An Historical Geography." Ph.D. diss., University of Oregon, 1974.

———. "Settlement and Subsistence in the Willamette Valley: Some Additional Considerations." *Northwest Anthropological Research Notes* 13, no. 1 (Summer 1979): 12–21.

———. "Changing Geography of Willamette Valley Woodlands." *OHQ* 83, no. 1 (Spring 1982): 66–87.

Tuan, Yi-Fu. *Topophilia: A Study of Environmental Perception, Attitudes, and Values.* Engelwood Cliffs: Prentice-Hall, 1974.

Turnbow, Alva Silas. *Robnett Family Record: A Genealogy and History of the*

Robnett Brothers and Sister Who Were Pioneers to Oregon in 1847 and 1851. Eugene: By the author, 1971.

Turnbow, Alva Silas, and Maude Ina Turnbow. *Charles Rice: His Ancestors and Descendants*. Eugene: Privately printed, 1957.

Unruh, John D., Jr. *The Plains Across: The Overland Emigrants and the Trans-Mississippi West, 1840–60*. Urbana: University of Illinois Press, 1979.

Wade, Richard C. *The Urban Frontier: The Rise of Western Cities, 1790–1830*. Cambridge: Harvard University Press, 1959.

Waggoner, George A. *Stories of Old Oregon*. Salem: Statesman Publishing, 1905.

White, Richard. "The Altered landscape: Social Change and the Land in the Pacific Northwest." In *Regionalism and the Pacific Northwest*, edited by William G. Robbins, Robert J. Frank, and Richard E. Ross. Corvallis: Oregon State Univeristy Press, 1983

———. *Land Use, Environment, and Social Change: The Shaping of Island County, Washington*. Seattle: University of Washington Press, 1980.

Williams, Ira A. "The Drainage of Farm Lands in the Willamette and Tributary Valleys of Oregon." *Mineral Resources of Oregon* 1, no. 4 (June 1914): 3–31.

Willis, Lois A. *The William Shields Family at the End of the Oregon Trail*. Hillsboro, Oreg.: By the author, 1970.

Works Progress Administration Writers' Program and the Linn County Pioneer Memorial Association, compilers. *History of Linn County*. N.p.: By the compilers, [1941]. Rpt. Portland, Oreg.: Boyce-Wheeler, 1982.

Young, F. Y. "The Oregon Trail." *OHQ* 1, no. 4 (Dec. 1900): 339–71.

Young, Stanley Paul. *The Wolf in North American History*. Caldwell, Idaho: Caxton Printers, 1946.

———. *The Wolves of North America. Vol. 1, Their History, Life, Habits, Economic Status, and Control*. Washington, D.C.: American Wildlife Institute, 1944.

Zucker, Jeff, Kay Hummel, and Bob Høgfoss. *Oregon Indians: Culture, History & Current Events*. Portland: Western Imprints, the Press of the Oregon Historical Society, 1983.

Index

Agriculture: and cessation of Kalapuya
burning, 124; in cis-Appalachia, 36;
effects of California gold rush on Willamette Valley, 106–107; and geese,
61–62, 124; Kalapuya, 15; wheat,
114, 115, 127, 115 table 3; in Willamette and Calapooia valleys, 57–59,
107–108, 114, 120–122, 124–128.
See also economy; plowing
Albany, 131, 132, 134, 144
Allen, Robinson and Company, 131–
132, 133
Alley, B. F., 152; quoted, 152–153
Allingham, David, 131
Andrews, James, 118
Applegate, Jesse, 13
Atkinson, George, 25, 88, 154; quoted,
25, 58, 88, 154
Ayers, James, quoted, 112

Baird, William C., 86
Barr, Silas V., quoted, 61
Bassett, Arnold, 130
Battue. *See* Kalapuya, and battue
Bears: bounties on, 63; Kalapuya and 16,
18; last grizzly in Linn County killed,
62; Willamette Valley settlers and, 62,
63, 140, 173 n. 32
Beaver, 16, 123
Benton Co., Or., 42, 127
Berries: elderberries, 17; huckleberries,

17; Oregon grape, 9; salmonberries,
17; snowberry, 9; thimbleberries, 17
Birds: cranes, 61, 123; curlews, 123;
ducks, 15, 61, 123, 126; geese, 15,
61, 123, 126; plovers, 123; snipes,
123; swans, 15, 61
Black Hawk War, 32
Blain, Elizabeth, 90, 91, 158
Blain, Wilson, xiii, 67, 83, 86–87, 91,
106, 130, 146, 148; aesthetic relation
to Willamette Valley, 76–79; attitude
toward Indians 86–87; attitude toward settlement 78–79, 87, 88–89,
90–91, 92, 93, 98, 146, 150; attitude
toward wilderness 86–87; biographi-
cal note on, 75; quoted, 47, 59, 64–
65, 66, 69, 76–77, 78, 79, 86, 88–
89, 90–91, 93, 106, 108, 146, 151,
155
Blakely, James, 100–102, 105, 106, 118,
119, 128, 129
Blakely, Sarah, 100
Bobcats, 16, 18
Bogue, Allan G., 31
Boston, Or., 134–136, 139
Boston Flour Mills, 108, 134
Bracken, 17, 125–126, 128
Brackenridge, W. D., 13
Bramwell, John Grath, quoted, 46
Brandon, Alexander, 134
British Royal Horticultural Society, 24
Brown, Clarissa, 63–64, 100, 104

203

Compositor: Huron Valley Graphics
Text: 10/13 Sabon
Display: Sabon
Printer and Binder: Braun-Brumfield, Inc.